Cursor Movement and Deleting Shortc

If you see a plus sign (+) between two keys, you must press and h
the second key, and then release both keys. If you see a comma
the first key, press and release the next key, and so on.

Press ...	*To move ...*
↑	Up one line
Ctrl+↑	Up one paragraph
Home, ↑	To the top of the current screen
Ctrl+Home, ↑	To the top of the current page
Home, Home, ↑	To the top of a document
↓	Down one line
Ctrl+↓	Down one paragraph
Home, ↓	To the bottom of the current screen
Ctrl+Home, ↓	To the bottom of the current page
Home, Home, ↓	To the bottom of a document
→	Right a character

Press ...	*To move ...*
Ctrl+→	To the beginning of the next word
Home, →	To the end of the screen
Home, Home, →	To the end of the line
←	Left one character
Ctrl+←	To the beginning of the previous word
Home, ←	To the beginning of the line
End	To the end of the line
Page Up	To the top of the previous page
Page Down	To the top of the next page

Deleting Text Shortcuts

Press ...	*To delete ...*
Backspace	Character to the left
Delete	Character to the right
Ctrl+Backspace	Current word
Home, Backspace	From cursor to the beginning of a word

Press ...	*To delete ...*
Ctrl+End	From cursor to the end of a line
Ctrl+Page Down	From cursor to the end of a page

Common Editing Tasks

If you want to ...	*Do this ...*
Highlight text	Press Alt+F4, use the cursor-movement keys to highlight the text. *Or*, using your mouse, click at the beginning of the text and drag to the end.
Insert a code so the date is always current	Pull down the Tools that menu, choose Date, and then choose Code.
Insert date text that stays the same	Pull down the Tools menu, choose Date, and then choose Text.
Start a new page	Press Ctrl+Enter.

If you want to ...	*Do this ...*
Check your spelling	Pull down the Tools menu, choose Writing Tools, choose Speller, and then choose Document.
Find a word	Pull down Edit the menu, choose Search, type the word, and press Enter twice.
Replace all occurrences of one word/phrase	Pull down the Edit menu, and choose Replace. Type the text to be replaced with another. Press Enter. Type the replacement text. Press Enter twice.

Common Formatting Tasks

If you want to ...	*Do this ...*
Make text bold	Press Ctrl+B, type the text, and press Ctrl+B. *Or* highlight the existing text, and then press Ctrl+B.
Underline text	Press Ctrl+U, type the text, and press Ctrl+U. *Or* highlight the existing text and then press Ctrl+U.
Make text italic	Press Ctrl+I, type the text, and press Ctrl+I. *Or* highlight the existing text, and then press Ctrl+I.
Indent a paragraph	Press F4 to indent on left side only. Press Shift+F4 to indent on left and right sides.
Center a line	Pull down the **L**ayout menu, choose **A**lignment, choose **C**enter, and type the text.
Right-justify text	Pull down the **L**ayout menu, choose **A**lignment, choose **F**lush Right, and type the text.
Add page numbering	Pull down the **L**ayout menu, choose **P**age, Page **N**umbering, and Page Number **P**osition. Choose a placement option. Choose OK in each of the dialog boxes.

If you want to ...	*Do this ...*
Change margins	Pull down the **L**ayout menu, and choose **M**argins. Choose the margin you want to change, type the margin in inches, and press Enter. Do this for each margin you want to change, and then choose OK.
Change line spacing	Pull down the **L**ayout menu, choose **L**ine, and choose Line **S**pacing. Type the spacing you want (**1** for single spacing, **2** for double spacing, and so on). Press Enter, and then choose OK.
Center a page	Pull down **L**ayout menu, choose **P**age, choose **C**enter Current Page, and choose OK.
Use a different font	Pull down the F**o**nt menu, and choose **F**ont. Choose **F**ont, highlight a font, and press Enter. Choose **S**ize, highlight a size, and press Enter. Choose OK.
Preview your document	Pull down the **F**ile menu, and choose Print Preview.

Getting Help from WordPerfect Customer Support

If you are stuck, you can call WordPerfect Customer Support. WordPerfect Customer Support operators can best help you if you are at your computer and in WordPerfect when you call. They can fix the problem more quickly if you can make the problem happen more than once and if you can tell them exactly when the problem occurs. (For example, the system freezes every time you try to print a document that has tables.)

If you're having a problem with ...	*Call ...*
Getting WordPerfect installed or running	800/533-9605
Printing on a laser printer	800/541-5170
Printing on a printer that isn't a laser printer	800/541-5160
Formatting a document	800/541-5096

If you're having a problem with ...	*Call ...*
Writing or using a macro	800/541-5129
Using graphics	800/321-3383
Anything before 7 a.m. or after 6 p.m. Mountain Time	801/222-9010 (Note that this one *isn't* a toll-free call)

I HATE WORDPERFECT® 6

Elden Nelson

I Hate WordPerfect 6

Library of Congress Catalog: 93-60612

ISBN: 1-56529-361-4

96 95 94 93 4 3 2 1

Interpretation of the printing code: the rightmost double-digit number is the year of the book's printing; the rightmost single-digit number, the number of the book's printing. For example, a printing code of 93-1 shows that the first printing of the book occurred in 1993.

Screen reproductions in this book were created by using Collage Plus, from Inner Media, Inc., Hollis, New Hampshire.

I Hate WordPerfect 6 is based on WordPerfect Version 6 for DOS.

Publisher: David P. Ewing

Associate Publisher: Rick Ranucci

Publishing Plan Manager: Thomas H. Bennett

Operations Manager: Sheila Cunningham

Dedication ... Sort of

I'm not going to dedicate this book to anybody. Does anybody *really* want a computer book dedicated to them? It's hard to imagine. Still, I guess it's possible ....

Rather than me dedicating this book to you, why don't you send me a letter telling me what you think of my book. The address is on the copyright page to your left.

Enjoy the book.

About the Author

Elden Nelson, a Title Manager at Que Corporation, has been a documentation writer for WordPerfect Corporation, where he wrote two macro manuals and contributed to several other manuals. Before that, Elden worked with WordPerfect's famed Customer Support team, where he learned to sympathize with the struggles of WordPerfect users and solve their problems. Most recently, Elden has been the Senior Writer for *WordPerfect Magazine*, a monthly how-to publication for people who use WordPerfect. Elden has written dozens of articles for this magazine and continues to write a monthly column. Other jobs he's had include being an insulation salesperson, a radio disc jockey, a newspaper humor columnist, and a singer in a rock band. Go figure.

When Elden isn't agonizing over a keyboard, he can be found on a pair of Rollerblades, alternatively whizzing down sidewalks at tremendous speeds and bandaging himself from his most recent injury.

Finally, Elden drives—and fanatically cares for—a red Mazda Miata, is a master of the barbecue grill, is 5'8" tall, has brown hair and eyes, speaks fluent Finnish, and has never been convicted of a felony. Any questions?

Credits

Title Manager:
Shelley O'Hara

Production Editor:
H. Leigh Davis

Copy Editors:
William A. Barton
Elsa M. Bell
Barb Colter
Jane A. Cramer
Phil Kitchel

Technical Editors:
Bob Beck
Chris Pichereau

Novice Reviewer:
Connie Burton

Editorial Assistants:
Julia Blount
Sandra Naito

Production Team:
Jeff Baker
Danielle Bird
Claudia Bell
Julie Brown
Laurie Casey
Brad Chinn
Brook Farling
Carla Hall-Batton
Bob LaRoche
Jay Lesandrini
Heather Kaufman
Wendy Ott
Beth Rago
Marcella Thompson
Joe Ramon
Caroline Roop
Linda Seifert
Sandra Shay
Tina Trettin
Michelle Worthington

Indexer
Michael Hughes

Cover Illustration by Jeff MacNelly.

Composed in *Goudy* and MCP*digital* by Que Corporation.

Acknowledgments

I acknowledged a whole *raft* of people in my last book, and I don't think it made even a little bit of difference in what I got for my birthday. Humph. See if I do *that* again. Still, a few people deserve to be acknowledged:

Thanks to Shelley O'Hara, Rick Ranucci, and Leigh Davis. Not only were they helpful in one way or another while I wrote this book, but they're my coworkers and would constantly cast sullen, menacing glances in my direction if I didn't acknowledge them.

Thanks to Dell Computers, particularly Denise McLaughlin, for providing me with a notebook computer while I wrote this book. Thanks also to my friends at *WordPerfect Magazine* for their support and to the Publications Department at WordPerfect Corporation for supplying me with all of the wonderful poems you'll read in this book. Yes, that's right. The same people who write and edit those boring technical manuals also write some of the most bizarre poetry on Earth.

And, thanks especially to Susan, my spouse, for far too many things to even begin mentioning. I was actually thinking of dedicating this book to her, but she let me know in no uncertain terms that she *didn't* want a hot pink book with an angry bird on it dedicated to her. Well, la-de-da. Aren't *we* hoity-toity?

Trademark Acknowledgments

Contents at a Glance

Table of Contents

I HATE WORDPERFECT 6!

I HATE WORDPERFECT 6!

II The On-Line Editorial Assistant 101

8 The Moving, Removing, and Other Handling (of Big Chunks of Your Document) 103

9 Using WordPerfect's Dictionary, Thesaurus, and Grammar Checker 115

12 Formatting Features You'll Use a Few Times Per Week 167

13 Formatting Features You'll Rarely Use 185

IV Files 199

14 More on Printing 201

I HATE WORDPERFECT 6!

I HATE WORDPERFECT 6!

I HATE WORDPERFECT 6!

Introduction

"Oh no! Not again!"

"This computer won't do what I want!"

"I *hate* WordPerfect!"

"Aaargh!"

Sound familiar? Welcome to the club. Computers are confusing. WordPerfect is confusing. But they don't have to be. If you hate WordPerfect, you'll love this book. This is a book about WordPerfect for people who don't want to read about WordPerfect. After all, you don't want to devote your life to your computer—you just want to type a letter.

The idea behind this book is that there's way too much in WordPerfect for any sane person to learn. This book has weeded out the bizarre, esoteric stuff and left you with the absolute essentials: bite-sized chunks of WordPerfect wisdom you can use to get your work done *now*. And as an extra bonus, it's actually fun to read, so you won't instantly fall asleep every time you flip the thing open.

What about Those Drawings in the Margin?

All the information in this book is *not* created equal. Occasionally, the book includes something more technical than the other stuff. This book uses icons (those are the funny drawings within the margins) to say things like, "Hey, this is technical stuff. You don't have to read it." The book has other icons that tell you when to be careful, alert you to some frustrating WordPerfect function that you'll have to deal with, and so on.

Here are the pictures and what they mean:

"I HATE THIS!"

This icon pops up whenever the book has to explain something frustrating or confusing about WordPerfect. It's a good idea to read the text next to this icon; it'll help you brace yourself for things to come.

TIP

You'll see this icon next to extra-helpful tips—things you can use to make your life easier.

CAUTION

"Beware! Warning! Don't do this!" is this icon's message. It can help you avoid WordPerfect pitfalls and potholes.

EXPERTS ONLY

If you're in the mood to read more detailed information on something about WordPerfect, seek out the material flagged with this icon. This is interesting, useful stuff, but it's more advanced, and you don't have to know this information in order to use WordPerfect well.

BUZZWORDS

BUZZWORDS

Computer people have made up hundreds of new words, as well as given strange new meanings to a lot of old words. This picture alerts you that one of these mysterious new terms is about to be explained.

PART I

A Crash Course in WordPerfect

Includes:

CHAPTER 1

The Very Basics
(Into the Wild Blue Yonder)

IN A NUTSHELL

- Get into WordPerfect
- Know where you are
- Type text
- Move around
- Correct mistakes
- Restore deleted text
- Use the function keys

So, you hate WordPerfect. Maybe you've tried to use WordPerfect a few times and feel frustrated at your inability to make it do what you want. Or maybe you've never even tried to use it; you just know you'll hate it and have managed to spare yourself the agony. (I myself have never tasted brussels sprouts for this very reason.)

In either case, you've somehow gotten yourself into a predicament: you have to use WordPerfect. What do you do now? Stop worrying. You've already made the right first move—you bought this book!

This chapter starts at the very beginning and guides you through the basics of WordPerfect. You learn how to start WordPerfect, write in WordPerfect, and then edit what you wrote. This chapter also teaches you how to get out of difficult situations.

Starting WordPerfect ("What's a nice person like you doing in a program like this?")

Starting WordPerfect isn't all that difficult. First, you turn on the computer. You see something like `C:\>` on-screen followed by a blinking underline. This "something" is called the *DOS prompt*, which is like being in the computer equivalent of Hell.

Type **CD\WP60**, and then press Enter. If the computer spits back `Invalid Directory` or something equally incomprehensible, try typing **CD\WP**. Then press Enter.

Your screen now reads either `C:\WP60` or `C:\WP`. To get into WordPerfect, type **WP** and press Enter.

BUZZWORDS

DOS

DOS (it rhymes with loss) is one of the three most-used buzzwords in the computer industry. (Never mind that I can't remember the other two right now.) DOS stands for Disk Operating System. DOS helps your computer talk to your keyboard, disk, monitor, and programs. In other words, your computer needs DOS to run WordPerfect and other programs. When you see that cryptic `C:\>` or `C>`, you can impress onlookers by glancing haughtily at the screen and exclaiming, "Ah, I see that we're at the DOS prompt."

Checklist

- If this procedure doesn't work, try asking someone more technically inclined (a coworker, your wife, the paper boy) to show you how to start WordPerfect. Be sure to write down the steps so that you can start the program yourself next time.
- When you turn on some computers, a list—rather than the DOS prompt—appears. If you turn on your computer and see a list, and if WordPerfect is on the list, you are one of the lucky few! Press the number or letter next to `WordPerfect` or `WP` on your screen. You're in!

TIP

You can perform some computer wizardry to make WordPerfect start whenever you turn on the computer. If you use WordPerfect almost every time you use the computer, this can be a helpful shortcut. Snare a computer-savvy friend

continues

continued

and try to bribe him into helping you. Here's the magic phrase you should use: "Will you please add WordPerfect to my AUTOEXEC.BAT file?" By the way, AUTOEXEC.BAT is pronounced "ought-oh-eggs-eck-dot-bat." Don't bother changing the AUTOEXEC.BAT file yourself. Because this file is vital to the proper functioning of your computer, only the technically enthusiastic should mess with it.

Getting into WordPerfect's New Look

The first time you start WordPerfect, it's not very attractive. In fact, it's downright plain. The letters are blocky and clumsy, and the blue-on-white motif has *got* to go. WordPerfect has a cleaner, easier-to-use graphic look that I think you'll like working with. Follow these steps:

1. Press and hold down the Alt key, then press V.

   A menu drops down from the menu bar at the top of the screen. You'll learn more about menus later in this chapter.

2. Press G for Graphics Mode.

   The screen flickers and changes. You now have a more modern, friendly look for WordPerfect. This different display means that your work on the screen will look much more like it will on the page.

Graphics Mode is just miserably slow!

This Graphics Mode isn't for everybody. If your computer is not very new, WordPerfect's Graphics mode may be too slow for you—or it may not work at all. If everything seems to take *forever* in Graphics Mode, you can speed things up by going back to Text Mode—just pull down the **V**iew menu and choose **T**ext Mode.

Or, it's possible that you'll try to turn on Graphics Mode and WordPerfect brings up a box that says something like `Not enough memory for graphics`. In this case, just press Enter and forget about Graphics mode—you can work in Text mode just fine.

If, for whatever reason, you work in Text Mode, you can still use this book. You won't be able to see certain things that you can see in Graphics Mode, and you'll have to use Print Preview to get an idea of how your text will look on the printed page (see "Print Preview" in Chapter 6). Also, your screen will look a little different than the pictures of screens in this book.

Looking around the WordPerfect Screen

WordPerfect. Heralded as one of the most powerful software tools ever created. Painstakingly detailed. Able to leap tall buildings in a single bound. So why is the screen practically blank? For the amount of money you've spent, wouldn't you expect something just a touch more exciting? Like maybe a three-day getaway in Cancun, or at least a VCR?

When you get to know it, however, you'll be pleasantly surprised at how useful WordPerfect is. Let's begin with a look at what's on-screen.

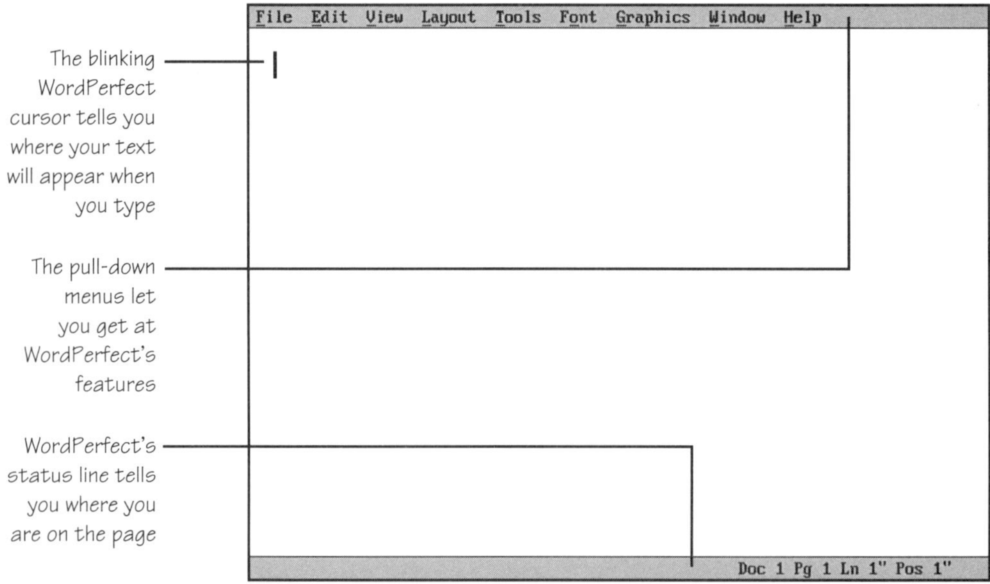

"What's That Blinking Thing?"

It's called a *cursor*. When you type words on the keyboard, they appear on-screen wherever the cursor is blinking. Think of the cursor as an on-screen "You Are Here" arrow.

Whenever you start WordPerfect, the cursor shows up in the upper-left corner of the screen. The cursor moves as you type, left to right, one space at a time.

"Who Typed That Row of Words at the Top of the Screen?"

Actually, nobody typed those words—and you don't have to worry about them showing up when you print things. That strip of words is called the WordPerfect *menu bar*, and each word represents a menu.

You can pull down any menu and see what that menu does—the same way you'd flip to a certain page in a restaurant menu. For example, the Layout menu has a bunch of commands that help you change the way your text looks on the page. You'll learn how to use the menu bar a little later in this chapter.

"What about those Hieroglyphics at the Bottom of the Screen?"

The bottom of the screen looks like this:

```
Doc 1 Pg 1 Ln 1" Pos 1"
```

These letters and numbers tell you where you are (technically, where your cursor is).

Decoding the Hieroglyphics

- `Doc` stands for "Document." *Document* is computer jargon for "Something you've typed." WordPerfect has the capability to let you work on two documents at once—like having paper in two typewriters at the same time. If you see `Doc 1` on-screen, you're working on the first document. If you see `Doc 2`, you're working on the second. WordPerfect lets you work on as many as nine documents at once. Will you ever work on nine things at once? Not unless you're writing the sequel to *Sybil*.
- `Pg` is not the rating of your document. Pg will not change to G when you write Disney stories, and it will not change to R when you write Madonna's next movie. Pg stands for "Page." If you see `Pg 1`, you're on the first page. `Pg 2` means you're on the second page. `Pg 972` means you're on page 972 and should consider being a tad more concise in your writing.

continues

Decoding the Hieroglyphics (continued)

- Ln means "Line." This number tells you how many inches you are from the top of the page. Because WordPerfect automatically sets up one-inch margins all the way around your document, this area shows 1" when you're at the top of a page. (***Note:*** You usually do not actually see the one-inch margin on-screen, but when you print a document, it will have a one-inch margin.)
- Pos means "Position." This number tells you how many inches you are from the left side of the page. Again, because WordPerfect automatically sets up margins of one inch all the way around your document, this area shows 1" when you're at the left edge of the page. Because this number changes with every character you type, it's an excellent thing to ignore.

EXPERTS ONLY

Pos can tell you a lot more about what's going on in WordPerfect than you want to know

- If Pos changes to POS, your Caps Lock key is turned on. Any text you type will appear in capital letters. Press the key again to turn off Caps Lock. POS changes back to Pos when you turn off Caps Lock.
- If Pos is flashing, your Num Lock key is on. Press the Num Lock key to turn it off.
- The color or look of the number to the right of Pos tells you whether you have selected bold, underline, italic, or other special features. On some computers, the appearance of the number will reflect the selected feature: 1" becomes *1"* when the italic feature is selected. On most computers, the 1" appears with some arbitrarily selected color background, and you are supposed to remember which color background represents each feature.

Typing Text (Writing the Great American Novel)

Typing in WordPerfect is a lot like using your typewriter but easier in lots of ways. First, you don't press Enter (on some old keyboards, Enter is called "Return") at the end of each line. WordPerfect automatically "wraps" the text to the next line. To see how WordPerfect knows when to go to the next line, type frantically at the keyboard for a minute. Try typing the following text without pressing Enter:

> **Judy, listening intently to the company president give the yearly review, realized she preferred Cocoa Puffs to Count Chocula.**

As you type, the cursor moves to the right, outrunning the letters. As you get to the end of a line, WordPerfect knows the line should end and zips down to the beginning of the next line. (The place where a line ends is called a *soft return*, but who cares?) Later, when you add text or make changes to the text, WordPerfect adjusts the line breaks.

You add text simply by typing it. As you type, everything in front of the cursor (the text you typed previously) is pushed down to clear space for the new text. This is perhaps the second most wonderful thing about using a word processor—and it's environmentally correct! Think of all the paper (and therefore trees) it saves; no more crumpled paper filling the garbage can!

The Multipurpose Enter Key

Don't completely forget about the Enter key. You still need it in certain situations—to separate paragraphs, for example. Simply press the Enter key when you want a paragraph to end.

You also use it to add blank lines between lines of text—and to end lines before they wrap to the next line. For example, a name or address usually doesn't go from margin to margin. Instead, type your name and press Enter. The cursor moves to the beginning of the next line, where you can type your address.

BUZZWORDS

HARD RETURNS

When you want to end a paragraph, you press Enter. The end of the paragraph is called a *hard return*, although there's nothing hard about it. This kind of line break will not be adjusted when you insert or delete text. *Soft returns* are inserted by WordPerfect and do adjust as you insert or delete text.

Other keys you need to know about when typing

- Press Tab when you want the first line of a paragraph indented. In fact, the Tab key works the same in WordPerfect as it does on a typewriter.
- The Caps Lock key makes letters capitals. It doesn't change a key's function like the Shift key.

Breaking Pages

After you type for a while, you fill up the screen (unless you're typing something remarkably short, like the New Year's resolutions you stuck to). At that point, the text you wrote earlier moves off the top of the

screen and makes room for new words at the bottom of the screen. DO NOT PANIC. The top line of your text hasn't fallen off the face of the earth; it's just moved off the top of your screen. You simply can't see it.

If you type long enough, you'll fill a page. WordPerfect can tell when the page you're working on doesn't have any more space, and it then gives you a new page. It separates the pages for you on-screen with a line.

Everything above the line is on one page; everything below the line is on the next page. As you fill up each page, a new line appears, signaling that you have begun a new page.

Sometimes you'll want to end a page before it's full of text, like after you've created a title page or when you want to end a book chapter. You can repeatedly press the Enter key until a page break appears, but this method is cumbersome and unnecessary. Besides (he said in an ominous voice), it can cause problems later.

A better method is to hold down the Ctrl key and press Enter. A page break appears at the position of the cursor. Look closely. This page break is not the same single line that separates your other pages. It's a double line.

BUZZWORDS

HARD AND SOFT PAGE BREAKS

The double line is called a *hard page break*, and the single line is called a *soft page break*. The location of soft page breaks change as you add and delete text so that the page contains the same number of lines. Hard page breaks, on the other hand, do not change when text is added or deleted; the page always ends at the position of the page break, no matter how few lines of text are on the page.

Cruising Around

You move the cursor by using the arrow keys. Look on your keyboard for a cluster of arrow keys pointing in different directions (up, down, left, and right). These keys show up in different places on different keyboards, in accordance with the computer manufacturer mandate that no two keyboards look or work exactly the same. On most keyboards, however, the arrow keys are in their own lonely little cluster just to the right of the letter keys.

Basically, the cursor moves in the direction indicated by the arrow. Press the down-arrow key. The cursor moves down one line of text (although not past the last word in the document). Press the right-arrow key. The cursor moves one letter to the right. You just press the arrow keys until the cursor is positioned where you need to edit text.

Amazing but true facts about moving your cursor

- You can't move the cursor past the end of the last word in the document. The cursor only goes as far as you've typed.
- If you hold down a cursor key, it goes completely berserk. For example, if you hold down the up-arrow key, the cursor begins rocketing toward the top of the document—you may even hear a very small sonic boom (then again, you probably won't). The cursor continues its mad ascent until you release the up-arrow key.
- If you press the left-arrow key when you're already at the left edge of the page, the cursor moves to the right edge of the page, one line up.

- If you have more than a screen of text and you press the right-arrow key when the cursor is at the right edge of a line, the cursor goes to the left side of the page, one line down.
- If the cursor is at the top of the screen and you press the up-arrow key, the text moves (computer types call this *scrolling*) down so that you can see text above it.
- Pressing the down-arrow key when you're at the bottom of the screen produces the opposite effect: the old text moves up so that you can see the text below it.

The Keys To Pressing Keys

Sometimes you'll have to press more than one key simultaneously. When that happens, there's a plus symbol (+) between the keys you're supposed to press. Press and hold down the key before the +, and then press the key after the +. Finally, let go of both keys.

If you want to get things done in WordPerfect, you've got to press a lot of keys. When you need to press a series of keys, they'll be separated by commas and spaces. For example, if you see instructions that say

"Press Home, Home, Up-arrow key, then press Shift+F8."

you would press your Home key twice, then press your up-arrow key, then hold the Shift key, press F8 (yes, there's a key on your keyboard that has an F8 on it) and let go of both keys. Ignore the commas and spaces.

Speed Movement Keys

When you start writing your great American novel (or at least creating long documents), you'll find that using the arrow keys to move your cursor through large sections of text is tooo slo-o-o-ow. WordPerfect has several difficult-to-remember keystroke combinations that quickly get you from one place to another. Although these keystrokes initially seem complicated, after some practice, your fingers will remember them.

Key or key combo	What the key or combo does
Home, Home, ↑	Moves the cursor to the top of your document. You press the Home key twice, and then press the up-arrow key.
Home, Home, ↓	Moves the cursor to the end of your document.
Ctrl+→	Moves the cursor to the beginning of the next word.
Ctrl+←	Moves the cursor to the beginning of the previous word. In case you were wondering, there are no key combinations to move to the end of the next or previous word.
Ctrl+↑	Moves the cursor to the beginning of the previous paragraph.
Ctrl+↓	Moves the cursor to the beginning of the next paragraph.

Key or key combo	What the key or combo does
Page Up	Moves the cursor to the beginning of the previous page. This key is sometimes labeled PgUp—kind of like reading shorthand.
Page Down	Moves the cursor to the beginning of the next page. This key is sometimes labeled PgDn.

Correcting Small Mistakes (Throw your White-Out in the trash)

I'm a lousy typist. I tend to hit the "C" when I meant to type "V" and it's pretty much a coin toss as to whether I land on the right key when I aim for the "M."

It's okay to be a miserable typist in WordPerfect, however. Cleaning up typos is no sweat. Removing an unwanted word is just as easy. You just have to become handy with the Backspace and Delete keys.

Pressing the Backspace key removes the character to the left of the cursor. The Backspace key is located in the upper-right corner of the letters part of your keyboard. Some Backspace keys are kind enough to be labeled with the word Backspace, while others have nothing but an arrow pointing left. Do not confuse this key with the left-arrow key, which does not delete text.

Pressing Delete removes the character to the right of the cursor. Use this key to delete text to the right of your cursor. Look for a key labeled "Del" or "Delete."

CAUTION

If you hold down the Backspace or Delete key rather than pressing it just once or twice, WordPerfect starts erasing at a furious rate. You often end up deleting a lot more than you wanted to. Don't hold down these keys unless you've got tons of text to erase.

Bringing Text Back from the Dead

When you're new to WordPerfect, you're bound to make a lot of little mistakes. As you get more practice, you'll find that your mistakes become much bigger. Just kidding. One mistake you might make—frequently—is deleting text you really wanted to keep.

When you delete text, it isn't really gone—at least, not right away. You can use the Escape key to "cancel" your most recent deletion. The Escape key is in the upper-left corner of your keyboard and might just say Esc instead of Escape on it.

Try experimenting with "undeleting" text. Type **The most important thing in the world**. Now press Backspace enough times to delete the entire sentence. You've just deleted The Most Important Thing in the World! Not to worry; you can bring it back. Press Esc. A box appears in the middle of the screen, with a couple of options: 1. Restore and 2. Previous Deletion. Press R for Restore and take a look at your screen. The Most Important Thing in the World is back!

Don't delay bringing back text that's been deleted. Do it as soon as possible. WordPerfect can only hold three deleted pieces of text, and it's easy to lose the one you want if you're not careful.

Ordering from the Menu

You're going to spend most of your time in this program just typing. Easy enough. But sometimes you're going to want to do something different, like change margins or set up new tab stops.

When you need to do something besides type in WordPerfect, you use the menu bar at the top of the screen. The menu bar looks like this:

```
File  Edit  View  Layout  Tools  Font  Graphics Window  Help
```

We're not in Kansas anymore!

So far you've been spared the tangle of screens, prompts, and menus that make up most of WordPerfect's features. Eventually, however, you'll feel brave and fearless and wander off into what is known as the "WordPerfect maze." One menu will lead to another and another until you're miles from home. And leaving bread crumbs won't help find your way back. (Trust me; I've tried.) To get back to the WordPerfect you know, press Esc until you return to the document screen.

Each of these words is a separate menu. As this book goes along, you'll use a few of the options in these menus ... and ignore most of them. Still, it's a good idea to know how to pull down a menu and choose an option. Press and hold down the Alt key. You should have two Alt keys on your keyboard—one on either side of your space bar. Then press the underlined letter from the menu you want to pull down.

For example, if you want to pull down the **H**elp menu, you press the letter H now. When you press the Alt+letter key combo, a list of choices drops down from the menu name, like this:

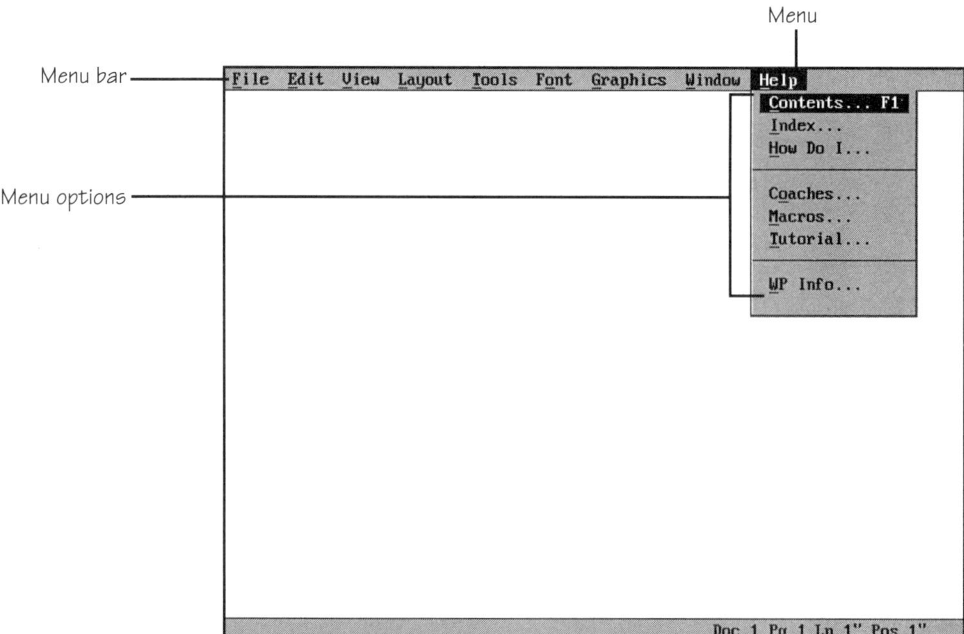

Press the different-colored letter from the menu option you want. For example, if you wanted to use the **H**elp **I**ndex, you would press I for Index.

▼ If your computer has a mouse and you like using it, you can use the mouse to pull down a menu. Just move your mouse around and you'll see an arrow moving around on your screen. Move this pointer to the menu you want to pull down, then click the left mouse button. The menu drops down. Then, click on the option you want.

▼ In the rest of this book, I'll word menu selections like this: "Pull down the **H**elp menu." This means you should press and hold down the Alt key, then press the bold letter—H in this case. Then release both keys. Or, use the mouse.

▼ If you pull down a menu and then decide you don't want it after all, you can make the menu disappear by pressing the Esc key twice.

EXPERTS ONLY

My mouse doesn't work!

If you have a mouse but nothing happens when you slide it around in WordPerfect, follow these steps to get the mouse to work:

1. Press Alt+F.
2. Press T, M, T, A.
3. Press Enter.

That ought to do it. You should be able to use your mouse now.

Those $#&! Function Keys

BUZZWORDS

FUNCTION KEYS

Function keys are labeled F1-F10 or F1-F12 and appear along the left or the top of your keyboard. These keys access features of a program. Every program uses the function keys in a different way.

Not everybody is a fan of the mouse. Some people don't have one, and some people don't like them. In WordPerfect, you can press function keys to get to any particular feature. For example, to start the Help feature, you press F1.

WordPerfect gives each key a "name." The F1 key is affectionately known as the Help key. F7 is the Exit key. WordPerfect prima donnas like to throw these names around to show off. You don't need to worry about the name.

You also shouldn't worry about memorizing the function of each key. First, there's nothing intuitive about which key does what. Why F1 for Help and F2 for Search? Why not? Second, there are at least 40 combinations of function keys. (You can press the function key itself, Shift and the function key, Alt and the function key, and Ctrl and the function key.) Most people are much better off using the menus. Still, if you stick with the function keys long enough, you'll get used to the keys you need.

TIP

When you want to use a function key combination (such as Alt+F2), press and hold down the first key (Alt). Then press the second key (F2). Release both keys.

Dealing with Dialog Boxes

Often, when you choose an option in a menu, a box appears—called a *dialog box*. Here's an example of what a dialog box looks like:

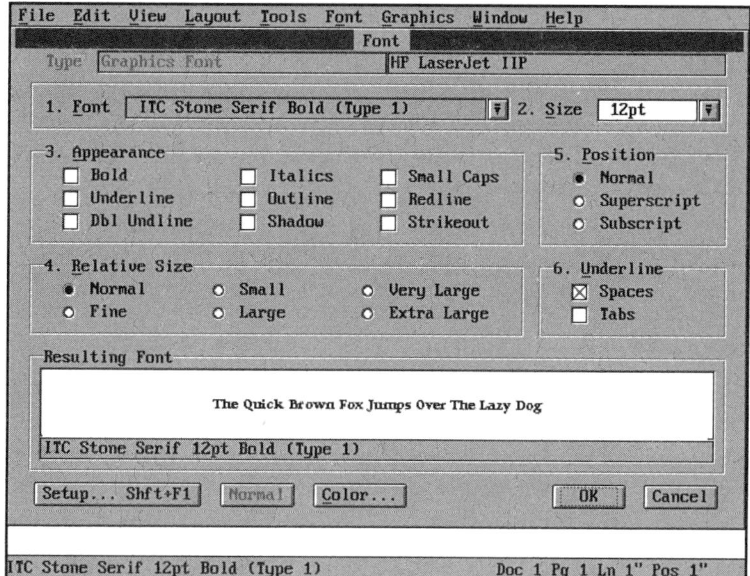

The WordPerfect Font dialog box.

Each dialog box has buttons; many have check boxes and places to type; and some have other strange bells and whistles. By doing various kinds of things in these boxes, you're turning on—and off—various WordPerfect features. You use different parts of dialog boxes in different ways, and it helps to know the tricks behind using them. Just skim over what dialog boxes do right now; when you need to use them later, you can come back.

Pressing the Right Buttons

Every dialog box has at least one button. You can "press" a dialog box button by clicking on it with your mouse or by pressing the letter on the button that's underlined. In this book, I'll tell you to *choose* the button you need to press.

You'll commonly see two buttons on dialog boxes. You'll see OK a lot—when you press this, it means that any other changes you've made in the dialog box are fine. OK is usually the *default* button, which means pressing Enter is the same as choosing OK. When you choose OK, the dialog box goes away. Choosing Cancel means you've changed your mind—the dialog box goes away and anything you've done in the dialog box is ignored. I'll tell you when to press any other button you'll ever need to choose.

Check It Out!

When you're marking off options you want in a new car, you put check marks by the things you want, and leave others blank. That's the idea behind check boxes in a dialog box. If you want to turn a feature on, you check the box. If you don't, you leave it blank.

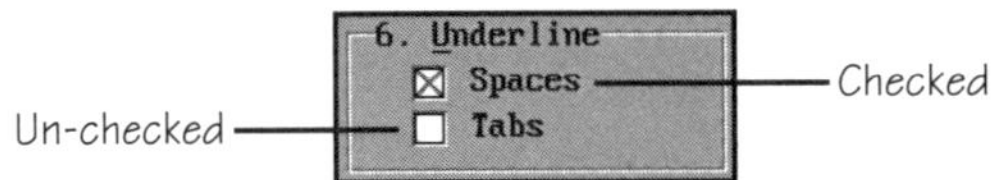

You check a box by clicking your mouse on it or by pressing the underlined letter in the text describing the check box. If you change your mind and want to un-check a box, you do it the same way.

Radio Buttons

Here's one of life's great truths: you can only listen to one radio station at a time. In a kinda-sorta similar way, there are certain features in WordPerfect that are mutually exclusive.

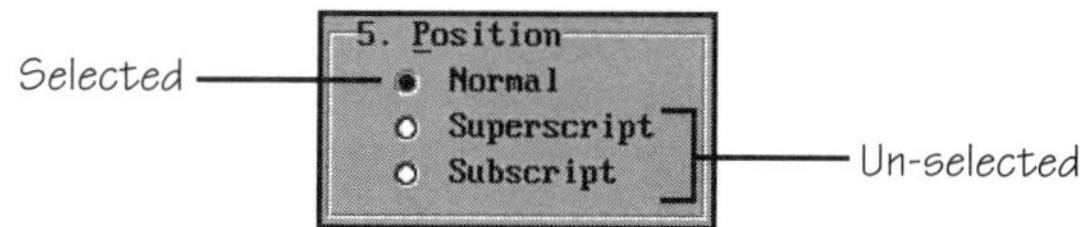

If you want the Font Position to be Normal, it can't *also* be Superscript. So, if you choose one radio button, all the others in that group are automatically turned off.

How do you choose a radio button? With a mouse, you click in the circle beside the text that describes the feature. With a keyboard, you press the underlined letter for that radio button.

Pop-Up Menus

Sadly, pop-up menus have absolutely nothing to do with Pop-Tarts. Pop-up menus have lists of options, and you choose one of them. You make the menu pop up by clicking the menu's down-arrow button, or—if you prefer the keyboard—press the underlined letter beside the menu. When the menu appears, double-click on the option you want, or use your arrow keys to highlight the option, then press Enter.

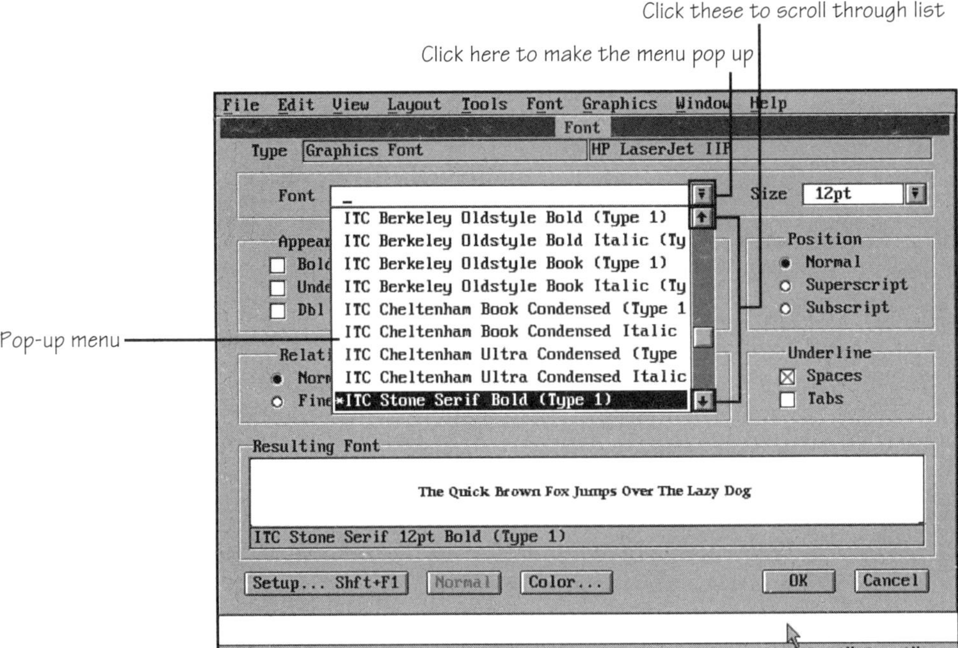

Some pop-up menus have more options than they can show. In this case, a *scroll bar* appears on the right side of the list. You can see more of the menu by clicking the up- and down-arrow buttons with your mouse, or use the up- and down-arrow buttons on your keyboard to achieve the same effect.

When you've chosen a pop-up menu option, either by double-clicking on it or highlighting it and pressing Enter, the menu disappears.

List Boxes

Some dialog boxes have large boxes in them, with several choices. When you need to choose one of those options, use your arrow keys to highlight it, then press Enter. Or, if you're using a mouse, double-click the item.

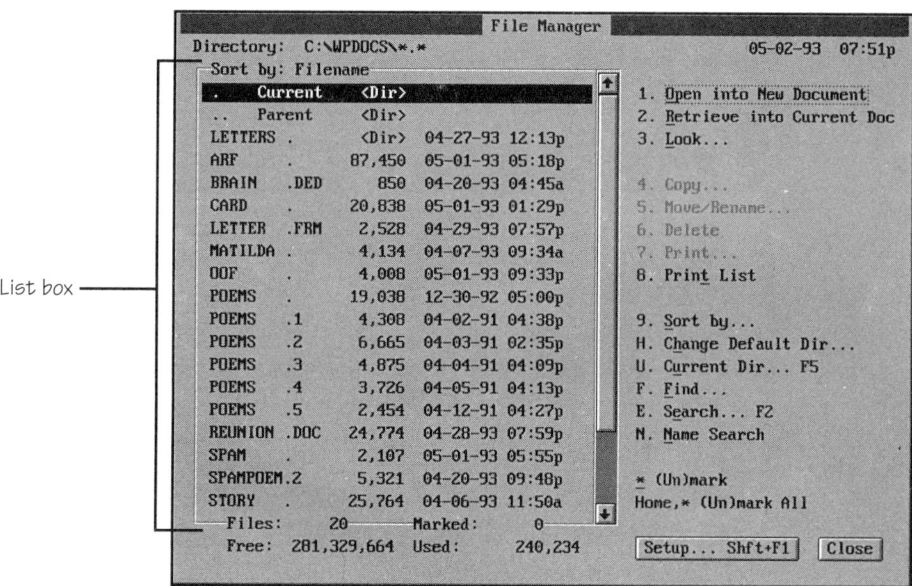

List boxes usually have more items in them than can be shown at once. When this happens, a scroll bar appears on the right side of the list. You can see more of the list by clicking the up- and down-arrow buttons with your mouse, or use the up- and down-arrow keys on your keyboard to achieve the same effect.

Text Boxes

Sometimes a dialog box needs to have you type a word or number. You type in what's called a *text box*. To begin typing in a text box, click the mouse where the text needs to go or press the underlined letter shown in the text beside where the text goes. If text is already highlighted in the text box you need to type in, just go ahead and type anyway—the old text disappears. When you're finished typing the text or number you need, press Enter.

When your cursor is in a text box, you can't just press a letter to choose other options in the dialog box—WordPerfect would just think you're typing. You need to leave the text box before choosing other options. You can leave the text box by pressing Tab or Enter.

Groups of Groups

Some of the dialog boxes in WordPerfect tend to get crowded. So, WordPerfect corrals similar features into *groups*—boxes drawn around sets of features. If you're using a keyboard to work in WordPerfect, you need to know about these groups. Before you can use a feature in a group, you need to choose that group.

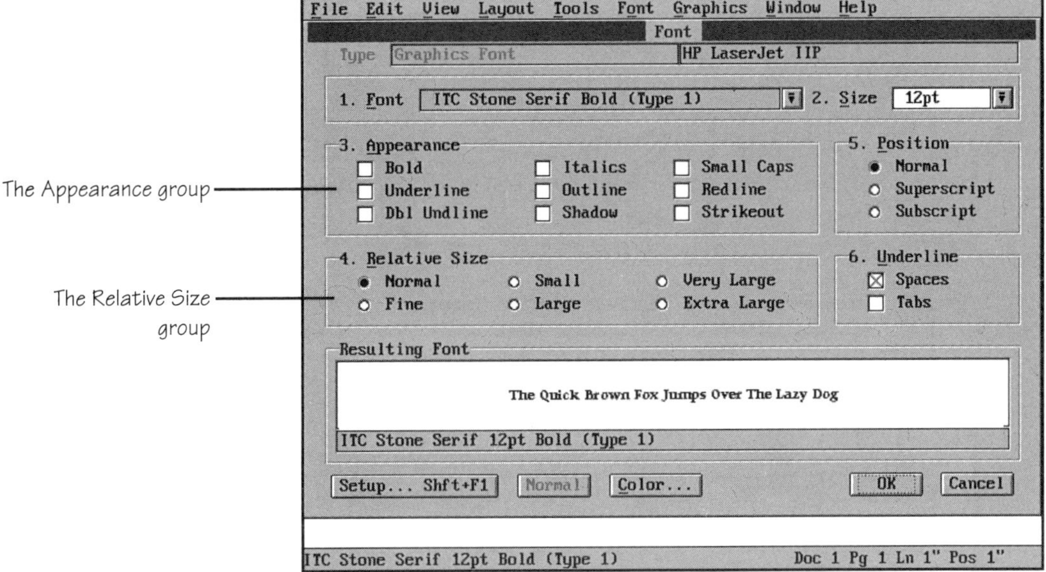

For example, before you can choose the Bold check box in this figure, you need to press A for **A**ppearance.

If you're using a mouse to choose options, you don't need to worry about choosing groups before choosing options—just click where you want to be. WordPerfect 6.0 is obviously biased toward mouse users, so you may as well go with the flow and learn to get comfortable with that rodent.

Some Options Look Dim!

Sometimes certain parts of a dialog box may be light gray, like one of the lightbulbs in the dialog box burned out. This doesn't mean something's wrong with WordPerfect; it just means that you can't use that feature right now.

SHOE
By Jeff MacNelly

Once upon...

a timeframe,

WHAT'RE YOU DOING?
WORKING.
© 1991 Tribune Media Services, Inc. All Rights Reserved

LOOKS LIKE YOU'RE SITTING.
I'M TRYING TO WRITE, IF YOU REALLY MUST KNOW.

WHAT'RE YOU WRITING?
NOTHING, SO FAR.

BUT THE COMPUTER MAKES WRITING A LOT EASIER, I'LL SAY THAT.

WITH JUST A FLICK OF THE FINGER...

I CAN WRITE REAMS OF NOTHING.
WHIRRRRR

I CALL IT "STREAM OF UNCONSCIOUSNESS."
7-21

CHAPTER 2

Editing Text
(Rewriting History)

IN A NUTSHELL

- ▼ Delete text
- ▼ Undelete text

WordPerfect is an editor's dream. With it, you can slash words, lines, or even pages with the greatest of ease. And if you change your mind, you can reverse the situation faster than you can say, "Oops!" This chapter shows you how to erase any amount of text at one time—from a single word to whole pages.

Deleting Text (Using that big WordPerfect eraser)

If you don't like the text you've written, delete it. The Delete and Backspace keys are great for deleting a few letters at a time, but they get really annoying when you want to erase a long word or a whole line. You have to either hold down the key and hope you let go before WordPerfect erases more than you want or tap the key over and over and over until you've gotten rid of the words you don't need.

You have some much faster—and more precise—tools at your disposal for erasing more than just a couple of letters.

Delete a Word

When you want to delete a single word, move the cursor so that it's anywhere in that word; then press Ctrl+Backspace. The word and the space after the word are gone.

EXPERTS ONLY

Fine-tooth distinctions you can skip

If you are boning up on your WordPerfect key-combination trivia, here are some additional alternatives:

- You can press Ctrl+Delete instead of Ctrl+Backspace. They both do the same thing.
- If the cursor is between two words when you press Ctrl+Backspace, the word closest to the cursor is deleted.
- If the cursor is in the middle of a word and you want to delete to the beginning of the word, press Home, Backspace.
- Press Home, Delete to delete from the cursor to the beginning of the next word.

Erase from the Cursor to the End of the Line

Sometimes you'll get really aggressive with your editing, and you'll want to get rid of whole strings of words. To delete from your cursor to the end of the line on your screen, just press Ctrl+End. Everything from the cursor to the end of the line disappears. If there's any text on that following line, it moves up to take the place of the deleted text.

TIP

Ctrl+End doesn't delete the whole line; it only deletes from the cursor to the end of the line. If you want to delete an entire line, press Home, Home, left-arrow key to move the cursor to the beginning of the line. Then press Ctrl+End.

Delete from the Cursor to the End of the Page

If you're disgusted with the latter half of a page of text, move the cursor to where you want the deletion to begin; then press Ctrl+Page Down. A box appears on your screen, with this message:

```
Delete Remainder of page
```

Under the message, you have two options, Yes and No. The **Y** and **N** are bold to show you which key to press, depending on your decision. Choose **Y**es. Presto! You have erased everything from the cursor to the end of the page.

TIP

If you prefer using the mouse, you can move the mouse pointer to the Yes button and click (with the left mouse button) on it once to do the same thing.

TIP

Pressing Ctrl+Page Down doesn't delete everything on the page—just everything from your cursor to the end of the page. If you want to delete everything on the page, move the cursor to the beginning of that page by pressing Ctrl+Home, then the up-arrow key. Now press Ctrl+Page Down, Y. Everything on the page is erased.

Erase Any Amount of Text

Deleting words, lines, and pages is all well and good, but sometimes what you want to get rid of doesn't fall neatly into one of these categories—you just want to erase a specific amount of text. You can delete a chunk of text—anything from a paragraph to several pages—most efficiently by using the Block feature.

The idea behind Block is that you mark a certain amount of text, just as if you were highlighting it with one of those fluorescent pink pens. Then you tell WordPerfect to delete the highlighted part. This is how you mark the text you want to erase:

1. Move the cursor to the beginning of the text to erase.

   Your cursor should be right under the first character that you want to take out of the document.

2. Pull down the **E**dit menu, then choose **B**lock.

   `Block On` appears in the lower-left corner of the screen. That's WordPerfect's way of telling you it's ready for you to mark the text.

TIP

If you'd rather use the mouse to select a command, just click on the **E**dit menu in the menu bar, then click on **B**lock. If you'd rather keep your hands on the keyboard, use the menus by pressing and holding the Alt key, then pressing the bold letter for the menu you want. For example, you would press Alt+E to pull down the **E**dit menu. When the menu appears, you choose an option from it just by pressing the bold letter. For example, if you want to choose **B**lock, just press B.

3. Use the arrow keys to move to the end of the text you want to erase.

   As you move the cursor, you see that everything from your beginning point to your cursor is highlighted. When you finish, your cursor should be right after the last character you want to delete.

4. Press Backspace or Delete.

The marked text disappears.

Other fascinating Block information

- If you'd rather use your function keys than pull things down from the menu, you can press F12 or Alt+F4 to turn on Block.
- If you start blocking text to delete and change your mind, press Esc to turn off Block. You also can press Alt+F4 or F12 to turn off Block.
- You don't have to start blocking at the beginning of the text to delete; if you want, you can start at the end and block to the beginning. WordPerfect is flexible. This flexibility is useful if your cursor is closer to the end of the text you want to delete than it is to the beginning.
- When the `Block On` prompt is on, you can't type text. If you decide you need to type something before you delete the chunk of text, press Esc to turn off Block, type what you need, and then start marking the text to be deleted.
- Blocking text is one of the things your mouse is best at. If you have a mouse, use it to move the *mouse pointer* (a little rectangle that moves on-screen when you move the mouse on your desk) to the place you want to begin deleting. Press and hold down the left mouse button, and then slide the mouse to position the mouse pointer where you want to stop deleting. Release the mouse button and press Delete.
- There's a lot more to learn about Block. In fact, Chapter 8 talks of nothing else.

Restoring Deleted Text for Fun and Profit

Any time you erase something, WordPerfect remembers it. In fact, WordPerfect remembers the three most recent things you've deleted—and you can get them back if you need them.

To get back the text you've deleted most recently, just press Esc, R.

You also can get back the two deletions before that as well. So if you block and delete a paragraph, then move down a couple of lines and delete a word, then move down to the bottom of the document and erase the whole last page, you haven't really lost anything. You can get back any of those three most-recent deletions.

This is how you get back your second or third most-recent deletion:

1. Move the cursor to where the deleted text ought to go.

   When you restore the text, WordPerfect plops it right at the position of the cursor.

2. Press Esc and then P for Previous.

   Your second most-recent deletion appears highlighted at the cursor position. If you want to see the third most-recent deletion, press P for Previous again. Make sure that the highlighted text is really the text that you want back.

3. Press R for Restore.

   The highlighted text gets put back into your document.

Checklist

- If you change your mind and don't want to bring the deleted text back, press Esc to cancel.
- You only get to restore your three most recent deletions; any deletions before those are gone. So it's important to restore text ASAP.
- What counts as a "deletion"? All of the text you delete until you do something else. If you delete an entire page before you move the cursor or stop typing, that whole page counts as a deletion. If you just erase one letter before you type or move, that single letter counts as a deletion.
- Deleting and restoring is a great way to move text from one point in your document to another. Just delete the text you want to move; then, before you do anything else, move the cursor to the new position for the text. Press Esc, R to place the text.
- If you're looking at the third most-recent deletion and press P for Previous again, WordPerfect doesn't show you the fourth most-recent deletion. Instead, it cycles back to the most recent deletion.
- You also can use the amazing Undo feature to bring back text you've just deleted—but you've got to use it *immediately* after you've erased your text. Just choose **E**dit, **U**ndo, or press Ctrl+Z to bring your deleted text back right where it was.

TIP

Oh, eye'm shure the speling's all rite

Just typing and editing your document isn't enough—you need to check your spelling and grammar, and WordPerfect can help. Chapter 9 has the lowdown on using WordPerfect's Speller and Grammar Checker.

CHAPTER 3

Save Your Work (Save Your Sanity)

IN A NUTSHELL

- Name your document
- Update your document
- Turn on the Automatic Backup feature
- Recover your document
- Clear the document screen
- Quit WordPerfect

After you create a work of genius, you have to save it. First, you name *and* save the document. Then, as you work, you just save (update) it. This chapter covers both tasks. You also learn how to clear the document screen *without* saving what you've written. After all, you'll write some things that you just won't want to keep—such as that sonnet about dental floss. Finally, you learn how to get out of WordPerfect.

What "Save" Means (Rescue 911)

If anything can make you hate WordPerfect (as well as computers in general), losing your hard work is it. Imagine that you've been working on a report. You're typing along faster than you ever have before—after all, you need to be finished in 57 minutes. Suddenly, lightning strikes and knocks out the power in your home. What happens to all your hard work?

The fact is, every time the computer is turned off—whether on purpose or by accident—it forgets everything. If there's a power failure or your computer unexpectedly "locks up" (refuses to budge because of some problem with the program), you could very well lose all your typing. You can't keep lightning from striking, so to prevent the loss of hours of work, you need to "save" your document often.

Save means to take the document you've been typing and store a copy of it on your hard disk. You never see your hard disk because it's permanently bolted into the insides of your computer—just think of it as a big filing cabinet inside your computer.

After you save a document, you can retrieve it and come back to your work another time.

BUZZWORDS

DOCUMENT

Unless you are in the legal field, you probably aren't used to referring to pieces of writing as *documents*. You probably wouldn't say, "Jane, get me the Company Picnic Document." In computerese, a *document* is any piece of writing—a poem, memo, letter, report. A document can be of any length—one line, a couple paragraphs or several pages.

Saving Your Document

To ensure that you never have to go through the agony of losing your work and having to retype it, get into the habit of naming your documents very soon after you start working on them. After that, you'll want to update your work after every few paragraphs you type. This is how you name a document:

1. Pull down the **F**ile menu, and then choose Save **A**s.

   As soon as you do this, a dialog box appears in the middle of the screen. The title of the box is Save Document *X* (*X* represents the number of the document you're working on). Your cursor is to the right of `Filename:` and inside a smaller box. You type the document's file name inside this box.

TIP

With the keyboard, you pull down a menu by pressing and holding down first the Alt key and then the bold letter for the menu you want. Because you want to pull down the **F**ile

continues

continued

menu for example, you press Alt+F. After you've pulled down a menu, you choose any of its options by pressing its bold letter. For example, you choose Save **A**s by pressing A.

With the mouse, move the pointer to the menu you want to pull down and click the left mouse button. Then move the pointer to the menu option you want and click again.

2. Type a file name, such as **MYFIRST.DOC**.

   You must follow some strict rules when naming files. You can use only 11 characters: an eight-character "first" name and a three-character "last" name (like "DOC" for a general-purpose document or "LST" for a list). A period separates the two names. You can't use spaces, and you shouldn't use punctuation (except the period). That leaves you with letters and numbers. Take a look at "The Name Game" section for the small print on these rules and regulations.

3. Choose OK or press Enter.

After you save your document, your work appears on-screen again, and you can get back to it. Meanwhile, the name you gave it (and some information about where it's kept) appears in the lower-left corner of your screen, like this:

```
C:\WPDOCS\MYFIRST.DOC
```

Checklist

- You can *change* the name of a document by using the steps for naming a document. When WordPerfect asks you for the name of the document (Step 2 in the preceding steps), type the new name. The new name replaces the old name.
- It's important to make your document names memorable. After a while, you'll have a lot of documents—each with a different name—and it's easy to confuse and forget names. You might want to name a document FRED if you're writing a letter to Fred.
- You can type the name in uppercase or lowercase. When the file name is displayed on-screen and in file lists, it will appear in all uppercase no matter how you type it.
- You might type a name that's already been used. If you do, a box appears, asking whether you want to replace the filename and giving you the options **Y**es and **N**o. This message means that you already have a file by the name you just typed. If you want to replace the file on-screen with the file you've saved previously, choose Y. If you don't or you are not sure, choose N for No; then type in a different name.
- You can press F10—the Save function key—instead of doing Step 1.

Knowing Where Your Files Are Kept (The path less traveled)

`C:\WPDOCS` is called the path. The path is like a road map pointing to where your file is kept. You can use your Little Orphan Annie secret decoder ring and the following items to decipher the message:

Checklist

- C: means the file is on your C drive, which is your hard disk. (If this reads A: or B:, the file is on one of your floppy disks.)

- \WPDOCS is the first directory. A *directory* is similar to a folder in your filing cabinet. You store related documents in one folder. Paths and directories are all part of that cryptic DOS program that everyone loves to hate. You actually can have another directory inside *this* directory, so you might have a path that looks like C:\WPDOCS\LETTERS. The path gives DOS directions so that DOS can find the file. The path essentially says: Start at the C: drive, look in the WPDOCS directory, and then go to the LETTERS directory; there you'll find the file. More about directories later.

The Name Game

DOS imposes some strict rules when it comes to file names. DOS is big on rules. If you don't follow these rules when you name your documents, you'll see an error message or WordPerfect will make up its own name (basically chopping off what won't fit).

Rules to keep in mind when naming documents

- The name can consist of two parts: a "first" name and a "last" name. You use a period to separate the two. In the file name BANANA.SPL, for example, BANANA is the first name, SPL is the last name, and the period separates the two names.

- The first name can have up to eight characters—but doesn't have to use all eight. The last name can have up to three characters, but it doesn't have to use all three. HOTFUDG.SUN is acceptable; CARAMELFUDGE.SUN is not because the first name is too long.

- The file must have the first name, but you don't have to add a last name. PARFAIT is OK.
- Don't use spaces. DILLY BAR won't work. WordPerfect will use only the characters before the space. So if you try this file name, WordPerfect will save the document as DILLY.
- Stick to using letters and numbers in your file names. Except for that period between the first and last name, avoid punctuation. #$!?CHUB won't work.

TIP

Use the file's last name, called the *extension*, to show how files are related. All LTR files might belong to the LETTER clan, for example, and all MMO files might be MEMOS.

Updating Your Document (Save early, save often)

Save your work regularly—every 10 minutes or three paragraphs. The document on-screen will change as you continue to work on it, but the document on-disk reflects only the work you did up to the point of the last save. You still have the potential to lose work unless you save often.

To update a document, pull down the **F**ile menu and choose **S**ave.

TIP

Besides updating your documents every few minutes, make sure that you save whenever you make a difficult or elaborate change that you just don't want to duplicate. Whenever I spend a long time struggling with how to explain a difficult idea and I finally get the wording right, for example, I update right away.

Setting Up Automatic Timed Backup (Better safe than sorry)

WordPerfect has a feature that was designed to make those inevitable disasters—blackouts, computer crashes, and clumsy electricians—a little more bearable. This feature is called Automatic Timed Backup. You tell WordPerfect to make a spare copy (*backup*) of your work every so often. If something ugly happens, you can use the backup.

You have to set WordPerfect to do automatic backups only once, so don't try to memorize the steps or worry about the menu options that pop up. Just follow these steps:

1. Pull down the **F**ile menu, choose Se**t**up, then choose **E**nvironment, **B**ackup Options, and then choose **M**inutes Between Backups. Your screen should look like the one on the next page.

   If your screen looks different, you probably took a wrong turn somewhere. Press Esc until you're back at the document screen, and then try again.

2. To decide how often you want WordPerfect to make a backup of your document, ask yourself this question: What's the greatest amount of work I could bear to lose? Half an hour? Fifteen minutes?

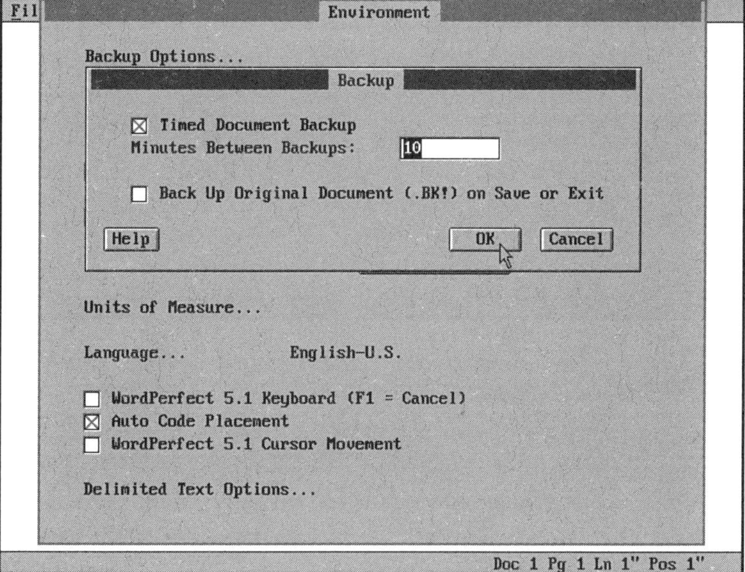

Here's where you tell WordPerfect to make automatic backups of your work.

The default is 10 minutes, which is a pretty good number. Just don't type 1 or 2—having WordPerfect back up your work that often would be more nuisance than it's worth because WordPerfect has to interrupt everything for a moment each time it does the automatic backup.

Type the number of minutes you want between backups, and then press Enter three times to get back to the regular editing screen.

Don't think that this Automatic Timed Backup system means you don't have to save your documents. Automatic Backup only makes copies periodically. If Murphy's Law goes into effect and your power goes off between backups, the backup won't include your most recent work. This work will reflect only the changes made up to the last backup. The bottom line is this: Still save and update your documents!

Disaster Strikes

"It" happens to everyone. You are cheerfully typing along when the unthinkable happens. The power goes out or the computer locks up. *Uh-oh.* I just hope you've been following the advice in this chapter!

Yes! I *Did* Set the Automatic Timed Backup

If you set the Automatic Timed Backup, you should be able to get most of your work back. First, start WordPerfect the way you usually do. Instead of jumping into the familiar editing screen, WordPerfect stays at the startup screen, with a large box giving you a lengthy and convoluted message that means, essentially, "Hey! Something happened last time you used WordPerfect!" At the bottom of this box are three buttons with these options: **R**ename, **D**elete, **O**pen.

Choose **O**pen (by clicking it with your mouse button or by pressing O) to bring the backup into your editing screen. This copy doesn't have a name, so make sure you name it, using the steps earlier in this chapter.

Oh No! I *Didn't* Set the Automatic Timed Backup!

If you didn't set the Automatic Timed Backup feature, you still can get the last version you saved. Chapter 4 fills you in on the fine art of opening a document. And if you didn't save the document, go directly to the start of this chapter. Do not pass Go. Do not collect $200.

Exiting Documents and WordPerfect (Get me outta here!)

You can type only for so long. Then your eyes stop focusing, you use adjectives where you should use adverbs, and your sentences read, "See Spot. See Spot run. See Spot run some more." It's definitely time to work on something else, or better yet, to take a break and go catch up with the Flintstones.

Before you can leave your document or turn off your computer, you need to exit WordPerfect. Remember how you had to master the art of getting into WordPerfect? Well, there's an art to getting out, too. You're going to need to ask yourself a few questions: Do you want to totally escape (exit WordPerfect), or do you just want to leave the current document and work on something else?

I Want Out!

OK. You want out. But you don't get off that easily (nothing's that easy in WordPerfect). You have to decide what to do with the stuff you've typed on-screen. Follow these steps:

1. Pull down the **F**ile menu and choose E**x**it WP. Make sure you choose E**x**it WP, not just **E**xit. This box appears:

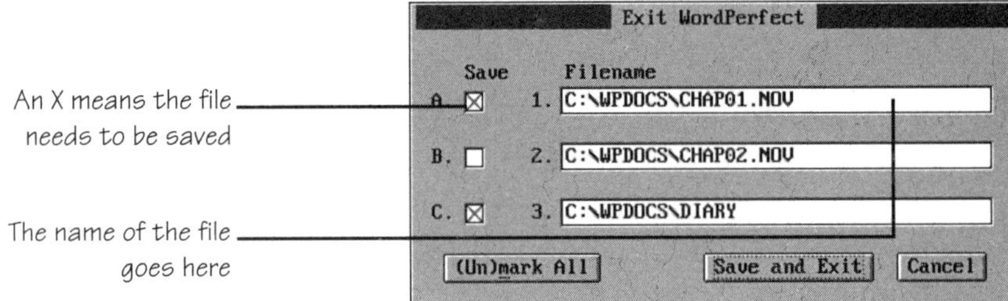

You need to tell WordPerfect whether to save the document. You do that with the Save boxes. Under Save, at the left side of the box, is a letter for the document (an A for the first document, a B for the second, and so on), and then a small square box. If there's an X in the box, changes have been made to the document since you last saved it—or you've never saved it at all (shame on you). Pressing the letter by the brackets makes the X go away if it was there or makes the X appear if it wasn't there.

2. If you don't want to save the document, remove the X. If you do want to save the document, make sure there's an X in the brackets.

3. If you've already named the document, skip to the next step. WordPerfect will save the document when you exit. If you haven't named the document, press the number (usually 1) next to the document, type a name for the document, and press Enter.

4. Press Enter to leave WordPerfect.

EXPERTS ONLY

Lots of documents

You can have more than one document open at a time in WordPerfect. When you want to leave WordPerfect, the Exit WordPerfect box will have a Save column and a Filename column for each document you have open. Make sure you have

an X in the box for each document you want to save as you leave. If you've already named all your documents, WordPerfect automatically puts an X by the documents that have been changed since you last saved them.

Oops! I Changed My Mind

Anytime during the exit's 20-questions process, you can tell WordPerfect that you've changed your mind and don't want to leave after all—just press the Esc key (if you're in the Exit WordPerfect dialog box, you may need to press Esc twice). The questions disappear, the interrogation ends, and you can get back to work.

I Want a Clean Sheet of "Paper"

Suppose that you're not quite ready to quit. You just want a new document on-screen. WordPerfect first makes you contend with the current document on-screen. Here are your choices:

Checklist

▼ **You *don't* want to save the document**
If you write a few sentences and want to give up and start over (rumple up that piece of paper and get a new one), you can clear the document window and start from a new, clean screen. Pull down the File menu, choose Close, then choose No at the `Save Document?` question.

continues

Checklist (continued)

- **You *do* want to save the document**
  If you've been working on a document, haven't saved it yet, and want to start working on something different, you've come to the right place. Pull down the **F**ile menu, choose **C**lose, choose **Y**es at the `Save Document?` question, and then type a file name for your document. Press Enter.

- **You've *already* saved the document**
  No more writer's block. You've finished one document, you're on a roll, and you're ready for the next document. Pull down the **F**ile menu, choose **C**lose. If your document is up-to-date, the document just disappears and you can get to work on your new document. If, on the other hand, you've made changes to the document since you last updated it, WordPerfect asks whether want to save the document—choose **Y**es.

CAUTION

Don't just turn off the computer when you're done typing for the day. It makes starting WordPerfect next time harder. Make sure that you *always* completely exit WordPerfect first.

CHAPTER 4

Opening Your Documents

IN A NUTSHELL

- ▼ See a list of files you've created
- ▼ Display a document on-screen (open it)
- ▼ Preview the document before you open it

When you name and save a document, the computer stores that document in a file on your hard disk. (Many people refer to a *document* as the text on-screen and a *file* as the text stored on disk, but the terms really refer to the same thing.)

When the document is on disk, you can "open" it—display it again on-screen so that you can make changes. This chapter teaches you how to do that.

Displaying Your Documents

Chapter 3 explains how to name and save your documents so that you can work on them again later. To help you find the document you want, you can display a list of documents and then choose one from that list. Here is how you display the list:

1. Pull down the **F**ile menu, and then choose **F**ile Manager.

   A dialog box appears in the middle of the screen. To the right of the word `Directory`, a message like this is highlighted:

   ```
   C:\WPDOCS\*.*
   ```

   This message tells you what set of files you'll be looking at. In this example, you'll be seeing all files that are in the WPDOCS directory.

TIP

To use the mouse to select a menu command, move the mouse pointer to the menu bar, click on the menu you want, then click on the menu option you want. If you like to keep your hands on the keyboard, press and hold down the Alt key, and then press the menu's bold letter. To pull down the **F**ile menu, for example, press Alt+F. Then, to choose an option from the menu, just press that option's bold letter—don't hold down the Alt key while you press the option's letter. For example, after you've pulled down the File menu, you choose **F**ile Manager by pressing F.

As a bonus, you'll notice that some menu options have function key combos listed by them. When you pull down the File menu, for example, right beside the Open option is F5. This means that in the future, if you can remember F5, you can skip using the menus and just press F5 in Step 1 instead.

2. Choose OK or press Enter.

A new box appears, filling the entire screen—the File Manager. There's a lot of stuff in this box, but you can ignore most of it. The important thing about this screen is that it shows a list of names (the documents you've saved) and numbers.

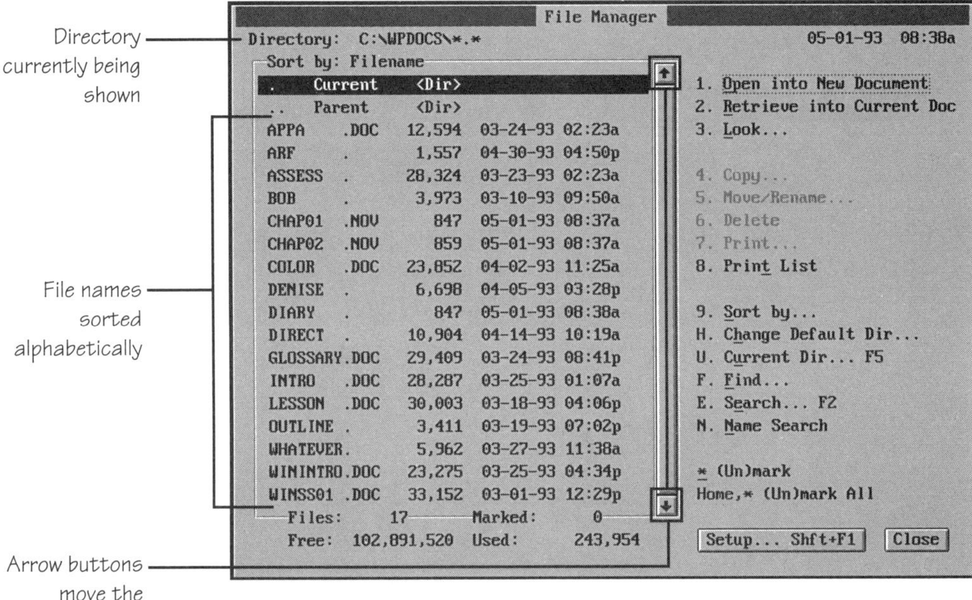

Managing the File Manager

- ▼ The left side of the list has the names of the files themselves. WordPerfect automatically alphabetizes these files.

- ▼ Beside each file name is a number telling you how big the file is. Ignore this number.

- ▼ On the right side of the list is the date and time the files were last worked on. This information can be helpful if you've got two versions of the same document and want to figure out which is the most current. Usually, however, you can just ignore this information.

- ▼ A bar highlights one file at a time. Use this bar to highlight the file you want to open.

- You can move around in File Manager the same way you move in a document. Press the down-arrow key; the bar moves down. Press the up-arrow key; the bar moves up.

- After you've highlighted a file, you can look at it to see whether it's the one you want (see "Using the Look Option"), or you can take a leap of faith and just open the file (see "Opening Documents in WordPerfect").

- After you've used WordPerfect for a while, you'll have more files than can show in the list at once. When that happens, use the arrow keys to scroll up and down in the list. Use the Page Up and Page Down keys to move up or down a whole screenful of files.

TIP

The File Manager can help you avoid some DOS tasks. You can move, copy, print, delete, and much, much more from this screen. In fact, just about everything you've ever had to do in DOS, you can do more easily in File Manager. If you're interested, Chapter 15 is completely dedicated to this magnificent feature.

Opening Documents (Fetch, Fido)

In WordPerfect lingo, *opening* means to bring a document you've worked on previously onto your screen. You *open* a document when you want to work on it again.

To open a document, follow these steps:

1. Pull down the **F**ile menu, and then choose **F**ile Manager.

A box appears, telling you which directory's files you're going to see listed.

2. Choose OK (or press Enter) to go to the File Manager.

See "Displaying Your Documents" earlier in this chapter for the exciting details of what these steps mean.

3. Use your arrow keys to highlight the file you want.

4. Choose **O**pen by clicking on it or pressing the letter O.

The document that you highlighted appears on-screen.

Bunches o' other ways to open the document

When you have the file you want in your sights, there are other cool ways you can open your documents to impress your friends and amaze your coworkers. Try these:

- Mouseketeers can move the pointer to the file you want to open and double-click on it. That is, you quickly click the left mouse button twice.
- Notice that the number 1 is beside **O**pen in the File Manager. You can press 1 (not F1, just the regular 1) to open the document.
- After you highlight the file, just press Enter to open it.

Checklist

- If you're in the File Manager and decide you don't want to open a file after all, press Esc to go back to the document screen.
- After you've opened the document, you can get to work editing it. Remember, however, that you have to save your changes.

EXPERTS ONLY

Confessions of a directory user

WordPerfect automatically goes to a certain directory each time you pull down the **F**ile menu and choose **O**pen, and then OK. If you want to go to a different directory, however, pull down the **F**ile menu, choose **O**pen, and then type a different directory name such as **C:\WPDOCS\LETTERS**. (The "full" name of the document, remember, is the path.) Press Enter when you're finished typing, and the list of files for that directory appears. More on directories later ....

Using the Look Option (Try before you buy)

Suppose that you can't find the file you want just by the name—a real dilemma if you don't use descriptive names. Have no fear. The Look option lets you peek at the file before you open it.

First, highlight the name of the document you *think* you want to work on. Then choose Look by pressing L or 3. The beginning of the document appears on-screen. You can use the arrow keys to move up and down through the document.

When you're finished looking at the file, press Esc to go back to the File Manager.

Checklist

- It's an almost overwhelming temptation to try to edit your document when you see it there in the Look screen. You can't. If you try, nothing will happen.
- If you're in the Look screen and find that you've picked the wrong file name, press N (for **N**ext) to look at the next file or P (for **P**revious) to look at the previous file.
- The top of the Look screen tells you the name of the document you're looking at.
- Look is only good for looking at text files, and it's only really good for looking at WordPerfect files. If you try to look at files made by another word processor, Look throws in some funny codes among the text. If you try to look at a graphics file or a program, Look will show you gobbledygook.
- Look gives you a pretty good idea of what your file contains, but if you're using fancy stuff in your files, like tables, columns, graphics, and fonts, they won't show up in Look.
- Exit the Look option by pressing Esc.

Opening Documents without Using File Manager (Express delivery)

If you know the name of the document you want to open, you don't have to dive into that cluttered File Manager screen; you can open the document from the comfort of your editing screen.

Here's how to open a document when you know its name:

1. Pull down the **F**ile menu, and then choose **O**pen.

   If you'd rather use function keys, press Shift+F10. The Open Document dialog box appears, where you type the name of the document you need.

2. Type the name of the document you want to open, then press Enter.

   The document appears on-screen. When it's on-screen, you can do any number of things: add text, change text, delete text, undelete text, or do the hokey-pokey and turn yourself around.

"I HATE THIS!"

It says File Not Found!

If you type the name of a file that doesn't exist, WordPerfect prompts you with this message:

`File Not Found -- `*`your file name`*

Your screen won't actually show the words *your file name.* Instead, you'll see the name you typed.

If you get this message, choose OK or press Enter to go back to the Open Document dialog box. Try typing the name again, and be sure that you type it correctly. Or press F5, Enter to go into the File Manager.

TIP

Most people who use WordPerfect tend to need the same file a few times in a row. Suppose that you start a report one day, finish it the next day, and want to make some changes to it the following day. WordPerfect remembers the four documents you've worked on for just this purpose. When it's time to open a document, pull down the **F**ile menu and choose **O**pen to bring up the Open Document dialog box. Press your down-arrow key, and lo! A list of the four documents you've used most recently pops down. Use your arrow keys to highlight the document you need, and then press Enter to open it.

EXPERTS ONLY

What if I've put my file in another directory?

If you want to open a document from somewhere other than the current directory, you have to type the path—the route to that document—and the document name at the Open Document dialog box. Suppose that you want to open FUSION.CLD from your C:\SCIENCE\EXPERMNT\MAD directory. You pull down the **F**ile menu, choose **O**pen, type **C:\SCIENCE\EXPERMNT\MAD\FUSION.CLD**, and press Enter.

Drag-and-Drop

The Cut, Copy, and Paste features in WordPerfect are as handy as can be, but they can also be a little bit cumbersome to work with—especially when you just want to move a little bit of text a little distance. First block it, then copy or cut it, then move your cursor, then paste it. It's almost easier to just retype it. WordPerfect's drag-and-drop feature helps eliminate some of those steps. It's great for moving a word, sentence, or paragraph to a different place on-screen. Here's how to use it:

1. Use your mouse to block the text that you want to move.

   If you're not familiar with blocking text by using the mouse, just click your mouse where you want the block to begin. Then, still holding down the mouse button, drag the mouse pointer to where you want the block to end. Your text should be blocked, and you can release the mouse button.

2. Move the mouse pointer so that it's pointing somewhere in the selected text.

3. Click and hold the mouse button, then move the mouse pointer so that it's where you want the blocked text to be.

   When you click the mouse, the mouse pointer changes shape, letting you know that click and drag is in effect.

4. Release the mouse button.

Your blocked text is moved from its old location to the new one.

Checklist

- You also can use drag-and-drop to make a copy of text that you want to use more than once in the document. Follow the preceding steps, but after Step 2, press and hold the Ctrl button. Don't release it until after you release the mouse button in Step 4. The blocked text remains where it was, but there's also a new copy where you release the mouse button.

- If you start dragging text and then decide that you don't want to move it after all, move the mouse pointer so that it's pointing somewhere in the blocked text; then release the mouse button. Your blocked text won't be moved or copied. You can turn Block off by clicking the mouse button somewhere in the screen or by pressing Esc.

continues

Checklist (continued)

- ▼ If you drag-and-drop some text and then decide you don't like it in its new place, pull down the **E**dit menu and choose **U**ndo. The text goes back to where it was before you started.
- ▼ Drag-and-drop is best for moving and copying small amounts of text—no more than a couple of paragraphs—across small distances. If you need to move a bigger chunk of text, use Cut, Copy, and Paste.

CHAPTER 5

Formatting Essentials (Looking Good)

IN A NUTSHELL

- ▼ Center a line
- ▼ Align text to the right margin
- ▼ Insert the current date
- ▼ Indent the first line of a paragraph
- ▼ Indent a whole paragraph
- ▼ Type **bold** text
- ▼ Type underlined text
- ▼ Type *italicized* text
- ▼ Add page numbers
- ▼ Double-space a document
- ▼ Take a peek at hidden codes

You can do hundreds of things in WordPerfect to make documents look good. This chapter focuses on those that you'll use most often. After you master these few tricks, you can easily fake your way to a nice-looking letter or report.

Front and Center

To center a line on a typewriter, you need a doctorate in mathematics: find the center of the page, count the number of characters in the title, divide by two, backspace that many times, cross your fingers, utter a few magic phrases, and type the title.

WordPerfect makes centering much easier. Follow these steps:

1. Move your cursor to the line where you want to type the title. This line should be blank.

2. Pull down the **L**ayout menu and choose **A**lignment.

TIP

> If you're using a mouse, just click on the **L**ayout menu, then click on **A**lignment. If you're using your keyboard, press Alt+L and then C.

3. Another menu, called a *submenu*, pops out.

   Choose **C**enter.

   Your cursor hops over to the center of the screen.

4. Type your title and press Enter.

   The cursor moves back to the left margin.

TIP

WordPerfect's menu is a fine thing, usually. Using the menu means you don't have to fiddle with that multi-colored function key strip that comes with the package. Every once in a while, however, the menu bar takes more effort than it's worth. Centering is one of those times. You can skip Steps 2-4 by just pressing Shift+F6.

Checklist

- If you've already typed your title and want to center it, move the cursor to the line that you want centered, press Home, Home, left-arrow key to go to the beginning of the line. Then press Shift+F6.
- This type of centering is only for single-line titles. If you follow these steps and then you type so much that your cursor jumps down a line, the second line of your title won't be centered.
- Chapter 11 tells you how to center multiple lines—even entire documents.

Aligning Text at the Right Margin

Another alignment choice in WordPerfect is right-alignment. For example, you might like your dates or your return address aligned with the right margin. To align text to the right, pull down the Layout menu, choose **A**lignment, then choose **F**lush Right (or just press Alt+F6). Your cursor jumps to the right side of the page. Now start typing. As you type, the cursor stays at the right side of the screen and text moves to the left. Press Enter and the cursor moves back to the left margin.

Date Stamp

It's always a good idea to put the current date on letters you type. That way, people can grumble at the postal service—instead of you—when it takes them so long to receive their mail. Here's how you add the current date:

1. Move your cursor to a blank line. This should be the line where you want the date to go.
2. Pull down the **T**ools menu, then choose **D**ate to bring up the Date submenu.
3. Choose **T**ext to insert the date.
4. Press Enter to go to the next line.

Checklist

- You can use function keys to insert the date, too. Just move to where you want the date, press Shift+F5, then press T.
- You can use these steps anywhere in a document where you want the current date to appear; the date doesn't have to be on a line by itself.
- You can do some other snazzy things with the Date feature. I'll keep you in suspense about them until Chapter 11.

Indenting Your Text (To tab or indent: that is the question)

When people read your documents, visual cues make reading easier. You may, for example, want to indent the first line of each paragraph to show clearly where the paragraph starts. Or you may want to call attention to a particular paragraph by indenting the whole paragraph.

File Edit View Layout Tools Font Graphics Window Help

New TV Show Ideas

by Howard J. Beighfey

Build A Better You

Use Tab to indent the first line of a paragraph

The American obsession with physical fitness wouldn't be so bad if we didn't have to spend 72 hours per week in the weight room to achieve the perfect body. A qualified panel of biophysicists, biochemists, and other scientists with the "bio" prefix will show you how–using everyday drugstore chemicals–to concoct amazing fitness-giving potions. Sample episodes might include:

Use F4 to indent the whole paragraph

Stir together a few household cleansers and Presto! an enzyme that converts your recently-eaten double cheeseburger with bacon into a fibrous, celery-like substance.

Whip up a chocolate shake containing a special acidic additive, and you've just performed a painless do-it-yourself liposuction. Give yourself a quick shot in the arm with your own home-made steroids, and watch the new you blossom in practically no time at all.

C:\WPDOCS\IDEAS.TV Doc 1 Pg 1 Ln 1" Pos 5.23"

Tabbing

To indent the first line of a paragraph, press Tab and type the paragraph. If you've already typed the paragraph, move the cursor to the beginning of the first line and press Tab. The first line will be indented one-half inch.

EXPERTS ONLY

Magically automatic paragraph indents

If you plan to indent the first line of all the paragraphs in your document, you may want to try a snazzy feature that will automatically do it for you. At the top of the document, follow these steps:

1. Pull down the **L**ayout menu, and then choose **M**argins.

   The Margin Format dialog box appears.

2. Choose **F**irst Line Indent.

   Your cursor appears in a box to the right of First Line Indent.

3. Type how far you want the first line indented, such as **0.5"**, then press Enter.

4. Press Enter to return to the document screen.

Now the first line in all the paragraphs in your document will automatically be indented. This feature is nice when you're typing long reports or other documents. If you're just typing a short letter or memo, it's probably not worth the effort.

Indenting

To indent the entire paragraph, press F4 and then type the text. If you've already typed the text, move the cursor to the beginning of the paragraph and press F4. All lines in the paragraph will be indented one-half inch.

TIP

The Indent (F4) feature is great for making numbered lists. At the beginning of a line, type a list number and period, such as **1.** Then press F4. Type the text for the list item, and then press Enter. Repeat these steps for each item in the list. Your text will be indented to the right of each number.

Adding *Emphasis* to Your Text (Make words scream for attention!)

One of the biggest disappointments of the written word is that you can't use hand and facial gestures. As I write this book, I'm waving my hands about and grimacing and occasionally sticking out my tongue. And you can't see any of it. Pity.

To show emotion in text, you can change the text style (or attribute) to **bold**, underline, and *italic*.

CAUTION

After you know how to use these emphasis tricks, you'll be tempted to use them all the time, and in combination. ***Don't.*** Too much emphasis defeats the purpose and makes your text look hyperactive.

Checklist

- Chapter 8 tells you how to emphasize text you've already typed.
- The next sections tell you how to use keyboard shortcuts to apply the emphasis. All of these text emphasizers are available from the Font menu—just pull down the menu and choose the emphasizer you want. When you're typing up a storm, it's often faster to use the keyboard.

Using Bold (Boldly going where no one has gone before)

Bold is great for titles and headings in your documents. It's not that great for emphasizing words in text. Too much bold makes it seem as though you are screaming, which in some cases might be true. Use italic for words that need emphasis.

To type bold text, first move the cursor to where you want to place the bold text. Then press Ctrl+B (or, if you're in a menuing mood, pull down the F**o**nt menu and choose **B**old).

Next, type the text.

When you're finished typing bold text, press Ctrl+B again. The same key that turns bold on also turns it off. If you want to use menus to turn off bold, pull down the F**o**nt menu and choose **B**old. But, I'm warning you; it's faster the other way.

Underlining Text (Text from down under)

Back when typewriters were the writing tool of choice, underlined text was your only emphasizer option. Most typewriters didn't have italic. Underlining is considered passe; use italic text instead.

But if you <u>must</u> use underlining, move the cursor to where you want to type the underlined text. Press Ctrl+U to turn on underline (or pull down the F**o**nt menu and choose **U**nderline), and then begin typing. Press Ctrl+U again to turn off underline. If you want to use menus to turn off underline, pull down the F**o**nt menu and choose **U**nderline.

Italicizing Text (The elegant emphasis)

One surefire way to improve the look of your documents is to use italic as your main method of emphasizing text. *Italicized text stands out when you read it, without detracting from the overall look of the page.*

TIP

As with any emphasis, don't overuse italic. If you italicize too many words, your documents will be difficult to read.

To use italic text, press Ctrl+I. Type your text. When you're finished typing, press the Ctrl+I again to turn off italic.

Adding Page Numbers

Anytime you type a document that is longer than a couple of pages, you probably should number the pages. Typing the page numbers yourself isn't the answer—they'll get shifted around anytime you edit your document.

Whenever your document needs page numbers, use WordPerfect's Page Numbering feature. You can put the page numbers on the left, center, or right side of the page, and you can choose to put the page number on the top or bottom of the page. And if that's not enough, you can alternate sides on even and odd pages.

Here's how you tell WordPerfect to number the pages for you:

1. Press Home, Home, up-arrow key to move the cursor to the beginning of the document.

The cursor must be in the first page for the page numbering to begin on the first page. That seems reasonable, doesn't it?

2. Pull down the **L**ayout menu and choose **P**age.

The Page Format dialog box appears.

3. Choose Page **N**umbering.

TIP

When you're in a dialog box, you can choose options by pressing the bold letter. For example, you choose Page **N**umbering by pressing N. If, on the other hand, you care to show off your prowess with the mouse, you can click anywhere on `Page Numbering` to get the same effect.

4. Choose Page Number **P**osition.

Another dialog box appears. Will this madness never end?

A list of possible locations for your page numbers appears in the left side of the box. On the right, a series of three "boxes" appear. They show you the various places that page numbers can appear on the page.

5. Press one of the numbers, 1 through 9 (or click any of the options in the left side of the list).

For example, if you want your page numbers to appear in the bottom center of each page, press 6. If you want page numbers to appear in the outside corner of alternate pages, like they do in books, press 4 (for the top corner) or 8 (for the bottom corner).

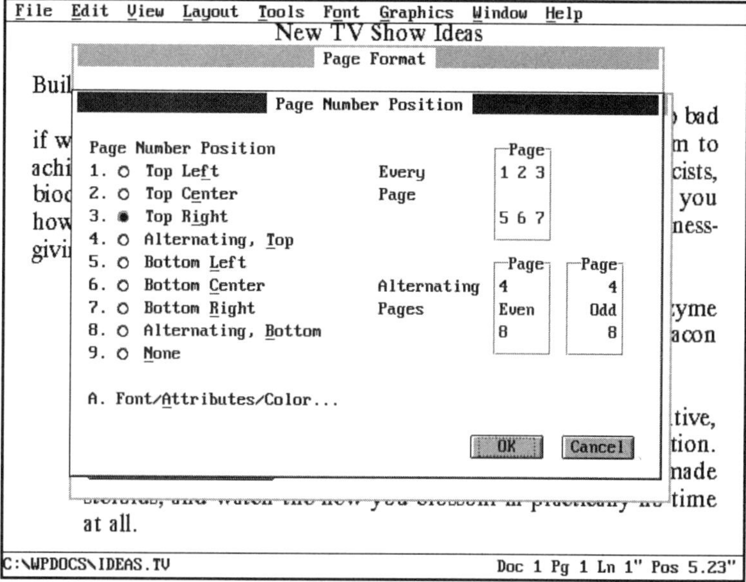

The Page Number Position dialog box.

TIP

Notice that when you choose one of the options in the list, a small black circle appears beside that option. This is to let you know that WordPerfect understands what you've done. You can still choose a different option, but only one item on the list can be selected at a time. If you choose a different option, the old one will be cleared.

6. Choose OK or press Enter.

This brings you go back to a dialog box that reads `Page Numbering`.

7. Choose OK twice (or press Enter twice) to go back to the document screen or press Home, F7.

Checklist

- The page numbers don't appear in your on-screen document, but they will appear when you print the document. You can see them if you preview the document, which is covered in the next chapter.
- The **L**ayout menu is the gateway to a plethora of features. So many, in fact, that Part IV of this book talks of little else.
- If want the current page number somewhere in your document text, just press Ctrl+P where you want the current page number to appear. Your page number appears on-screen.

Page numbering etiquette

Some writing styles say that the first page of letters and other documents shouldn't have a page number—instead, page numbering should start on the second page. If that's the way you work, follow these steps:

1. Go to the top of the document by pressing Home, Home, up-arrow key.
2. Pull down the **L**ayout menu, then choose **P**age.
3. Choose S**u**ppress, choose P**a**ge Numbering, and then choose OK (or press Enter).
4. Press Home, F7.

Changing Your Line Spacing

Sometimes you need double-spaced documents; sometimes you need 1 1/2 spacing. Changing line spacing isn't really all that hard. Here's how you do it:

1. Move the cursor to the place where you want the new line spacing to take effect.

2. Pull down the **L**ayout menu, and then choose **L**ine.

   The Line Format dialog box appears.

3. Choose Line **S**pacing.

   Your cursor is in a box about midway down in the dialog box. The number highlighted by your cursor indicates the line spacing in effect right now. You don't have to delete this number; it will disappear when you type a new one.

4. Type a number for the line spacing you want; then press Enter.

   For example, if you want double spacing, type **2**; if you want 1 1/2 spacing, type **1.5**. Remember to press Enter after you've typed the number.

5. Choose OK or press Enter to return to your document.

   This new line spacing is in effect from here to the end of the document—or to the next place you change line spacing.

You can have several line spacing changes in a single document, but it looks terrible. Your documents will look more consistent and professional if the line spacing does not change several times throughout.

Line spacing is the perfect feature to use if you need to subtly alter the length of your document. If you're supposed to have a three-page paper and it only goes for 2 1/2 pages, go to the top of the document and change your line spacing to `1.3`, instead of `1`. The extra space between lines gets an instant half page for you. You can make long-winded documents appear shorter in the same way—just decrease the line spacing.

Reveal Codes (WordPerfect's sinister underworld)

Each time you make a formatting change, WordPerfect inserts a special code into your document. Most of the time, you don't even have to know the codes are there. But if your formatting starts to go haywire, you may need to travel to the Underworld where these hidden codes dwell.

To display the hidden codes, pull down the View menu, then choose Reveal Codes (or press F11 or Alt+F3).

The screen splits, and you see two versions of your document: the regular, normal document and the hidden, secretive codes that lurk below. Quickly press F11 or Alt+F3 again to turn off Reveal Codes.

Don't worry about Reveal Codes now. Chapter 12 helps you travel through this world to troubleshoot any formatting problems.

BUZZWORDS

REVEAL CODES

Reveal Codes are the hidden codes that WordPerfect inserts into your document for formatting changes. The codes can be singular (such as `[Tab]`) or can come in a set (such as `[Bold On]` and `[Bold Off]`). Usually you can guess from the name of the code what the code does.

CHAPTER 6

Printing Basics

(Getting It Down on Paper)

IN A NUTSHELL

- Use Print Preview
- Print the entire document
- Print the current page

You've really got to use your imagination when you're typing in WordPerfect. You can't see your page numbers or how the text will look on the page. You don't know for sure how the document will look on paper ... until you see it on paper.

This chapter explains how to get a sneak preview of the document by displaying a close approximation of how it will look when printed. You also learn how to print a document.

Using Print Preview (Coming soon to a printer near you)

When you're typing a document, it's difficult to tell how the final document will look. To really see the document—with all its special enhancements—you have to print it. Then you've got to make corrections, print it again, make more corrections, print it again, scream in frustration, print it again, develop an ulcer, print it again.

You can save a lot of time, frustration, and trees by using the Print Preview feature. It gives you a good idea of how your document is going to look when it comes out of the printer, and it's much faster than printing your file.

I'm not quite telling the truth when I say you can't see the margins and so forth while you edit. You can, but only if you're willing to put up with WordPerfect being quite a bit slower. WordPerfect has a Page Mode that lets you see everything on the screen pretty much as it will print.

If you really want to see everything as it will print, pull down the **V**iew menu, and then choose P**a**ge Mode. You'll be able to see all items the way they will print—page numbers, margins, everything. The trouble is that this feature reduces the speed of even the mightiest computers to a snail-on-Valium pace. You can return to the Graphics mode by pulling down the **V**iew menu and choosing **G**raphics.

To preview a page, move the cursor to the page you want to preview. Pull down the **F**ile menu, then choose Print Preview.

Depending on the speed of your computer, you may have to wait anywhere from 1 to 20 seconds for Print Preview to come on. (Be patient—this is serious magic at work.) Then, looking like a Polaroid snapshot of your page, up comes a preview of your document!

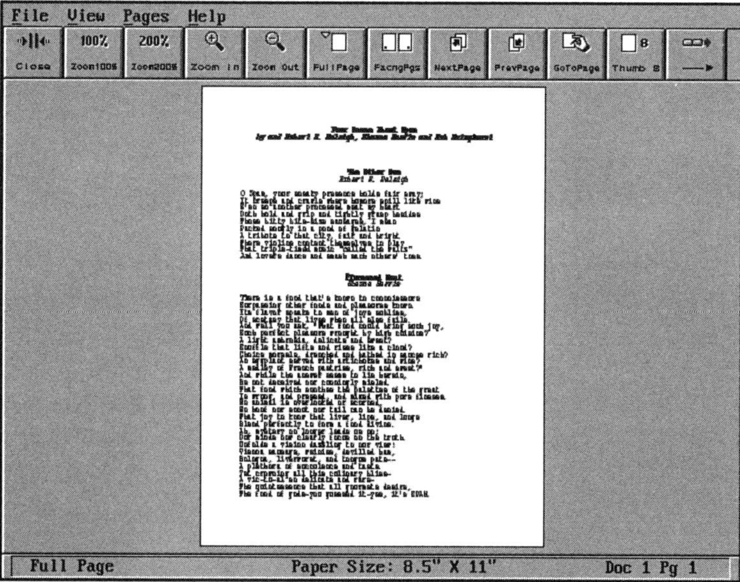

Pull down the **F**ile menu and choose Print Pre**v**iew to see a preview of how your page will look on paper.

Look at the Print Preview screen. Do you see any changes that you need to make to the document—center the footer, add the date, tighten up that seven-line title? When you're finished previewing the page, pull down the **F**ile menu, and then choose **C**lose (or, if you have the rare talent of being able to remember which function key does what, press F7) to go back to the document screen.

Preview fun

- At the top of the Print Preview screen, you'll notice a strip of buttons called the Button Bar. If you have a mouse, you can perform the tasks in this list quickly by clicking with the mouse on the correct button; the buttons are shown in the margin.

- If the full-page view is too dinky for you to see details of your document, pull down the **V**iew menu and choose **1**00% to change the view to 100%. You won't be able to see the whole page at a time, but you can see different parts of the page by pressing Home, and then the up- or down-arrow key.

- If you want to enlarge the view, pull down the **V**iew menu and choose **2**00%.

- If you want to see the whole page again, pull down the **V**iew menu and choose **F**ull Page.

- Press the Page Up key to view the previous page; press the Page Down key to go to the next page.

- If you want to jump to a certain page, press Ctrl+Home, type the page number you want (such as **15**), and press Enter.

- But wait, there's more! WordPerfect's Print Preview can do a lot of things that I just don't feel like writing about right now. To learn about all the gee-whiz things you can see in Print Preview, see Chapter 14.

Nothing happens!

Suppose that you're at a document screen, you try to preview, and nothing happens or you get a baffling error message. Any number of things could have caused the problem. You probably have a screen (monitor) that won't work with this feature. My advice is to call WordPerfect Customer Support (toll-free) at 1-800/541-5096 and tell them you can't get Print Preview to work. They'll be able to help you.

Print the Entire Document (I can't believe I printed the whole thing!)

It's a great feeling to be finished with a document and ready to print. One of the few times people truly appreciate computers is when they see the results of their work on paper. But getting to that point isn't as easy as it sounds.

Turning On the Printer

Before you print your document, make certain that your printer is turned on and ready to print. There are more than a thousand different types of printers, so there's no one set way to turn on a printer. Try flipping the biggest switch you can find on the printer. If something lights up, the printer is probably on. If nothing happens, be sure that the printer is plugged in. Or try a different switch.

You also might need to put the printer *on-line* (ready to go). Look for an On-Line button. If it's lit, you're probably OK. If it's not, try pressing it. If there isn't one, you probably don't need to put the printer on-line.

If you can't get the printer on and on-line, put on your best pathetic face and ask some computer-savvy friend to help you.

Printing the Document

Next, open the document you want to print (if it's not on-screen already). Chapter 4 covers the delicacies of opening a document. After the document is on-screen, you're set to go. Pull down the **F**ile menu, then choose **P**rint—or, if you're a function key fanatic, just press Shift+F7. With the Print dialog box on-screen, choose **F**ull Document, then choose P**r**int.

Cross your fingers. With any luck, your document begins printing.

"I HATE THIS!"

My printer won't print!

There is a veritable cornucopia of reasons why your document may not print. Sometimes it's the computer's fault, sometimes it's the printer's fault, sometimes it's the fault of the cable that connects the two, sometimes it's the fault of WordPerfect, and sometimes it's the fault of Congress. Solving printing problems is one of the hardest things you can do in WordPerfect, and I suggest you try to get somebody else—the local WordPerfect guru or a WordPerfect Customer Service Rep—to go through the grief. If you haven't done so yet, now might be a good time to make friends with a nearby computer guru.

After you follow these steps, WordPerfect goes back to the document screen and you're free to get back to work. You can continue typing, editing, whatever. WordPerfect will continue to print. In fact, there's no reason for the document to even be on-screen anymore. You can go ahead and clear it; WordPerfect will print it just the same.

If you do try to work while WordPerfect is printing, don't use Print Preview. For some reason, WordPerfect can't print and use Print Preview at the same time (it's the WordPerfect equivalent of trying to pat your head and rub your stomach at the same time). If you do go into Print Preview while you're trying to print a document, WordPerfect will wait until you come back out before it finishes the print job.

Don't exit WordPerfect or turn off the computer until all your print jobs are finished printing. Although you can keep working while a document is printing, the document will not continue printing if you exit WordPerfect or turn off your computer.

Print the Current Page (One at a time, please)

You might want to print a single page—not the whole document. To print a single page from the document you're working on, first make sure that your printer's ready to go. Then:

1. Move the cursor to anywhere on the page you want to print.

Use your Page Up and Page Down keys to move quickly from page to page.

2. Pull down the **F**ile menu, and then choose **P**rint.

3. Choose **P**age.

4. Choose P**r**int.

WordPerfect starts printing the page and takes you back to the document screen, where you can get back to work—or get back to your nap, whichever you prefer.

CHAPTER 7

Help Me!

IN A NUTSHELL

- Look up a topic
- Get help on the feature you're using now
- Let WordPerfect guide you through a task
- Go to WordPerfect school

With a program like WordPerfect, you need all the help you can get. After all, it has exactly 9.3 bazillion features in it. Not to mention the well-known fact that between menus, mice, function keys, and shortcut keys, there are so many ways to get to any feature that it's statistically impossible to remember any of them.

But wait a minute before you break down into helpless sobs. After all, you've got this book, which helps you safely ignore most of those features and strange access methods. In addition, WordPerfect gives you the Help feature, which is designed to answer your questions while you use WordPerfect. You can get an overview of the feature you're currently using, look up how to accomplish certain tasks, and even have WordPerfect give you an interactive lesson. This chapter shows you how.

Look It Up

If you know the name of the feature you need help with, WordPerfect can give you the steps for using it. Just follow these steps:

1. Pull down the **H**elp menu, then choose **I**ndex.

   A mile-long list of topics appears. The information you need is almost certainly in there, if you dare to look it up.

2. Choose **N**ame Search, and then begin typing the name of the feature or topic you want help with.

   As you go, WordPerfect highlights the closest item to what you've typed so far. After you've typed the first few letters of the topic, you should be able to see whether it's in the list. If it is, you can use your up-and down-arrow keys to highlight it.

As soon as you press an arrow key, WordPerfect leaves Name Search and you're on your own to finish highlighting the topic you want. But, you can always go back into Name Search mode by choosing **N**ame Search again.

3. After you've got the topic you want highlighted, choose **L**ook to read WordPerfect's information on it.

   If you're still in Name Search mode when your topic is highlighted, you'll need to press Enter before the **L**ook button appears.

   The Help text for your topic appears.

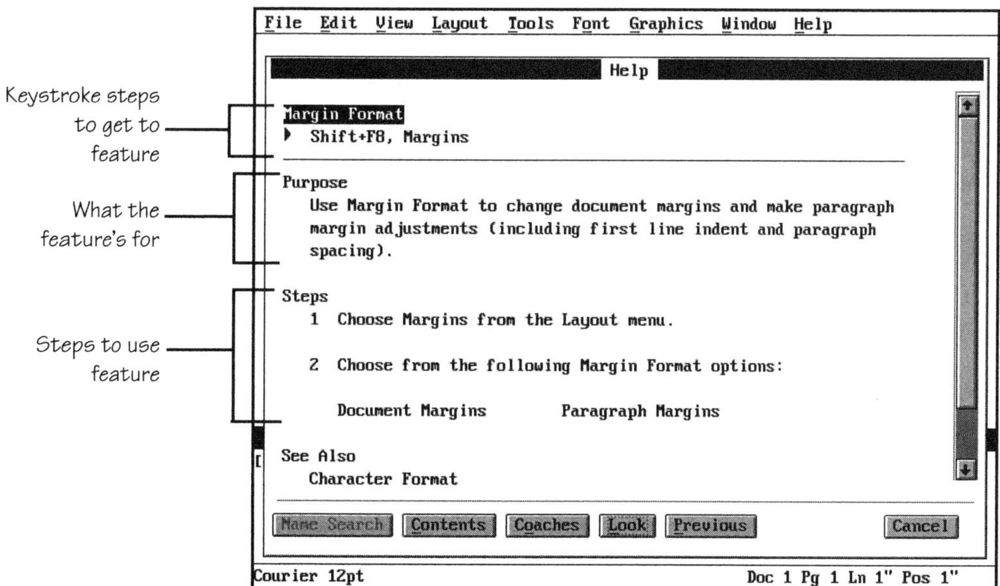

Help using help

- There's probably more to the help topic than will fit on your screen. Use your down-arrow key to scroll through more of the text.
- When you're finished looking at the help text, press Esc to leave the Help system.
- If you want to look up something else, choose **P**revious. This takes you back to the index and you can go through the whole thing again.

I can't find what I need!

With such a huge index of topics, you'd think that every possible thing you'd ever need help on would be listed. *Wrong.* In fact, it sometimes seems that WordPerfect has cleverly anticipated what you'd try to look up then indexed everything *except* that. Try thinking of another way to look up the same task. Or try looking things up in this book instead.

Anywhere, Anytime

You never know when a WordPerfect dilemma may rear its ugly head. It could be while you're changing your line spacing or deciding where your page numbers should go. With a single keystroke, you can get help on the feature you're using: Just press F1. A box appears with instructions on how to use the feature you're using. Press Esc when you're finished with the Help box and want to return to the task you were working on.

Checklist

- There's probably more to the help topic than will fit on your screen. Use your down-arrow key to scroll through more of the text.
- You'll notice that some of the words in the help text are bold. You can double-click these terms with your mouse (or use your arrow keys to highlight the topic, and then press Enter) to get information on that topic. When you're done, press Esc to leave Help or choose **P**revious to go back to the Help topic you were looking at before.
- Some terms in Help are underlined. If you highlight one of these terms and choose **L**ook, a definition pops up. Choose OK to return to the Help screen when you're finished reading the definition.

Hey, Coach!

There are a few things that everybody needs to do once in a while, like making bulleted lists, making outlines, and using bold and italic. WordPerfect's Coach feature guides you, step-by-step, through these tasks. To get WordPerfect to coach you through something, follow these steps:

1. Pull down the **H**elp menu, and then choose C**o**aches.

   A list of tasks appears—these are the things WordPerfect can coach you through. Use your arrow keys to scroll through the list.

2. Highlight one of the items in the list, and then choose Select.

If you're using a mouse, you can just double-click the item instead.

The coach asks you questions about what you want to do, and then guides you through doing it.

"I HATE THIS!"

No coach!

There's a limited number of Coach topics—you may not find what you're looking for. If you can't find the topic you want, choose Cancel to leave the Coaches dialog box.

A Quick Trip to WordPerfect U

If you're feeling extra-ambitious someday, you might want to go through some of the interactive tutorials that come with WordPerfect. They take you through some of the same features that you learned in the first part of this book and may help you get a better handle on how WordPerfect works. Follow these steps to get a few hands-on lessons from Professor WordPerfect:

1. Pull down the **H**elp menu, and then choose **T**utorial.

   The WordPerfect 6.0 Tutorial dialog box appears.

2. Choose OK.

   The program asks whether you'll be using a mouse.

3. Choose **Y**es if you want to practice using your mouse during the tutorial, or choose **N**o if you want to work on your keyboard skills.

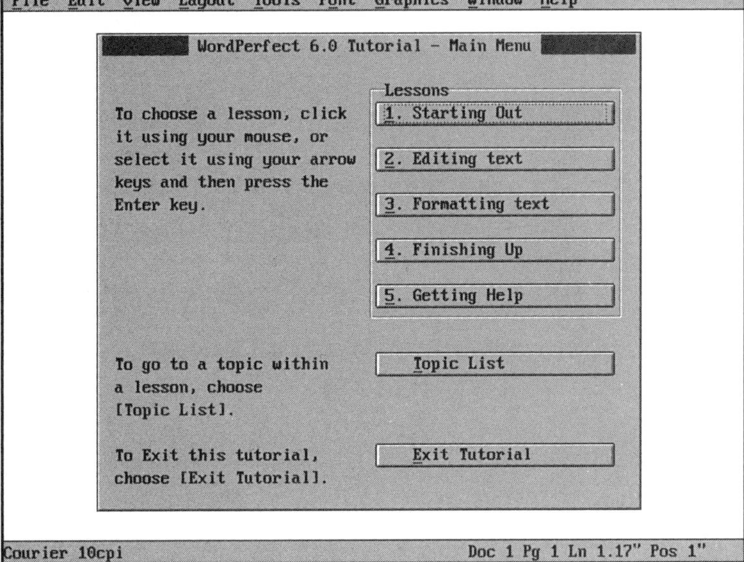

The WordPerfect Tutorial helps you bone up on your editing, formatting, and document-saving skills.

4. Choose one of the lessons, and follow WordPerfect's instructions.

Checklist

- ▼ There are five lessons, and you can start with whichever one you want—you don't have to do them in order.
- ▼ If you get tired of the lesson, you can leave anytime by choosing the Exit button. If you do this, a box appears containing two options: **R**eturn to Lesson and **G**o to Main Menu. To leave the lesson, choose **G**o to Main Menu, and then choose **E**xit Tutorial. You can't exit by pressing Esc.

PART II

The On-Line Editorial Assistant

Includes:

8: The Moving, Removing, and Other Handling (of Big Chunks of Your Document)

9: Using WordPerfect's Dictionary, Thesaurus, and Grammar Checker (Getting It Right)

10: Finding and Replacing Text (The WordPerfect Swap Meet)

CHAPTER 8

The Moving, Removing, and Other Handling (of Big Chunks of Your Document)

IN A NUTSHELL

- Highlight text
- Highlight a sentence, paragraph, or page
- Delete highlighted text
- Move highlighted text
- Make copies of highlighted text
- Save highlighted text in file
- Print highlighted text
- Make highlighted text bold, underlined, or italic
- Alphabetize highlighted text

If you've ever drawn a circle around a paragraph and then made an arrow from the circle to where the paragraph should go, you al ready understand the idea behind WordPerfect's Block feature.

The idea behind WordPerfect's Block feature is to highlight a chunk of text and then do something with it. This chapter shows you the ways you can highlight a block of text, and then it shows you what you can do with the block.

Blocking Text (The electronic highlighter)

Blocking refers to highlighting (selecting) a chunk (block) of text—a word, line, paragraph, whatever. After you highlight the block, you can do just about anything with it: make it bold, move it to a different page, and much, much more!

You can use one of two methods to block text: the arrow keys or the mouse.

Block Text by Using the Arrow Keys

First, move the cursor to where you want to begin the block. The cursor should be at the left of the first letter you want in the block. Pull down the Edit menu, and then choose Block. WordPerfect lets you know that Block is on by showing the following at the bottom-left corner of the screen:

```
Block On
```

Use the arrow keys to move the cursor after the last character you want in the block. As you move the cursor, everything between the starting point of your block and your current position is highlighted.

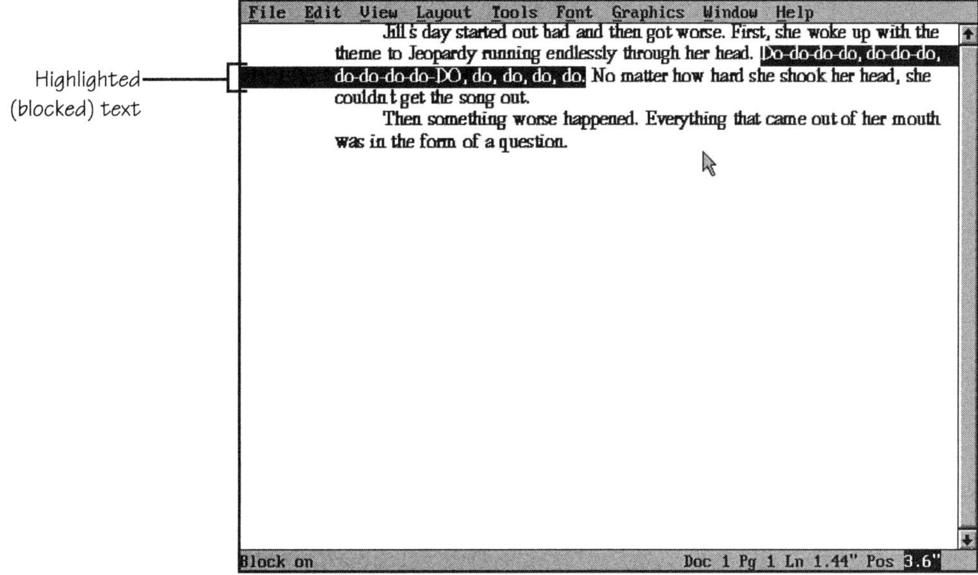

Checklist

- If you've got a section of text blocked and then decide you don't want to block text after all, press Esc to turn off Block.
- Besides using your arrow keys, you can use the other cursor-movement keys to highlight text. After Block is on, for example, you can block to the end of the document by pressing Home, Home, down-arrow key. You also can use other cursor-movement keys, such as Page Up and Page Down.
- You also can press Alt+F4 or F12 to turn on Block.

TIP

When you turn on Block, you're automatically in Instant Search mode. That means that WordPerfect will jump to the next character you press. You can use this tip to highlight text quickly.

First, move your cursor to where you want the block to begin. Press F12 or Alt+F4 to turn on Block. Then press the character you want the block to jump to. If you want to jump to the end of the sentence, for example, you could press the period (.). WordPerfect would move the cursor *after* the next period it finds. If you want to block the next two sentences, press the period twice (..).

Block Text by Using the Mouse

Even if you don't like it for most things, you should try blocking text with the mouse—it's what the mouse was born for. Use the mouse to move the mouse *pointer* (a little arrow that doesn't appear until you move the mouse) on-screen so that it's directly over the first character you want in the block.

Press and hold the left mouse button. While holding down the mouse button, move the mouse so that the pointer is where you want the end of the block.

As you move the mouse, text is highlighted. If you move the mouse pointer so that it's at the bottom of the screen, text scrolls up. When the text is highlighted, release the mouse button.

Block Sentences, Paragraphs, and Pages—Fast!

You'll commonly need to block sentences, paragraphs, and pages. WordPerfect makes it a quick matter to block them.

Move your cursor so that it's anywhere in the sentence, paragraph, or page you want blocked. Pull down the **E**dit menu and choose **S**elect.

A list of options appears in the **S**elect submenu. Choose **S**entence, **P**aragraph, or **P**age, depending on how much you want blocked.

Everything from the beginning of the sentence to the beginning of the next sentence is blocked. The same thing goes for paragraphs and pages.

Deleting a Block of Text

If you don't like something you've written, you don't have to scribble through it. Instead, block the text to be annihilated. Then press Backspace. Poof—there's a small puff of smoke, and the block is gone.

Checklist

- If you decide you didn't want to delete the text after all, pull down the **E**dit menu, and then choose **U**ndo (or just press Ctrl+Z if you'd rather use the keyboard).
- Deleting a block of text also can be used as a tricky way to move your information. Just delete the block of text you want to move, and then move your cursor to where you want to insert the text. Press Esc, and then R to place the text in its new home. WordPerfect remembers only the three most-recent deletions, so make sure that you restore the deleted text right away.

Moving Text

As you write documents, you'll probably notice from time to time that a certain sentence would make more sense a couple of paragraphs later, or your introduction works better as a conclusion. And hey, wouldn't point C be clearer if it came between points A and B?

WordPerfect lets you freely move blocks of text. Here's how:

1. Highlight the text you want to move.

2. Pull down the **E**dit menu, and then choose Cu**t**.

   The block of text disappears. This is called *cutting* because you snipped a chunk of text right out of your document—just as if you had used scissors. That text is now silently lurking in the dark recesses of your computer's memory, waiting for you to need it again.

3. Move the cursor to where you want to insert the block of text.

4. Pull down the **E**dit menu, and then choose **P**aste.

   The block of text is pasted in its new place.

Checklist

- WordPerfect holds your text in its memory until you cut another block of text or exit WordPerfect. Make sure that you paste (put) the text into a new position in the document before you exit WordPerfect. If you don't, the text will be gone forever.

- After you've cut text, you can paste it any number of times into as many places as you like. To paste text again, just pull down the **E**dit menu and choose **P**aste.

- ▼ You may need to go to the beginning or end of the pasted text and put in some spaces or hard returns (which you make by pressing Enter) to make it look right.

- ▼ You'll find you use these editing tools all the time, so you should take the time to learn the shortcut keys: press Ctrl+X to cut and press Ctrl+V to paste.

Copy Cat Text

Suppose that you want to use the same text more than once. You want the original to stay where it is, but you want to use that same block of text again somewhere else. That's called *copying and pasting*, and this is how you do it:

1. Block the text you want to copy.

2. Pull down the **E**dit menu, and then choose **C**opy.

   The highlighting disappears, but a copy of the block is safely tucked away in WordPerfect's memory.

3. Move the cursor to where you want to place a copy of your block of text.

4. Pull down the **E**dit menu, and then choose **P**aste.

   The copy of your block appears.

Checklist

- WordPerfect holds your text in its memory until you copy or cut another block of text or exit WordPerfect. Make sure that you paste (put) the text into a new position in the document before you exit WordPerfect. If you don't, the text will be gone forever.
- After you've copied text, you can paste it any number of times into as many places as you like. To paste text again, pull down the **E**dit menu, and then choose **P**aste.
- You may need to go to the beginning or end of the pasted text and put in some spaces or hard returns (which you make by pressing Enter) to make it look right.
- If you plan to do a lot of copying, it's a good idea to know the shortcut keystroke, so you don't always have to use the menus. To copy blocked text, press Ctrl+C. To paste the text, press Ctrl+V.

Saving Text You Use All the Time

Chances are, you often say the same stuff again and again in a document—particularly in letters. You can save part of a document and then insert that part in another document. For example, you might get tired of typing the following:

> **We are sorry that your Roy Orbison wig caught fire. We thought we had thoroughly tested the wig's flammability. Please accept our sincere apologies and this coupon for $5 off our Liberace wig.**

You can save this block of text and use it again and again. It's a two-step process: save the text in a new file, and then insert the text.

Saving the Text

To save the text, block the part of the document you want to save as its own file. Then pull down the **F**ile menu and choose Save **A**s. You see the Save Block dialog box in the center of the screen.

Type a name for the document (the block); then choose OK. Make sure that you follow the rules for document names—eight letters or fewer, with an optional period and three more letters. No spaces. (Take a look at the section The Name Game in Chapter 2 for more details about naming files.)

After the block of text has been saved, the text is no longer highlighted.

Inserting the Saved Text

To put that saved block of text into another document, move the cursor to where you want the block. Pull down the **F**ile menu and choose **R**etrieve to bring up the Retrieve Document dialog box. In the box, type the name you gave the block, and then choose OK.

Print a Block of Text (Prints Charming)

If you've just written a couple of paragraphs and want a chance to take an old-fashioned red pen to them, you don't have to print the whole document. You can print just the part you need. Make sure that your printer is turned on and ready to print. Guess what you do next. Did you guess that you have to block the part of the document you want to print?

Congratulations. You're getting the hang of it.

After you block the text, pull down the File menu, and then choose Print. The Print dialog box appears. If you look very carefully, you'll notice that the Blocked Text option is selected.

Choose Print. The block prints—right in the same position as it would if you had printed the whole page. Headers, page numbers, and other gadgets like that are printed, too.

Adding Oomph to Blocked Text

If you want to make a section of text really stand out, make it bold, italic, or underlined.

First, block the text that you want to emphasize. Then do one of the following:

- Press Ctrl+B to make the blocked text **bold**.
- Press Ctrl+U to underline it.
- Press Ctrl+I to make it *italic*.

The text takes on the appearance that you applied, and Block is turned off.

Alphabetizing Text

Alphabetizing text is a sort of quasi-block function. It will come in handy when you need to sort something like a list of names. First, block the list of names. Next, pull down the Tools menu and choose Sort. A funky box appears at the bottom of the screen. This is the Sort dialog box, the complexity of which has driven many people completely mad. Avert your eyes and choose **P**erform Action quickly—or if you can't find the **P**erform Action button in all this mess, just press Enter, which will do the same thing. The list is sorted by the first word in each line.

Sorting out sort guidelines

- Each list item should be only one line long. This kind of alphabetizing doesn't work with list items that take two or more lines.
- Each item should end with a hard return (press Enter).
- Don't block any part of the document that isn't part of the list. If there's an introduction before the actual listing of the names, for example, that introduction shouldn't be included.
- If your list looks mangled after WordPerfect tries to sort it, all is not lost. Pull down the **E**dit menu and choose **U**ndo to restore the list to the way it was before you tried sorting it.

Shoe®
BY JEFF MACNELLY
THIS BEEPING PILE OF PLASTIC JUST AIN'T A TYPEWRITER.

WHERE'S THE DING?

IN THE GOOD OLD DAYS OF NEWSPAPERING YOUR TRUSTY TYPEWRITER WOULD HELP YOU EXPRESS YOURSELF...
EDITOR

YOU COULD POUND THE KEYS HARDER WHEN YOU WERE MAD...

AND PLAY THAT UNDERWOOD LIKE A PIANO WHEN YOU FELT POETIC.

MOST IMPORTANT, THOUGH, WAS THE WAY YOU COULD BLOW OFF STEAM WHEN YOU MADE A MISTAKE...
TAPPA... TAPPA... TAPPA... PATTA....

YOU COULD RIP OUT THE PAPER, CRUMPLE IT UP AND HEAVE IT ACROSS THE NEWSROOM.
ZIP!

SOMEHOW IT MADE YOU FEEL A LOT BETTER WHEN YOU DID THAT...

BUT TODAY, WITH THESE WORD PROCESSORS AND COMPUTERS,... WELL, IT JUST AIN'T THE SAME...
10/9

BUT IT'S STILL PRETTY SATISFYING.
EDITOR
MACNELLY
© Jefferson Communications, Inc. 1983
Distributed by Tribune Company Syndicate, Inc.

CHAPTER 9

Using WordPerfect's Dictionary, Thesaurus, and Grammar Checker

(Getting It Right)

IN A NUTSHELL

- ▼ Check the spelling in your document
- ▼ Check the spelling in a single page
- ▼ Check the spelling in a block
- ▼ Look up a word's spelling
- ▼ Add new words to WordPerfect's dictionary
- ▼ Find synonyms for words
- ▼ Find antonyms for words
- ▼ Use Grammatik to check your grammar

It's incredibly tempting to start this chapter with a crack about the various possible spellings of *potato*. But I'm not going to. *Most* of us are lousy spellers. And the few of us who are gifted with spelling make typos anyway. It comes down to this: we all make spelling mistakes.

WordPerfect can be a real lifesaver when it comes to checking your work for spelling errors. WordPerfect can look through your document and flag any possible mistakes; then, it lets you decide how to correct them. You also can polish your writing by finding *precisely* the word you need with WordPerfect's thesaurus and using Grammatik to wade through your document and point out various writing mistakes you've made.

"I HATE THIS!"

The work of a proofreader is never finished.

Don't let WordPerfect take the place of a careful proofreader. WordPerfect can check only your spelling—it can't tell whether you're using words correctly. You could spell check a document that says, "Their, they're now deer. Don't you cry." WordPerfect would think that sentence is just dandy. After you finish checking your spelling, read through your document again and look for words that are used in the wrong way.

Revving Up the Speller

Before you can check your document's spelling, the document must be on-screen. The position of the cursor doesn't matter. Then follow these steps:

1. Pull down the **T**ools menu, and then choose **W**riting Tools.

A little bite-sized dialog box pops out with five options. For right now, the only one that matters to you is Speller.

2. Choose **S**peller.

The Speller dialog box appears with a whole slew of options. Luckily, WordPerfect has considerately anticipated what you need to do by highlighting the option you need.

TIP

If you want to get to the Speller in a hurry, just press Ctrl+F2.

3. Choose **D**ocument.

A box appears in the middle of your screen, telling you that WordPerfect is checking your document. You may see a little train of dots chugging along in this box to keep you entertained while WordPerfect looks for mistakes. (Or you may not, depending on how fast WordPerfect finds a mistake.)

When WordPerfect finds an error—or a word that it *thinks* is an error—that word is highlighted in the top half of the screen, and a giant dialog box fills the bottom half of your screen. The top half of the screen still shows your document, but the bottom half is reserved for suggestions the Speller will make while it's checking your document. Your screen looks like this:

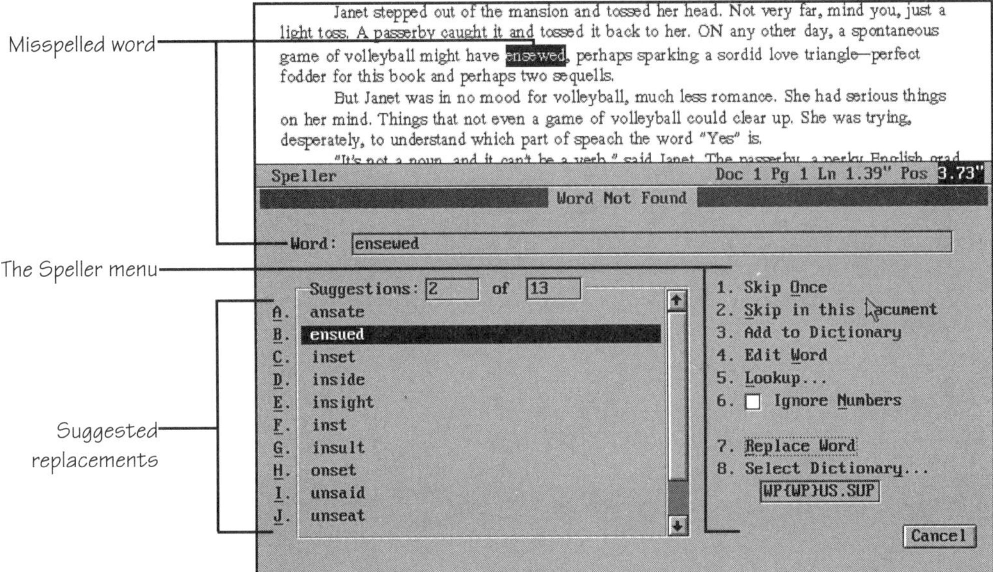

After you make a correction, WordPerfect moves to the next misspelling.

Checklist

- If you just want to check the spelling for one page, move your cursor to the page you want to check, press Ctrl+F2, and then choose **P**age.
- You also can check from where your cursor is to the end of the document. Just move your cursor to where you want to begin checking, press Ctrl+F2, and then choose **F**rom Cursor.

Correcting Mistakes

You have lots of choices about how to handle a word that WordPerfect flags:

Checklist

- If the correct spelling is in the Suggestions list box, highlight the correct spelling and choose **R**eplace Word (or press Enter). If you prefer, you can use your mouse to double-click on the correct spelling instead.

- The Suggestions list box can show only 10 suggested spellings at a time, and WordPerfect might have more in mind. If you don't see the correct spelling right away, try scrolling down through the list to look at other suggestions.

- WordPerfect doesn't know every word in the world. When it comes across a word it doesn't know—like a name or a specialized term you use—WordPerfect highlights the word and assumes that it's spelled wrong. If you plan to use that word frequently, you can add it to WordPerfect's dictionary by choosing Add to Dictionary. From now on, WordPerfect will know the word and won't flag it as being misspelled.

- If WordPerfect stops on a word it shouldn't, but you don't want to add the word to the dictionary, choose Skip in this Document. WordPerfect will ignore the word from now on whenever you check this document—but it will still flag the word in *other* documents. You also can have WordPerfect skip the word just once by pressing 1, but I can't think of any reasons you would want to do that.

continues

Checklist (continued)

- If WordPerfect stops on a misspelled word but none of its suggestions are what you want, choose Edit **W**ord. Your cursor jumps up to the misspelled word and you can fix the mistake yourself. When you're done, press F7 or Enter to tell WordPerfect to start checking again.
- WordPerfect thinks any word with a number in it is wrong. If you use words that contain numbers, choose the Ignore **N**umbers check box to turn off number checking.

Double Double Words

If you have the same word twice in a row (such as "up up and away!"), WordPerfect counts that as a problem, too. The second of the two words is highlighted and the Duplicate Word Found dialog box appears. You can skip past the double word by choosing **S**kip Duplicate Word. You can get rid of one of the occurrences of the word by choosing **D**elete Duplicate Word. If you want to tidy things up yourself, choose **E**dit Word, do your editing, and press F7 to get back to checking your spelling. If you want WordPerfect to ignore double words, choose Disable Duplicate Word **C**hecking (but I wouldn't do that if I were you).

wRONG cASE

WordPerfect also checks to see whether you've gone a little crazy with your Shift key. If you've got unusual capitalization in a word, such as the first two letters being capitalized, WordPerfect brings up the Irregular Case dialog box.

Choosing **S**kip Word makes WordPerfect skip past the word. If you want to change the word to more ordinary capitalization, highlight the way you want the word to look in the Suggestions list box and choose **R**eplace Word. If you choose **E**dit Word, the cursor goes to the word and lets you fix things yourself. Press F7 when you're ready to continue with spelling checking. Choose **D**isable Case Checking if you want WordPerfect to stop looking for unusual capitalization.

Stop the Speller

If you decide to stop checking your spelling before WordPerfect is finished, choose Cancel or press Esc. A prompt appears, telling you the spell check is completed. Choose OK to make the prompt disappear.

The Spell Check Is Finished

After WordPerfect has finished, it shows a prompt telling you so. Choose OK to make the prompt go away.

Things To Hate about the Speller

WordPerfect's speller isn't perfect. Here are a couple things it won't do:

Checklist

- WordPerfect's "dictionary" is really nothing more than a long list of words. If you want a definition of a word, you're going to have to get out the old-fashioned paper dictionary and look up the word.

continues

Checklist (continued)

▼ WordPerfect is not a proofreader. When WordPerfect checks your spelling, it looks only for correctly spelled words. It has no way of telling whether you used the words in the right way. If you write "pane" where you should write "pain," WordPerfect won't see a problem because the word is spelled correctly. So, use WordPerfect to check you're spelling, but make sure you *reed* your document carefully *two* make sure it makes *cents*.

TIP

WordPerfect comes with Grammatik, which is designed to check your grammar. You can learn how to use this program at the end of the chapter.

Spelling Check Shortcuts

You don't have to check the entire document. If you checked a document before and have just added a paragraph, you can check just that paragraph. Or you might want to check just one word.

To check a block of text, press F12 or Alt+F4; then move your cursor to where you want the spelling check to end. The section you want to check should be highlighted. Press Ctrl+F2 to start the Speller. WordPerfect checks only the block.

To check just one word, move the cursor so that it's on the word you want to check, press Ctrl+F2 to start the Speller, and then choose **W**ord. If you got the word right, WordPerfect doesn't do anything but move the cursor to the next word and bring the Speller dialog box back up. If you got the word wrong, WordPerfect highlights the word and shows some suggestions. Make the change, and then choose Close to leave the Speller.

Looking Up a Word

There are certain words people just cannot remember how to spell. *Definitely* is *definately* one of them. If you need to write a word that you just don't know how to spell, you can look it up. Here's how:

1. If you've already typed the word, move your cursor so that it's anywhere in that word. Otherwise, move your cursor so that it's where you want to put the word you want to look up.

2. Press Ctrl+F2.

   The Speller dialog box appears.

3. Choose **L**ook up Word.

   The Look Up Word dialog box appears with your cursor in a text box at the bottom of the screen. If your cursor was in the middle of a word when you started, that word is highlighted.

4. Type your best guess for the word; then press Enter.

   But how are you supposed to try to type a word you don't know how to spell? Just take a wild guess. WordPerfect will then take a couple of guesses at what it thinks you meant to type.

TIP

If your best guess for the word is already in the box, you don't have to type it again in Step 4—just press Enter.

5. Scroll through the list until you've highlighted the word with the correct spelling, and then press Enter.

If you decide you just want out without choosing any of the words, choose Cancel to return to the Speller dialog box, and then choose Close.

Checklist

- **If your cursor was in a word when you began**
  That word is now highlighted and WordPerfect asks whether you want to replace it with the word you've chosen from the list. Choose **Y**es if you want to put this new word in place of the old one or **N**o if you don't. If you choose **N**o, WordPerfect will ask whether you want to insert the word into text. Choose **Y**es to put the word in your document at the cursor or **N**o if you don't need the word in your document right now.

- **If your cursor wasn't in a word when you began**
  WordPerfect asks whether you want to insert the word you chose into the document. Choose **Y**es if you want the word at your cursor or **N**o if you were just looking up the word for future reference.

- When you're done looking up words, just press Esc until you're back at the document screen. Depending on where in the Speller's Lookup feature you are, you may need to press Esc once or twice.

TIP

If you really have no idea how part of the word is spelled, just put an asterisk (*) in place of that part. The asterisk means "I'm not sure how this chunk of the word is spelled." Suppose that you need to use the word *hematophagous* (and I hope you never do) but don't have a clue what comes between the *hem* and the *us*. Just press Ctrl+F2, L; type **hem*us**; and press Enter. Among several other very obscure words, *hematophagous* shows up.

Cheating at crossword puzzles

Yes, you can use WordPerfect's spelling checker to cheat at crossword puzzles. If you know how long the word should be and know at least a couple of its letters, you can probably get WordPerfect to figure out the rest.

To use the "Cheat-At-A-Crossword-Puzzle" feature, press Ctrl+F2, and then choose **L**ook Up Word. Type the word you need, using a question mark for every letter you don't know. For instance, if you need a nine-letter word for indigestion and you know "d" is the first letter, "e" is the fifth and "i" is the eighth, you would type ***d???e??i?***. This is called a word *pattern*.

After you type the pattern, press Enter. WordPerfect lists all the words it knows that fit in the pattern you've set—including *dyspepsia*. If there are more words that fit the pattern than will fit on-screen, you can press Enter to see another screenful of words.

When you're done, you're ready to cheat at another word by choosing **W**ord or Word Pattern and typing a new pattern in the text box, or you can go back to your document by pressing Esc three times.

Finding the Right Word

If you've ever stared blankly at your computer for ten minutes, wishing you could come up with the perfect word, WordPerfect's Thesaurus may be just the brainstorming tool you need. The Thesaurus gives you a list

of *synonyms* (words that have the same—or at least similar—meaning) for a selected word. This same feature also lists *antonyms*, words with the opposite meaning as what you pick.

To find a synonym or antonym for a word in your document, move the cursor so that it's touching the word you want to check. Pull down the **T**ools menu, choose **W**riting Tools, and then choose **T**hesaurus to start the Thesaurus feature.

A box with three columns appears at the bottom of the screen. The word you're looking up is highlighted at the top of the screen, and a series of synonyms and antonyms appears in the first column. After the synonyms comes a separator line; then any antonyms are listed. There will probably be more synonyms and antonyms than will fit on the screen, so you can scroll through the column for more words.

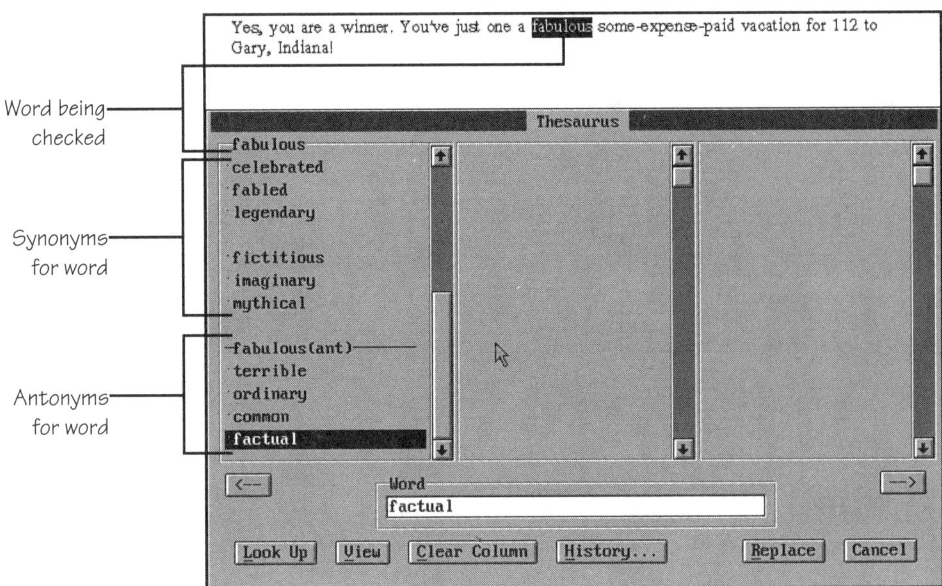

"I HATE THIS!"

What's a synonym for 'moronic'?

WordPerfect doesn't know synonyms or antonyms for every word. If it doesn't have any suggestions, WordPerfect will bring up a `Word not found` message. Choose OK to make the prompt disappear and WordPerfect gives you a chance to look up a different word. You can press Esc to turn off the Thesaurus or look up a different word by typing a word and pressing Enter.

Replacing the Word

If you see a word you like better in the replacement list, highlight the word, and then choose **R**eplace.

Press the letter corresponding to the word you want. The Thesaurus box disappears and you can get back to writing.

To leave the Thesaurus without picking any words, choose Cancel.

CAUTION

Don't take WordPerfect's word for it! If WordPerfect says a word is a synonym for a word you're looking up, but you're not very familiar with the word, look it up in the dictionary. Make sure that it means what you need it to mean.

Looking Up Synonyms of the Synonyms

You can look up synonyms—and antonyms—of the words that are in the Thesaurus columns. Use your mouse or arrow keys to highlight a word you're interested in, and then press Enter or double-click on the

word. A column containing synonyms and antonyms for the word appears to the right of the column.

Checklist

- ▼ If a word doesn't have a dot by it, don't bother trying to look it up; WordPerfect doesn't have any synonyms or antonyms for it.
- ▼ If you fill up all three columns, you can still look up synonyms. The old columns of synonyms just move off to the left. You can review the old columns by moving the highlight bar to the leftmost column and continuing to press the left-arrow key. Your old columns of words will come back onto the screen.
- ▼ If you don't need a column of words, move the highlight bar to the column and choose Clear Column.
- ▼ If you want to look up a word that isn't in your text, pull down the Tools menu, choose Writing Tools, choose Thesaurus, choose Look Up, type the word you want to check for synonyms, and then press Enter.

Fixin' Yer Grammer

Grammatik is a tool that comes with WordPerfect and can point out grammar problems your documents have. You can then go through your document and use the suggestions or skip them. To check your document's grammar, follow these steps.

1. Save your document.

This isn't absolutely necessary, but it's a good idea because the grammar checker is going to put a *lot* of remarks in your document, and it's nice to be able to have a copy of your work *before* those remarks are inserted.

2. Pull down the Tools menu, and then choose Writing Tools to make the Writing Tools dialog box appear.

3. Choose Grammatik.

Don't be too concerned that you're about to use a grammar checker that can't even spell "grammatical" correctly.

A different screen appears, telling you you're using Grammatik 5.

4. Pull down the Checking menu, and then choose Mark.

Grammatik starts checking your document, counting mistakes as it goes. The grammar checker doesn't work like the spell checker; instead, it marks all the mistakes it finds at once.

After Grammatik is done, it returns to the screen you saw earlier.

5. Choose Quit Grammatik.

This brings you back to your document screen, with grammar suggestions all over the place. The suggestions are in all uppercase, enclosed in a strange combination of dashes and parentheses:

```
¦--(THIS, FOR INSTANCE, IS WHAT A GRAMMATIK REMARK LOOKS LIKE)--¦
```

Checklist

- When you're back at the document screen, read Grammatik's suggestions, and then make the changes you want to the document, in the same way you would edit any document.
- Remember that Grammatik is much more picky than human readers; you don't have to do *everything* the grammar checker suggests. In fact, if you make some of the changes, your writing will start to look incredibly stilted.
- After you're finished looking over the changes Grammatik suggests, pull down the **T**ools menu, choose **W**riting Tools, and then choose **G**rammatik to bring up the grammar checker. From the Grammatik screen, pull down the **C**hecking menu, and then choose **U**nmark. It takes Grammatik just a moment to take out its remarks, and then it tells you it's finished. Press Esc to make the box go away, and then press **Q** to go back to the WordPerfect editing screen.

CAUTION

As you're making changes to your document, don't delete the markers at the beginning and end of the Grammatik comments:

¦--(LIKE THE ONES AROUND THIS PHRASE)--¦.

If you do, you might lose some of your document when you have Grammatik remove its comments.

CHAPTER 10

Finding and Replacing Text (The WordPerfect Swap Meet)

IN A NUTSHELL

- Find a word
- Find formatting "codes"
- Replace one word or phrase with another—one at a time
- Replace one word or phrase with another in one fell swoop

Suppose that you are at the end of a long chapter in your novel and you can't remember the fate of Aunt Matilda. Something happened to mean, old Aunt Matilda somewhere in the chapter, but you can't remember where or what. Did they find the dead man in her cellar and give her the electric chair? Or did she escape on motorcycle?

WordPerfects Search feature can help with these types of dilemmas. Rather than read through the entire chapter, you can use the Search feature to look for specific text—such as *Matilda*—in your documents.

WordPerfect's companion feature, Replace, is another great editing tool. Suppose that your real Aunt Matilda calls and says that on second thought, she *is* going to include you in her will. You better change all references from mean, old Aunt Matilda to mean, old Aunt Helga. You can do so with Replace.

Searching for Text (Where, oh, where has my little text gone?)

Use Search whenever you need to find a certain word or phrase. The search begins from your cursor and stops when it finds the text you need. You can search backward or forward through the document.

Here's how you search for specific text:

1. Move the cursor to wherever you want to begin the search.

   Remember that you can search in either of two directions: from the cursor toward the beginning of the document or from the cursor to the end of the document.

TIP

If you want to search through all the text in the document, press Home, Home, up-arrow key before you begin the search. This moves the cursor to the top of the document.

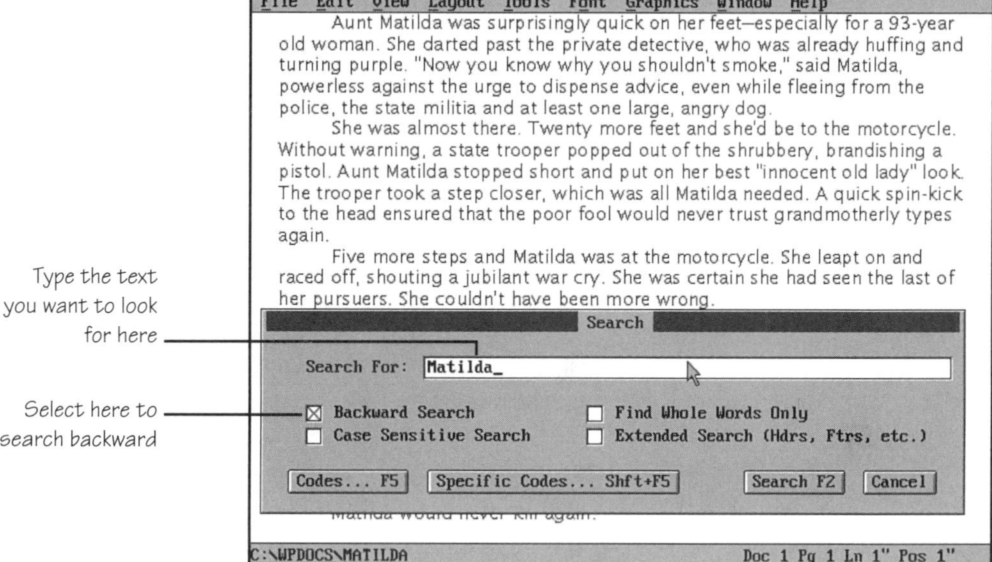

2. Pull down the **E**dit menu, and then choose Searc**h**.

3. Type the word or phrase you want WordPerfect to find.

4. Choose Search to make WordPerfect look for the text.

- You also can display the Search dialog box by pressing F2.

- If you want to search from the cursor toward the top of the document, you need to choose the Backward Search check box so that it has an X in it. You can make WordPerfect automatically have this check box selected when the Search dialog box appears by pressing Shift+F2 to bring up the dialog box.

- Sometimes you may want to find "car" but not "card," "streetcar," or "reincarnate." Ordinarily, if you search for "car" WordPerfect will stop at any of these, because they all have "car" in them somewhere. You can make WordPerfect ignore things like this by choosing the Find Whole Words Only check box.

- If WordPerfect can't find the text you want, a `Not Found` box appears on your screen. Choose OK to make the prompt go away. If you get a `Not Found` message and you're sure that the text is there, try again. Make sure that you're typing exactly what you're looking for. Don't add any extra spaces or punctuation at the end of the word. If you still get a `Not Found` message, try searching in the other direction.

- If you press F2 or Shift+F2 and text from a previous search appears, just type the new text. The old text will disappear.

- You can change the direction of the search even after you've started typing the text you want to search for. Just press the up-arrow key if you want to search from the cursor up through the document, or press the down-arrow key if you want to search down through the document.

- If you press F2 or Shift+F2, and then decide you don't want to search for anything after all, press F1 to go back to the document screen.

▼ If the text you want to find is in a header, footer, footnote, or endnote, this process won't find it unless you choose the Extended Search check box. Get all the details in the following Experts Only sidebar.

TIP

After you find the text you're looking for, you may want to look for the *following* appearance in the document. Press F2, F2. If you want to find the *preceding* occurrence, press Shift+F2, F2.

EXPERTS ONLY

The case of a sensitive search

When WordPerfect searches for text, it usually matches the text you type to both lowercase and uppercase letters. So, whether you type **nacho**, **Nacho**, **NACHO**, or **NaChO** as your search text, WordPerfect would think *nacho, Nacho, NACHO,* or anything in between is a match and would stop.

If you want WordPerfect to find a match only when the text in the document *exactly* matches your search text, right down to how you capitalize the text, choose the Case Sensitive Search check box. For example, if you choose the Case Sensitive Search check box and type **Frijole** for your search text, WordPerfect will count *Frijole* as a match, but not *frijole, FRIJOLE,* or anything else.

EXPERTS ONLY

What if the text is in some strange place like a header?

When you do a normal search, WordPerfect hunts through the regular text only. It doesn't look at headers, footers, foot-notes, and endnotes. If you want to include these text

continues

continued

elements in your search, plus all the regular text, you need to do what WordPerfect calls an *extended search*. To do an extended search, choose the Extended Search check box in the Search dialog box.

If the text you want is in a header, footer, or some other fancy part of the program, WordPerfect will take you right to it. This means that when the search is done, you'll be sitting who-knows-where. After you've done what you need to do, press F7 until you get back to the document screen.

Searching for Formatting Codes

You also can search for WordPerfect *formatting codes*, which are the things that make your text look the way it does. (The wacky world of formatting is covered in Part III of this book.)

For example, if you want to search for the next place that bold formatting occurs, pull down the **E**dit menu, and then choose Searc**h** to bring up the Search dialog box. Now choose the Codes button (or press F5) to bring up the list of codes.

Scroll through the list until you find **Bold On**. Highlight it, choose Select, and `[Bold On]` appears in the Search For text box. You can search for other formatting things, like Tabs, Enters (called `HRt` in this list, which stands for Hard Return), line spacing changes, and so forth. Just scroll through the codes list, highlight the code you want to search for, and choose Select. When you're ready to begin the search, choose Search.

Using the Replace Feature (Pulling the ole switcharoo)

Say that a while back you wrote a letter about toxic waste to President Bush. (You're against it.) You were so pleased with the results (a printed form letter thanking you for your concern) that you want to send the same letter to President Clinton. Do you have to retype the letter?

Not with WordPerfect's Replace feature. The Replace feature is perfect for making wholesale changes to your documents. You can use it to change every instance of a word or phrase into another, or you can pick and choose.

TIP

You should start by replacing text one incident at a time. That way, you can be sure that the search is going as planned. You don't want to turn a search and replace into a search-and-destroy mission.

1. Move the cursor to where you want to begin replacing text.

   You will generally want to begin at the top of the document; you can move there by pressing Home, Home, up-arrow key.

2. Pull down the **E**dit menu, and then choose Replace to bring up the Replace dialog box.

3. Type the text you want to replace; then press Tab to move your cursor into the Replace With text box.

   For your letter, you would type **bush**, which is the text that needs to be replaced.

File Edit View Layout Tools Font Graphics Window Help

Aunt Matilda was surprisingly quick on her feet—especially for a 93-year old woman. She darted past the private detective, who was already huffing and turning purple. "Now you know why you shouldn't smoke," said Matilda, powerless against the urge to dispense advice, even while fleeing from the police, the state militia and at least one large, angry dog.

She was almost there. Twenty more feet and she'd be to the motorcycle. Without warning, a state trooper popped out of the shrubbery, brandishing a pistol. Aunt Matilda stopped short and put on her best "innocent old lady" look. The trooper took a step closer, which was all Matilda needed. A quick spin-kick to the head ensured that the poor fool would never trust grandmotherly types again.

Search and Replace

Search For: Matilda

Replace With: Helga

[X] Confirm Replacement
[ ] Backward Search
[ ] Case Sensitive Search
[ ] Find Whole Words Only
[ ] Extended Search (Hdrs, Ftrs, etc.)
[ ] Limit Number of Matches:

Codes... F5 | Specific Codes... Shft+F5 | Replace F2 | Cancel

C:\WPDOCS\MATILDA Doc 1 Pg 1 Ln 1" Pos 1"

Type what you want to look for

Type what you want to replace it with

Choose this to have WordPerfect ask each time before it replaces

4. Type the replacement text.

For the letter, type **clinton**. That's the text you want to insert in place of the text in Step 3.

5. Choose Replace.

WordPerfect zooms through your document, making your changes. When it's done, it tells you how many times the text was found and replaced. Choose OK to make this message go away.

Checklist

- Sometimes it's not such a hot idea to replace *every* instance of your text. If you want to pick and choose, read "Replacing One by One," later in this chapter.

- If you look at your document after the Search and Replace is done and notice that something went horribly wrong (you just replaced all occurrences of the letter "t" with the letter "m" in an important report), you can return the document to how it was before the Search and Replace by pulling down the **E**dit menu and choosing **U**ndo.

- The Replace feature is terrific for cleaning up irregular capitalization in documents. For example, if you sometimes forget to capitalize *American*, you can fix the problem in one pass. For the search text, type the word you forget to capitalize, leaving the whole thing in lowercase (**american**). For the replacement text, type the word with its correct capitalization (**American**).

- Your documents will look their best if you have only one space at the end of each sentence. (Two spaces at the end of each sentence went out with the typewriter.) You can get rid of those habitual extra spaces by using the Replace feature. For the search text, press the space bar twice. For the replacement text, press the space bar once.

- If the text you want to replace is in a funky place (header, footer, footnote, endnote), press Home, Alt+F2 in Step 2. WordPerfect will then include this text in the search.

- You can use the Replace feature to remove all occurrences of a word or phrase and replace the word or phrase with nothing. Just make sure there's no text in the Replace With text box before you choose Replace.

- If you want to replace text in a certain part of your document, move the cursor to the beginning of that part, press Alt+F4, and then move the cursor to the end of the section. After the section is selected (*blocked*), use Replace as you normally would. Only text in the block will be replaced. (Chapter 8 tells you all about the Block feature.)

- You can have the Search and Replace start from your cursor and work toward the beginning of the document if you like. Just choose the Backward Search check box before choosing Replace.
- WordPerfect usually searches and replaces only in the main part of your document. If you want WordPerfect to be more thorough and look through headers, footers, endnotes, and other dusty corners of WordPerfect, choose the Extended Search check box.
- Sometimes you may want to find "car" but not "card," "streetcar," or "reincarnate." Ordinarily, if you search for "car" WordPerfect will stop at any of these, since they all have "car" in them somewhere. You can make WordPerfect ignore things like this by choosing the Find Whole Words Only check box.
- If you wonder what the Case Sensitive Search check box is for, you should read "The case of a sensitive search" sidebar, earlier in this chapter.

Replacing One by One

You might not want WordPerfect to go hog-wild and automatically replace every occurrence of a word or phrase with another. Suppose that in your letter to the president you include this sentence:

> I'm tired of being relegated to the bush leagues.

If you did a blanket Search and Replace, WordPerfect would change this sentence to

> I'm tired of being relegated to the clinton leagues.

When you want WordPerfect to ask you each time before it replaces text, follow the same steps as in the previous set of instructions, but make sure you choose the Confirm Replacement check box before you choose the Replace button in Step 5. When the Search and Replace begins, WordPerfect stops each time it finds the text you're replacing and brings up a box asking:

```
Replace Match Number X?
```

Choose **Y**es if you want to change the old text to your replacement text. Choose **N**o if you want to skip this one. If you get tired of answering each time and are pretty sure you want to replace the rest without having WordPerfect ask you, choose **R**eplace All.

If you get partially through the Replace process and decide you want to stop, choose Cancel. A message box appears, telling you how many occurrences were found and replaced. Choose OK to get rid of the box. Remember, however, that the replacements that have already been made will remain changed. You can change them back by pulling down the **E**dit menu and then choosing **U**ndo.

PART III

The Pretty Stuff

Includes:

CHAPTER 11

WordPerfect Formatting Features You'll Use Every Day

IN A NUTSHELL

- Use Tab to indent the first line of a paragraph
- Indent the first line of paragraphs *automatically*
- Indent a paragraph
- Center text
- Align text along the right margin
- Add emphasis to your text by making it bold, underlined, or italic
- Choose exotic, exciting new fonts
- Change the margins
- Add page numbers
- Change the line spacing
- Put today's date in the document
- Put an automatically updating date in the document

Wow. What a list of topics. Think of this part of the book as a menu of *formatting changes*. (This chapter contains the chef's selections.) Browse through the formatting changes you can make, and pick and choose what works for you. Some sections have a lot of steps. Don't let that intimidate you. This chapter is essentially a set of formatting recipes; you can just follow along.

Using Tabs and Indents

To make a document more readable, tabs show where one paragraph starts and the next begins. You can do this with the Tab key, or WordPerfect can do it automatically for you. To call attention to a particular paragraph, use the Indent feature.

Tabbing

When you want the first line in a paragraph to start a bit further to the right than the rest of the paragraph, just press Tab. Then type the paragraph. If you've already typed the paragraph, just move the cursor to the beginning of the paragraph and press Tab.

Checklist

- If you want the first line indented even more, press Tab twice—or as many times as you want.
- Don't press Tab at the beginning of each line when you want an indented paragraph. That's what the Indent feature is for.
- By default, each time you press Tab, your cursor moves 1/2 inch. You can change this distance; read "Changing Your Tab Stops" in Chapter 12.

Automatic Tabbing

If you plan to have a tab at the beginning of each paragraph throughout your entire document, WordPerfect can put them in for you. That way, all you have to do at the end of each paragraph is press Enter, and WordPerfect automatically indents the first line of your paragraph. Follow these steps:

1. Move your cursor to the top of the document by pressing Home, Home, up-arrow key.

   You do this because the auto-indent feature applies only from where your cursor is when you turn on auto-indent. If you *want* the auto-indent feature to begin somewhere else in the document, move your cursor to that point.

2. Pull down the **L**ayout menu, and then choose **M**argins.

   The Margin Format dialog box appears. The part you're interested in right now is toward the bottom of the box and looks like this:

   ```
   7. First Line Indent:     0"
   ```

3. Choose **F**irst Line Indent.

   Your cursor moves into the text box. Here's where you type how far you want the first line of each paragraph to be indented.

4. Type the amount of space (in inches) you want the first line of each paragraph to be indented, and then choose OK.

Because the standard tab distance in WordPerfect is 1/2 inch, you may want to type **0.5**. One-quarter of an inch also looks good, so you may want to use **0.25**. It's up to you. After you choose OK, the dialog box disappears. From this point on in the document, the first line in each of your paragraphs will be automatically indented.

You can use this technique on documents that already exist, too. Just follow the steps—existing paragraphs will automatically have their first line indented.

Indent a Paragraph

It's always impressive to quote an expert when you need to give your opinion some backing:

> *Dr. Spock agrees that you should not swing a toddler around by his ankles after he has eaten an entire bag of Iced Animal Cookies.*

When a quote is more than three lines long, it belongs in a paragraph of its own. The entire paragraph should be indented to set it apart from regular text.

To indent a paragraph, move the cursor to where the paragraph will begin. (If you've already typed the paragraph, move the cursor to the beginning of it.) Pull down the **L**ayout menu, choose **A**lignment, and then choose **I**ndent to make the whole paragraph jump one-half inch to the right. Or, if you want to indent the faster-but-harder-to-remember way, just press F4.

Use the Indent feature to make lists. At the beginning of a line, type a list number and a period, such as **1.** or **2.** Or, if you prefer bullets (•), press Ctrl+2, and then press the asterisk key (*) twice to make a bullet. Next, pull down the **L**ayout menu, choose **A**lignment, and then choose **I**ndent to start indenting. Type the text for the list item; then press Enter twice. Repeat these steps for each item in the list. Your numbers or bullets appear in a column to the left of the indented text—just like in the lists in this book.

Checklist

- If you want to indent further to the right, follow the steps for indenting more than once. You can get a good idea of where the left side of the paragraph will be by looking at the Pos measurement in the status line.
- You can indent both the left and right sides of a paragraph. Pull down the **L**ayout menu, choose **A**lignment, and then choose I**n**dent.

For Bibliographies Only

Once in a while, you may want to indent everything but the first line of a paragraph. This is called a *hanging indent* and is useful for bibliographies.

To make a hanging indent, move the cursor to the beginning of the paragraph, pull down the **L**ayout menu, choose **A**lignment, and then choose **H**anging Indent. The first line of your paragraph won't be indented, but every other line in the paragraph will be. Here's how it will look:

> Spock, Dr. "The Dangers of the Swinging Toddlers and Iced Animal Cookies." *Pediatric Care*, no. 7 (July 1988): 12-63.

TIP

If you want to make the headings in your document stand out from the rest of the text, try this technique. Press Shift+Tab, type the heading, and then press Enter. You might also want to make the text bold and big, which you learn about later in this chapter.

Centering Text (Stuck in the middle with you)

If you've ever had to center a line of text using a typewriter, you'll be pleased to know that WordPerfect will not make you participate in the same kinds of mathematical gymnastics. In fact, telling WordPerfect to center a title is simple.

Center One Line

To center only one line, move the cursor to the beginning of the line where you want your centered text. This line should be empty. Pull down the **L**ayout menu, choose **A**lignment, and then choose **C**enter from the mini-menu that pops out beside **A**lignment. The cursor jumps to the middle of the line. Type the text you want centered. As you type, the line automatically adjusts so that the text stays centered. You can edit the line later and it will *still* stay centered. Pretty amazing. Press Enter to end the centered line.

Checklist

- This doesn't work with text that's more than one line long. If you type so much that the cursor wraps to the next line, neither line will be centered.

- You can use these steps to center a line that you've already typed. Move the cursor to the beginning of the line, pull down the **L**ayout menu, choose **A**lignment, and then choose **C**enter. The text jumps a little to the right and becomes centered.
- If you consider yourself a master of the function keys, you can press Shift+F6 to turn on Center. Good luck remembering that.
- If you want to center large chunks of text (10 or more lines), use *center justification*. This scary-sounding but rather simple, concept is explained in Chapter 12 in the section "Justifying Text."

"I HATE THIS!"

I have to squint to make the text look centered!

The Center feature doesn't center your text between the left and right edges of the page. Instead, WordPerfect centers text between the left and right *margins*. What's the difference? Well, if your left and right margins are the same size—each 1 inch, for example—there's no real difference. If your margins are different—say you have a left margin of 3 inches and a right margin of .5 inch—then, the center between your margins is different than the center between the edges of the page. Your "centered" text won't look centered at all. What does all this mean? If you're going to use Center, you ought to have even-sized margins.

Centering a Bunch of Lines

Sometimes a title has several lines and you want them all centered. Go ahead and type them normally, pressing Enter at the end of each line. Now you can use the Block feature together with Center to center the whole thing at once. Move the cursor to the beginning of the first line

you want centered, pull down the **E**dit menu, choose **B**lock, and then move the cursor to the end of the last line you want centered. All the lines you want centered should be highlighted now. Pull down the **L**ayout menu, choose **A**lignment, and choose **C**enter. Each line of the block of text jumps to the center of the page.

Aligning Text at the Right Margin

Many business-letter writing styles call for the date at the right margin; a few also call for the return address at the right margin. This section tells you how to right-align text that you type.

Aligning One Line

To align one line at the right margin, move the cursor to a new line. This line is where you want to place the right-aligned text. Next pull down the **L**ayout menu, choose **A**lignment to make the Alignment submenu appear, and then choose **F**lush Right. The cursor jumps to the right side of the screen, showing you it's ready for you to type the text.

Type the text. Notice that as you type, the cursor stays at the right side of the screen, and text you've already typed moves left. In other words, the thing you last typed is always up against the right margin. Press Enter to go to a new line. The cursor jumps back to the left side of the screen.

Checklist

- You can use a fast function key to turn on right alignment by pressing Alt+F6.
- You can make text that you've already typed align with the right margin. Move the cursor to the beginning of the text you want to

flush right, pull down **L**ayout, choose **A**lignment, and choose **F**lush Right. The text jumps to the right side of the page.

▼ The text you type shouldn't be more than one line long. If it is, the second line won't be flush with the right margin.

Aligning Lots of Lines

You can make several existing lines flush with the right margin. First, you block the lines; and then you use the Flush Right feature.

To block the lines, decide what text you want flush right. Then move the cursor to the beginning of the first line of the text, pull down the **E**dit menu, choose **B**lock, and then move the cursor to the end of the last line. Next, pull down **L**ayout, choose **A**lignment, and choose **F**lush Right. In the blink of an eye, your blocked text becomes right-aligned.

TIP

If you want to make a large part of your document flush right, *don't* use the Flush Right feature. Instead, use the Justification feature. Take a look at the section "Justifying Text" in Chapter 12 for more about the Justification feature.

Using Bold, Underline, and Italic (Adding oomph)

Bold, underline, and italic text can help you add special emphasis to important words. Here's how you type a word—either bold, underline, or italic—that stands out from the crowd:

1. Move the cursor to where you want to type the emphasized text.

2. Depending on whether you want bold, underline, or italic, press one of these keystrokes:

   - Press F6 or Ctrl+B to make text **bold**
   - Press F8 or Ctrl+U to make text underlined
   - Press Ctrl+I to make text *italic*

3. Type the text you want emphasized.

   The text appears, emphasized the way you chose.

4. Turn off the text emphasizer by pressing the same key you used to turn it on.

Checklist

- F6 and F8 turn on the bold and underline emphasizers because that's the way WordPerfect's always done it—they don't have a better reason than that. You'll find it easier to remember to press Ctrl and the first letter of the emphasizer you want to use.
- You can add emphasis to existing text. First, block the text by moving the cursor to the beginning of the section you want to emphasize, pressing F12 or Alt+F4, and then moving the cursor so that it's after the last character you want emphasized. Next, just press the keystroke combo shown in Step 2.
- You may decide to remove the emphasis from text. To do this, block the text by moving the cursor to the beginning of the section you want to de-emphasize by pressing F12 or Alt+F4 and then moving the cursor so that it's after the last character you want the emphasis removed from. Pull down the Font menu and choose Normal to make plain ol' text again.

Giving Your Documents a Font Lift

Back in the old days, when the IBM Selectric typewriter reigned supreme, the part of the machine that actually struck the page was a little metal ball covered with letters and numbers. If you wanted your documents to have a different look, you could remove one ball and stick in a different one. The different balls had the same letters on them, but the letters looked different.

That's the idea behind computer *fonts*. You've always got the same letters and numbers available, but you can give those letters and numbers a different look. In other words, a computer font is just the electronic version of one of those typewriter balls.

With a computer, however, it's easy to change the font in your documents. Here are some different fonts:

Times

Helvetica

Palatino

Courier

What fonts you have depend on your printer. Different printers let you print different fonts. Experiment with different fonts to see which ones look good where.

Choosing a Font

Here's how you choose a new font:

1. Move the cursor to where you want the new font to begin.

This new font will apply from your cursor to the end of the document, or until you change the font again. If you want the font in effect for the whole document, press Home, Home, up-arrow key to move the cursor to the beginning of the document.

2. Pull down the Font menu, and then choose Font.

3. Choose Font to make a list of your fonts appear.

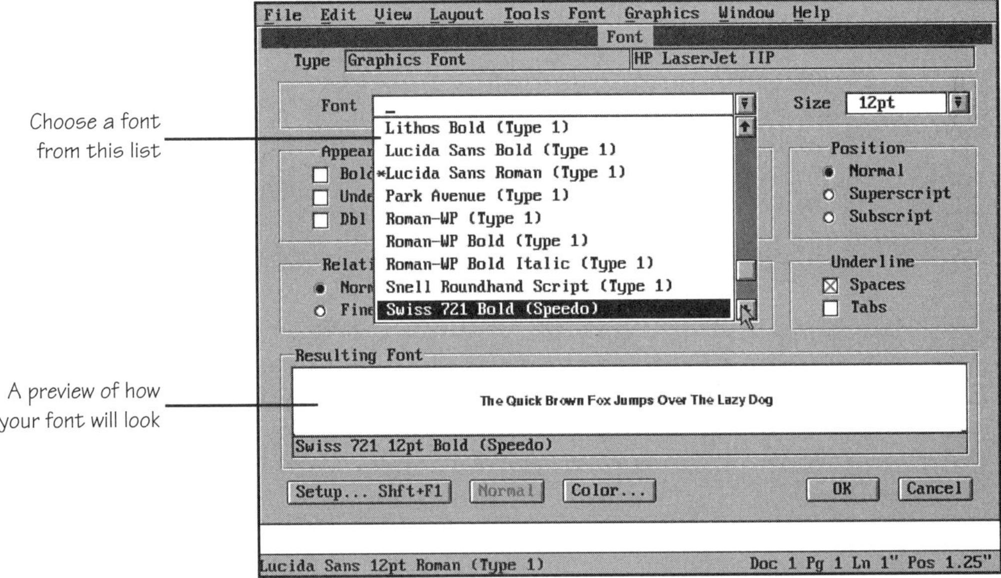

Your list of fonts might only contain two or three fonts—or it might contain dozens. It all depends on your printer. You may need to scroll through the list to see all your fonts.

4. Use arrow keys to highlight the font you want to use; then press Enter.

If you like using a mouse, just double-click on the font you want—that way you won't have to press Enter to select the font.

TIP

Any time you highlight a font, the Resulting Font box gives you a preview of how it will look when printed. This helps take the guesswork out of choosing a font.

5. Choose Size, and then type a number—the bigger the number, the bigger the font. Type **12** for normal-size text, **24** for titles, or **36** for really big, 1/2-inch-high titles. You also can type larger or smaller numbers. Press Enter when you've typed the number you want.

   The Resulting Font box shows how large the font will be—if the size fits into that box.

6. Choose OK to close the dialog box and accept the font.

"I HATE THIS!"

One size fits all

Not all fonts *let* you choose a size. These fonts come in just one size. When you try to follow Step 5 with these kinds of fonts, a menu appears, showing only one number. That's the one you have to work with. Press Enter to accept the number. If you need a larger or smaller size, try using a different font—WordPerfect comes with a few fonts you can use to pick different sizes.

BUZZWORDS

POINT

A measurement, like inches, but much smaller. There are 72 points per inch.

Pontificating on fonts

- When the list of fonts appears, an asterisk is beside the font that's currently in use.
- If you are in the Font dialog box and decide you don't want to select a font after all, press Esc to return to your document screen.
- If you want to change the font for only part of a document, move to the beginning of where you want the new font, turn on Block (pull down the **E**dit menu, and choose **B**lock), move your cursor to where you want the new font to end, and follow Steps 2-6.
- Some fonts in your Font list may have Bold, Italics, or even Bold Italics as part of the font name. It's not a good idea to select these as your font. Instead, choose the plain version of the font, and then choose the check boxes in the dialog box for the emphasizers you want to use.
- Experiment with mixing fonts before you use them in documents. Some font combinations work well; others can make you dizzy.
- If you need to add emphasis to your text, you can take care of that the same time you're changing your font. Before you choose OK, choose any of the text emphasizers in the Appearance part of the dialog box.

CAUTION

After you get used to the Font feature, you'll be tempted to use it all over the place. If you use too many fonts in a document, your text will look like one of those anonymous threats people tie to bricks and throw through windows.

Adjusting Your Margins (Corral your text)

Margins are the white space that surrounds the text on a page. WordPerfect sets up standard 1-inch margins all the way around the page. These settings work for most documents. If you need to tinker with the number of words on the page—cram more text or less text—change the margins.

Here's how you set new margins:

1. Move your cursor to where you want the new margins to begin.

   New margin settings apply from the position of the cursor when you change the margin to the end of the document—or to the next place you change the margins. You usually want to be at the top of the document when you change margins so that the new settings apply for the entire document. To get to the beginning of the document, press Home, Home, up-arrow key.

TIP

When you set new top and bottom margins, they apply from the page your cursor is in right now. When you set new left and right margins, on the other hand, they apply from the *paragraph* you're in right now. So, if you want your new left and right margins to apply from the beginning of the page, make sure your cursor is at the beginning of the page when you begin these steps.

2. Pull down the **L**ayout menu, and then choose **M**argins.

   Up comes the Margin Format dialog box.

3. Choose any of the following: **L**eft, **R**ight, **T**op, or **B**ottom margin.

It doesn't matter which margin you set first.

4. Type a measurement for the margin, and then press Enter.

Use decimals for your measurements. For example, if you want a 1 1/2-inch margin, type **1.5**. If you want a 3/4-inch margin, type **.75**. You don't have to type the inch marks after the numbers. WordPerfect puts them in for you.

5. Repeat Steps 3 and 4 for any other margins you want to change.

6. Choose OK to close the dialog box.

"I HATE THIS!"

But my cursor is on the page! Why isn't the margin changed?

When you set the top and bottom margins, make sure that the cursor is positioned at the *top* of the first page that the margins apply to. If the cursor isn't at the top of the page, your new margin settings won't take effect until the next page, unless Auto Code Placement is active.

TIP

Changing margin settings is a good way to increase or decrease the amount of text that fits on a page. If you need more room to fit all your text on a page, make smaller margins—say, 0.75-inch margins instead of 1-inch margins.

College students take note: If you need a document to take up more pages, make your margins a little bigger. Most college professors can't tell the difference between a 1-inch

margin and a 1.25-inch margin. Most college professors can, however, tell the difference between a 1-inch margin and a 2-inch margin, so don't take this little deception to the extreme.

No 0-inch margins allowed!

If you're using a laser printer, you can't set margins of 0 inches because laser printers can't print to the edge of the paper. If you try to set margins of 0 inches, WordPerfect will automatically adjust them to your printer's minimum margin capabilities.

Adding Page Numbers

Page numbers are vital for keeping a document in order. Suppose that you copy a 22-page report. Suddenly the copier takes a disliking to the report and spits the pages out in a scrambled order. Without page numbers, all the kings horses and all the kings men won't be able to put the report back together again.

Setting the Page Number

One of the cardinal sins of WordPerfect is numbering pages yourself by typing them at the top (or bottom) of the page. After all, if you have to edit the document, your page numbers can wind up in the wrong places, and even on the wrong pages. Instead, use WordPerfect's automatic page numbering system. Here's how you do it:

1. Move the cursor to the page you want your page numbering to begin on.

   There's one exception to this rule. If you want page numbering to begin on page two, you should still move your cursor to the beginning of page one and follow these steps; then follow the steps in the first item in the "Page 2 on Page Numbers" checklist, below.

2. Pull down the **L**ayout menu, and then choose **P**age to retrieve the Page Format dialog box.

3. Choose Page **N**umbering to go to the Page Numbering dialog box, and then choose Page Number **P**osition.

   The Page Number Position dialog box has a list of options where the page numbers can go, along with three boxes. These boxes are supposed to be like pages, and the numbers in the boxes show where in the pages you can have page numbers.

4. Choose an option corresponding to the part of the page that will have page numbers. For example, choose Top R**i**ght if you want page numbers in the upper-right corner of your pages. Choose Bottom **C**enter if you want page numbers in the bottom center of each page.

5. Choose OK to go back to the Page Numbering dialog box.

6. Choose OK in the next two dialog boxes to go back to the document screen.

You're all set, page-numbering-wise. The page numbers aren't visible while you type. You won't see them until you either print your document or use the View Document feature.

Page 2 on Page Numbers

There are lots of things you can do to tinker with the placement of page numbers. Here are some ideas:

Checklist

- You may not want page numbering to begin until the second page—that's the way things usually work in letters and reports. To start page numbering on the second page, go to the top of the document (press Home, Home, up-arrow key), pull down the **L**ayout menu, choose **P**age, choose S**u**ppress, choose **P**age Numbering, and then choose OK twice to get back to the document screen.
- You can add text next to the page number. For example, the page number could read *Page 3* rather than just 3. To add text, follow Steps 1 through 5 in the basic steps. Before you do Step 6, choose Page Number **F**ormat. Your cursor will be at the beginning of `[page #]`. Type the text you want by the page number, such as **Page**. Press the space bar so that there'll be a space between your text and the page number. Press Enter when you're done; choose OK to close this dialog box, and choose OK again to return to your document.
- You can make automatic page numbering part of a WordPerfect header or footer. For instructions (as well as an explanation of "headers" and "footers"), see "Creating Headers and Footers" in Chapter 13.
- If you want to insert the page number within the text of your document, move your cursor to where you want the number, and then press Ctrl+P.
- If you want automatic page numbering, but need to start at a number different from 1, follow Steps 1 through 5; then choose Page **N**umber to bring up the Set Page Number dialog box. Choose New **N**umber, type the number you want to start with, and then press Enter. Choose OK in what seems like dozens of dialog boxes until you're back to the document, or press Home, F7.

Changing Line Spacing

You might have only a 9-page report and need it to be 10 pages. You can either go through the report, adding lots of adjectives and maybe a couple of witty anecdotes, or you can take the easy way out—*increasing* your line spacing. You also can try *decreasing* your line spacing to fit more on a page. Here's how you change line spacing:

1. Move the cursor to where you want to change line spacing.

   If you want to change your line spacing right from the beginning of the document, press Home, Home, up-arrow key. If you want to change line spacing starting with a certain paragraph, move the cursor to the beginning of that paragraph.

2. Pull down the **L**ayout menu, and then choose **L**ine to go to the Line Format dialog box.

3. Choose Line **S**pacing.

   Your cursor jumps to the text box containing the current Line Spacing number—probably something like **1.0**.

4. Type the new spacing number, and press Enter.

   Type numbers like **2** for double spacing and **3** for triple spacing. You also can use decimals, like **1.5**, **2.2**, **1.18** and so forth.

5. Choose OK to return to the document screen.

Your new line spacing shows up.

TIP

You can have more than one line spacing change in a document. Each line spacing change stays in effect from where

you make the change until the end of the document—or until the next line spacing change.

Putting the Date in Your Document

No need to look at that wall calendar anytime you need to put the date in your document. WordPerfect has a feature that plops the date in as fast as you can say "What time is it?" You can put in today's date, or you can put in a special date code that automatically updates itself every time you open the document.

What Day Is It?

When you write a letter or report, you usually want to include the current date. That way, if you ever open the document again, you can see when you wrote the letter.

To insert the current date into your document, first move the cursor to where you want the date to appear. Next, pull down the **T**ools menu, choose **D**ate, and then choose **T**ext from the Date submenu. The date zips into your document and looks like this:

```
July 4, 1993
```

January 1, 1980. Am I in a time warp?

If the wrong date appears, your computer's clock needs to be set. Find someone who's not afraid to brave the dangers of DOS and ask this person to fix your computer's clock. (Computer time is handled by the DOS monster, not by WordPerfect.)

After you've inserted the date using this technique, the date is just normal text. You can edit it or delete it just like you would any other text in your document.

Insert a Date that Automatically Updates

WordPerfect lets you insert a date that is updated every time you open the document. This little feature might come in handy on a report or memo you are writing. You want the date you *finish* the document to show up—not the date you started it.

When you want an auto-updating date, move the cursor to where the date should go. Pull down the **T**ools menu, choose **D**ate, and then choose **C**ode from the Date submenu. The date appears (in the July 4, 1993 format). This date will update itself anytime you open or print this document.

Checklist

- WordPerfect uses the computer's clock to figure out the date. If the wrong date appears, you should find someone familiar with updating the computer clock to set the proper date for you.
- Although this date *looks* like regular text, it's really a special computer code. You can't edit the automatically updating date. If you want to delete it, move your cursor so that it's right after the date, and then press Backspace once.

CHAPTER 12

Formatting Features You'll Use a Few Times Per Week

IN A NUTSHELL

- Justify your text
- Change your tab stops
- Change the font used for all new documents
- Insert symbols and letters from international alphabets into your document
- Center your text between the top and bottom margins
- Create headers and footers
- Type and print an envelope

Fold down a corner on this page. Or stick a Post-It on one of the edges. This chapter covers stuff that you'll need to do every few days—not enough that you should bother memorizing the procedures but often enough that you'll want to be able to find these pages quickly.

The features included here can make your documents look really polished and professional. For example, you learn how to make your text line up on both margins—like it does in newspapers and magazines. Or make your text centered—for an invitation or poem.

You learn to make the distance between tab stops larger or smaller. You find out how to make your text centered between the top and bottom margins, which is handy when you're making a cover page. You create a *header*, which is a line or two of text you want to be at the top of the page. (By the way, a *footer* is the same thing, only it shows up at the bottom of the page.) All this, and we'll even throw in a free Ginsu knife.

Justifying Text (Text to the left, text to the right)

Different types of documents need different "looks." A letter to an old high school chum should have a different look than an official memo to your employees. A party invitation should have a different look than a company report. Using different *line justification* is a good way to give your document a look that matches its message.

JUSTIFICATION

Justification describes how words line up with the left and right margins. If you have left justification, words line up at the left margin but not at the right. *Right justification* has words line up at the right margin but not at the left. *Center justification* centers lines between the two margins, and *full justification* has text lined up on both the left and right margins, the way text looks in newspapers and some magazines.

Examples of how each type of justification looks.

Left-justified text:	Right-justified text:
Dear Elden , You may already be a winner. Yes, you have been selected as one of the finalists in the Hocus-Pocus Sweepstakes.	Betty McDaniel 1300 South Street Augatuck, MI 60788 (212) 555-6011
Center-justified text:	**Full-justified text:**
You are hereby invited to The Nelsons' Second Annual Clam-Bake	**Tabloid Journalists Kill Elvis!** Four tabloid journalists were apprehended today for the murder of Elvis Presley. Apparently, the King really was alive and had recently announced his intentions of coming out of hiding.

Changing Your Justification

When you use this feature, the new justification is in effect from your cursor position to the end of the document—or until you make another justification change, whichever comes first.

This is how you change your text's justification:

1. Move the cursor to the beginning of the line where you want the new justification.

You can set the justification and then type the text, or set the justification in front of text that already exists. If you want the justification to take effect at the very beginning of the document, press Home, Home, up-arrow key; this moves the cursor to the beginning of the document.

2. Pull down the **L**ayout menu, and then choose **J**ustification.

   The Justification submenu appears.

3. Choose the type of justification you want.

All the text from the cursor to the end of the document now appears in the new justification.

Justifying justification

▼ You can have more than one justification setting in a document. For example, you might want to have a part of a document center-justified, and the rest left-justified. To apply different justifications at different parts of the document, just follow the steps above at each point you want a justification change.

▼ WordPerfect's default justification is Left. If your document is going to have left justification throughout, you don't need to do anything.

▼ Don't use this technique to change the justification for just a line or two. There's a much easier way, which you can learn about in Chapter 11 in the "Centering Text" and "Aligning Text at the Right Margin" sections.

Centering a Page between Top and Bottom Margins

When you make a cover page for a report, you usually want the text centered between your top and bottom margins. To center everything on a page between the top and bottom margins, follow these instructions:

1. Move the cursor to the page you want centered between the top and bottom margins.

2. Pull down the **L**ayout menu, and then choose **P**age.

   The Page Format dialog box appears.

3. Choose **C**enter Current Page.

4. Choose OK to return to the document screen.

On the document screen, the page won't look centered between the top and bottom margins. Don't worry; it is. If you don't trust WordPerfect, you can preview the document, which is explained in Chapter 6.

Checklist

- ▼ These steps make only the *current* page centered from top to bottom margins. If you want to center *all* the pages in the document, go to the top of the document (Home, Home, up-arrow key), pull down the **L**ayout menu, choose **P**age, choose Center **P**ages, and then choose OK.

- ▼ Steps 1-4 center the page between the top and bottom. If you also want to center between the left and right margins, go back to the section "Justifying Text." That section teaches you about center justification—centering between the left and right margins.

Changing Your Tab Stops

If you aren't particular about where tabbed text lines up, use the default tab settings (a tab stop every half inch). If you want the text indented more than 1/2 inch, press Tab again to move over another half-inch. Keep pressing Tab until the text is indented as far as you want it.

If you *are* picky about the place the tabs line up and you *don't* like extraneous tabs in the text (you want a tab at 2.8 inches and you want one—and only one—tab stop), you can change the tab settings. Groups of tab stops are called *tab settings*.

You can have several different tab settings in a document, and each setting applies until you change tab settings again or until the end of the document—whichever comes first.

Making the Switch

Here's how to set a new tab setting:

1. Move the cursor to the beginning of the line where you want the new tab setting to begin.

   If you want the tab setting to be in effect for the whole document, press Home, Home, up-arrow key to move the cursor to the beginning of the document.

2. Pull down the **L**ayout menu, and then choose Ta**b** Set.

   The menacing Tab Set dialog box appears on your screen.

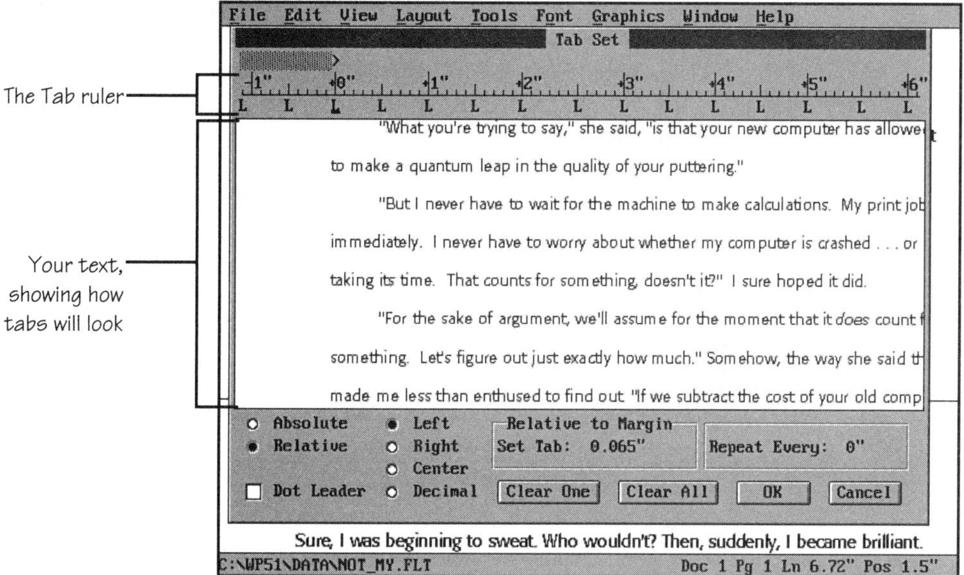

3. Make any changes to your tab setting; then choose OK twice to return to the document screen.

Decoding the Tab Set dialog box

- In the ruler, each L stands for a left-justified tab stop.
- The numbers (such as 0", +1", +2", and so forth) stand for the distance from the left margin. If you have a 1-inch left margin, the 1-inch tab would be 2 inches from the left side of the page, because the 1-inch left margin *plus* 1 inch from the left margin is 2 inches, total.
- You can use the left- and right-arrow keys to move the cursor along the tab ruler.

continues

Decoding the Tab Set dialog box (continued)

- To remove a tab, move the cursor under the tab and press Delete.
- Choose Clear **A**ll to remove all the tabs from the ruler.
- Create a new tab by moving your cursor to the location you want the tab stop and then choosing **L**eft.
- To create a new tab in a *specific* place, type the distance from the left margin you want the tab to be, and then press Enter.
- To put a tab stop at a certain position on the page, type that position and press Enter. For example, if you want a tab stop 3.7 inches from the left margin, choose **S**et Tab, type **3.7**, and then press Enter. A new tab stop appears where you specified.
- To put tab stops at regular intervals on the tab ruler, first choose **S**et Tab, type where you want the first tab of the set to be, and then press Enter. Next, choose Re**p**eat Every, type the distance that should be between each tab stop, and then press Enter again. Suppose that you want tab stops every quarter-inch (0.25") and want the first one to begin right at the left margin (0"). Choose **S**et Tab, type **0"**, press Enter, choose Re**p**eat Every, type **0.25"**, and then press Enter. (It's really easy once you get used to how WordPerfect thinks.)

TIP

You can drag an existing tab stop to another position. Use the arrow keys to move the cursor under the tab stop you want to move. Then hold down the Ctrl key while you press the left- or right-arrow key to move the tab to its new position. As you move the tab stops, the text below the ruler moves

too, so that you can see how the text will look with the new setting. Note, however, that you cannot move a tab past an existing tab.

Using Fancy Tab Stops

All those Ls on the tab ruler stand for *left tabs*. Left tabs are the most common type of tabs. You can set several other tabs. You put other tabs on the tab ruler by moving the cursor to where you want the tab stop, and then choosing the type of tab you want. You can set these types of tabs:

Choose this	Important stuff about the tab
Left	This is the normal type of tab. When you tab to a left tab stop, text that comes after the tab flows to the right.
Center	When you tab to a center tab stop, the text you type is centered over that tab—not centered between the margins. Use this type of tab for column headings.
Right	When you tab to a right tab stop, the text you type flows to the left, which means the *end* of your text is at the tab stop. Use this type of tab for headings that appear above columns of numbers.

continues

Choose this	Important stuff about the tab
Decimal	Use this type when you need to type a column of numbers with decimals. All of your numbers will line up on the decimal point, making things easier to add.
Dot Leader	This type of tab stop can be used with any of the other types. After you've created a left, center, right, or decimal tab, choose this to make the tab a dot leader tab, as well. By doing this, a row of dots appears from your previous position to the beginning of the tab, like this: `Recipes for Success......123`

TIP

If you type columns of numbers in your text and those numbers use decimal places, you can use a feature to align the decimal points like this:

```
 12.55
101.77
  2.99
```

From the document screen, rather than press Tab, press Ctrl+F6. You see a prompt that says **Align Char = .** This means the text will be aligned on the period key, which is what you want. Type the number, and press Enter. Do the same for the next number.

Changing the Default Font (Hooked on fonts)

When you don't specify a font, WordPerfect picks one for you—generally a typewriter-like concoction that may or may not be to your liking. This font is called the *default*. Fortunately, you can specify a different default font. This font will be the one all your documents use, whenever you don't pick a different one. Luckily, you won't have to go through these steps very often.

To change the font WordPerfect uses for all new documents, follow these steps:

1. Pull down the **L**ayout menu, and then choose **D**ocument.

   The Document Format dialog box appears.

2. Choose Initial **F**ont to bring up the Initial Font dialog box.

3. Choose **F**ont to see a list of fonts you have available.

   You may have more fonts available than you can see right now. Use the arrow keys to scroll through the list.

4. Highlight the font you want, and press Enter.

   If you've currently got a firm grip on your mouse, you can just double-click the font you need.

5. Choose All **N**ew Documents.

6. Choose OK in both dialog boxes to go back to your document screen.

Now, when you create a document and don't specify a certain font, WordPerfect will automatically use the font you just selected. You aren't locked into this font, however; you can still choose other fonts when you need them. (Flip back to Chapter 11 in the "Giving Your Documents a Font Lift" section for the dirt on changing fonts.)

Putting Interesting Characters into Your Documents (What a character!)

If you occasionally need to type a word or phrase in a foreign language, you'll also need to be able to put those accent marks and squiggly things over certain letters. You may even need to make an upside-down question mark (¿) or exclamation point (¡).

If you pretty much stick to English in your documents, you may still want to know how to put a • character (for making lists) or a happy face ☺ (to show people what a cheerful person you are) into your document. WordPerfect lets you add all these funky characters easily.

First, press Ctrl+2; then type certain characters or numbers, and press Enter. It's that easy.

This chart shows you how to create some basic characters:

To make this character	Press Ctrl+2, then press . . .
Anything with an accent over it, like á, é, í	The letter, followed by an apostrophe, like **a'**
Anything with a tilde over it, like ñ	The letter, followed by a tilde, like **n~**
Anything with umlauts, like ä, ö, ü	The letter, followed by quote marks, like **a"**
ç, Ç	**c,** **C,**
æ Æ	**ae** **AE**
¡	**!!**
¿	**??**
¼	**/4**
½	**/2**
©	**co**
™	**tm**
®	**ro**
■	******
¢	**c/**
—	-- (this makes an em-dash which is good for separating phrases)
–	**n-** (this makes an en-dash, which is used to separate parts of phone numbers)
☺	**5,7** then **Enter**
☹	**5,26** then **Enter**
⊠	**5,25** then **Enter**
£	**4,11** then **Enter**
¥	**4,12** then **Enter**
§	**4,6** then **Enter**
♪	**5,9** then **Enter**

Creating Headers and Footers

A *header* is text that shows up at the top of every page in a document. A *footer* is the same kind of thing, but it shows up at the bottom of the page rather than the top. The main purpose of headers and footers is to

give your documents continuity. You might, for example, include your company name or the title of your report in the header. The footer might include the date or page number.

Headers (Heads up)

Here's how to put a header in your document:

1. Move the cursor to the first page that you want to have the header.

   If you want the header to start on the first page, press Home, Home, up-arrow key.

2. Pull down the **L**ayout menu, and then choose **H**eader/Footer/Watermark.

   The Header/Footer/Watermark dialog box appears. Don't worry about what a "watermark" is—they're for secret agents only.

3. Choose **H**eaders, and then choose Header **A**.

   If you're using a mouse, you can simply click on Header **A**.

   Another dialog box appears. Its options let you decide which pages the header should appear on. You'll almost always want it on all pages, which is the default—so you don't have to change it.

4. Choose **C**reate to place the header on every page.

   An editing screen appears that looks a lot like the regular document screen.

5. Type the header text.

   The title of your document, the date it was created, your name, and a page number code are common things to put in a header.

6. After you're done creating the header, press F7 to return to the document screen.

You won't be able to see the header while you're writing your document. You need to print the document, use the slow and mysterious Page mode, or use Print Preview to see the header or footer.

Footers

You do just about the same thing to create a footer:

1. Move the cursor to the first page that you want to have the footer.

   If you want the header to start on the first page, press Home, Home, up-arrow key.

2. Pull down the **L**ayout menu, and then choose **H**eader/Footer/Watermark.

3. Choose **F**ooters, and then choose Footer **A**.

   If you're using a mouse, you can simply click on Footer **A**.

   Another dialog box appears. Its options let you decide which pages the footer should appear on. You'll almost always want it on all pages, which is the default—so you don't have to change it.

4. Choose **C**reate to have the footer appear on every page.

   An editing screen appears that looks a lot like the regular document screen.

5. Type the footer text.

   The title of your document, the date it was created, your name, and a page number code are common things to put in a footer.

6. After you're done creating the footer, press F7 to return to the document screen.

You won't be able to see the footer while you're writing your document. You need to print the document or use Print Preview to see headers and footers. (Or, if you're adventurous and have a fast computer, you can try Page mode instead.)

Header and footer ideas

- If you want the current page number in your header or footer, move your cursor to where you want the page number and press Ctrl+P.

- You can have the current date as part of the header or footer. Just pull down the **T**ools menu, choose **D**ate, and then choose **C**ode from the Date submenu. Press Shift+F5, C to insert the date. This date updates automatically whenever you open or print the document.

- If you decide you want to make changes to a header or footer you've already created, follow the same steps—except in Step 4, choose **E**dit instead of **C**reate. This takes you into the editing screen where you created the header or footer. Make the changes you need, and then press F7.

- If you don't want a header or footer to appear on the first page of a document, pull down the **L**ayout menu, choose **P**age, choose **Sup**press, choose **H**eader A or **F**ooter A, and then choose OK in each of the dialog boxes.

- You can have headers and footers on each page in your document. You're not restricted to having one or the other.

Easy Envelopes

The word "envelopes" has always struck fear into the hearts of word processor users—with good reason. They've been a hassle to set up—until now. WordPerfect 6.0 has a built-in Envelope feature so slick, so easy to use, you'll finally be able to get rid of that typewriter once and for all.

You can use the Envelope feature in a couple of ways. First, if you already have written the letter and it's on-screen, WordPerfect can create the envelope from that. Second, you can create an envelope any time, for any address. Follow these steps whenever you want to print an envelope:

1. Pull down the **L**ayout menu, and then choose En**v**elope.

   The Envelope dialog box appears. If you've already written the letter, the mailing address is automatically entered in the Mailing Address box. If you want to make any changes, choose **M**ailing address, and edit the address.

   If you're creating an envelope from scratch, choose **M**ailing Address, type the address for the person you're sending the letter to, and then press Exit (F7).

2. If you want your return address on your envelopes, choose **R**eturn Address, type your address, and then press Exit (F7). Choose **S**ave Return Address as Default and that address will automatically be used in the envelopes you create in the future.

3. Set WordPerfect to print the envelope size you want.

At the top of the dialog box, by 1. Envelope size, you can see what size of envelope WordPerfect is set to print—the default size is the standard business-size envelope. If you need to change that, choose Envelope Size, highlight the envelope size you want to print, and then press Enter.

4. Place an envelope in your printer.

5. Choose Print.

Out comes your envelope, formatted as nice as can be.

CHAPTER 13

Formatting Features You'll Rarely Use (But Are Still Nice To Know)

IN A NUTSHELL

- Make your text larger or smaller
- Keep certain parts of your document together on the same page
- Insert footnotes and endnotes into your documents
- Clean up your document with the Reveal Codes feature

In WordPerfect, there are a good handful of features that you need to use all the time, and dozens of features that you may never need to use at all. The features in this chapter fall somewhere in between. You probably won't need them often, but when you do, you'll be glad WordPerfect includes them.

Make Your Text Larger or Smaller

Certain parts of your documents need to stand out. For example, you want your titles and section headings to reach out of the paper, grab your reader by the lapels, and scream "Look at me!" Most books (including this one) showcase titles and headings by making them bigger. WordPerfect has a way of achieving this effect.

If you are a lawyer and like lots of small print, or if you are writing for Munchkins, you can use these same steps to make the text small.

This is how you tell WordPerfect what size to make the text you are about to type:

1. Move the cursor to where you want to type the different-sized text.

2. Pull down the Font menu, and then choose Size/Position.

   A submenu of different size options appears. The sizes listed are all relative to how big your font is in the first place. Flip back to the "Giving Your Documents a Font Lift" section in Chapter 11 if you want to learn more about choosing a font.

3. Choose one of the options, depending on how large you want your text.

For document titles, choose **V**ery Large or, if you want something *really* big, choose **E**xtra Large. For section headings, **L**arge is about right. If you're writing a contract and need some teeny print, choose **F**ine.

TIP

Superscript and Subscript are both the same size as Fine, but Su**p**erscript is higher than usual and Su**b**script is lower than usual. Both of these settings are good for mathematical equations. When you're done typing superscripted or subscripted text, pull down the F**o**nt menu, choose Si**z**e/Position, and then choose **N**ormal Position to go back to the way your text looked before.

4. Type the text.

5. Pull down the F**o**nt menu, choose Si**z**e/Position, and then choose Normal Si**z**e to return to normal-sized text.

Checklist

- To change the different-sized text back to normal-sized text, first move the cursor to the left of the first character that's the different size, and then turn on block by pulling down the **E**dit menu and choosing **B**lock. Block the text by moving the cursor so that it's after the last character that you want to be normal-sized. Then, pull down the F**o**nt menu, choose Si**z**e/Position, and choose Normal Si**z**e to return to normal-sized text.

- You can change existing text to a different size. Move the cursor to the beginning of the text you want to change, pull down the **E**dit menu and choose **B**lock, and move the cursor past the end of the text. Then follow Steps 2-3.

Keep Text on the Same Page (All together now)

Once in a while you'll have a pair of paragraphs that you want together on the same page—no matter what. Or you might have a list as part of your document and want to make sure that the items don't get split between pages. Here's what you do:

1. Move your cursor to the beginning of the section that you don't want split.

2. Pull down the **E**dit menu, and then choose **B**lock.

3. Move the cursor past the end of the section you want to keep together.

   The entire section you want to keep from being divided should be highlighted.

4. Pull down the **L**ayout menu, and then choose **O**ther.

   The Other Format dialog box appears.

5. Choose **B**lock Protect.

6. Choose OK.

If WordPerfect would usually have put a page break somewhere in the middle of the area you blocked, the page break now comes before the block so that the section isn't split between pages.

Using Footnotes and Endnotes (For scholarly types only)

Footnotes and endnotes are those superscripted numbers (like this[1]) with corresponding messages that appear later in the document. You usually see footnotes in academic papers.

What's the difference between footnotes and endnotes? *Footnote* messages are located at the bottom of the same page as the numbers that refer to them at the *foot* of the page. *Endnotes*, on the other hand, are all collected at the *end* of the document.

Here are the steps for putting endnotes or footnotes into your documents:

1. Move the cursor to where you want the footnote or endnote reference.

   The footnote or endnote *reference* is the little number that goes into your document. The footnote or endnote itself is the message at the bottom of the page or document.

2. Pull down the **L**ayout menu, and then choose **F**ootnote or **E**ndnote.

   A submenu appears. The only options you should ever have to worry about are the top two: **C**reate and **E**dit.

TIP

Don't mix footnotes and endnotes in a single document. Pick one format or the other and stick with it.

---

[1]*This is what a footnote looks like, just in case you're curious.*

3. Choose Create to create the note.

   An editing screen appears, looking a lot like the one you use to type your documents. There are a couple of differences, however. The bottom-left corner of the editing screen tells you which kind of note you're creating, and the number of your note appears in the upper-left corner.

Don't erase this number! If you do, when you print the document, your note won't have a number beside it.

4. Type the note.

5. Press F7 to return to the document screen.

The note number appears just left of the cursor. The number is superscripted (raised a little higher than the other text).

Notes on footnotes

- You won't be able to see your footnotes or endnotes in the normal document screen. If you want to verify that they're really there, use the Print Preview feature (explained in Chapter 6), print the document, or use Page mode.

- WordPerfect automatically numbers and organizes your footnotes and endnotes. If you suddenly remember that you need to put a note between two you've already created, just follow the ordinary steps. WordPerfect puts your note in the right place and renumbers the other notes.

- If you need to edit a footnote or endnote, follow Steps 1-3, and then choose **E**dit. A prompt appears, asking for the note you want to edit. Type the number and choose OK (or just press Enter). You're taken to the editing screen, where you can fix your note. When you finish, press F7 to go back to the document screen.

- To erase a footnote or endnote, move the cursor so that it's to the left of the number you want to delete. Press Delete. The number disappears and WordPerfect renumbers the other notes in the document for you.

- The reference numbers to both endnotes and footnotes are superscripted. The corresponding numbers in footnotes are also superscripted, but the corresponding numbers in endnotes aren't—they're normal-sized numbers with a period.

Erasing Unwanted Formatting

Reveal Codes. What an ominous term—well-named because it *is* ominous.

When you make formatting changes—make words bold or italic, change margins, add headers and footers—WordPerfect is putting codes into your document.

These codes are notes WordPerfect makes to itself: "Start bold here and end it here. Put a header here. Change the margins here." Usually you can't see these codes; they'd just get in the way of your work. But when you turn on Reveal Codes, you can see all the codes that have been inserted into your document.

Why Look at the Dark World of Reveal Codes?

When would you want to see your codes? When you want to get rid of one, mainly. Some formatting features are hard to remove from your document unless you can see the code that creates it. In that case, you have to travel into the dark world of Reveal Codes.

Turning on Reveal Codes (Brace yourself!)

To turn on Reveal Codes, pull down the View menu and choose Reveal Codes.

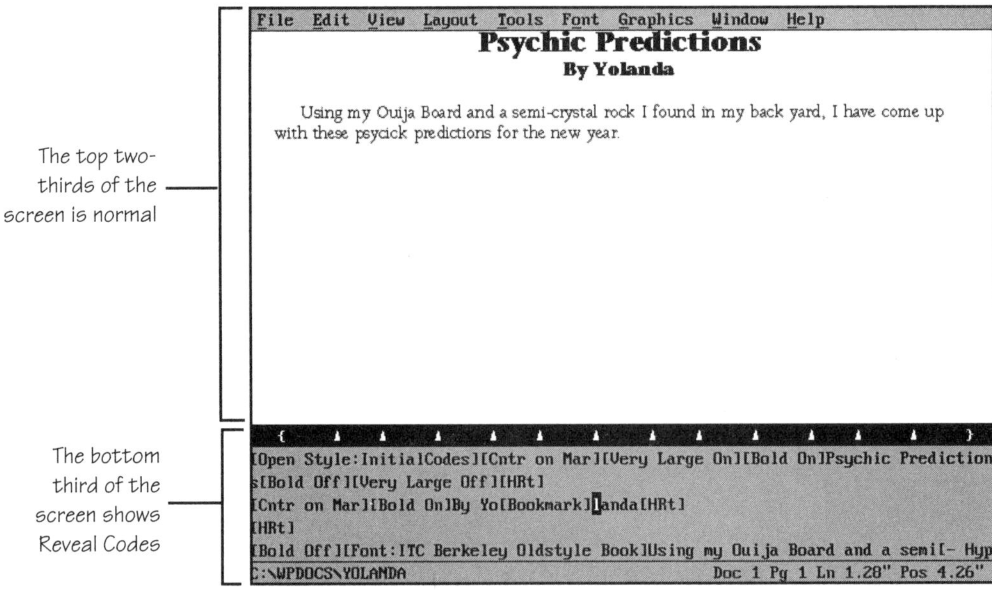

When you turn on Reveal Codes (F11 or Alt+F3), a bar splits the screen in two. The top part of the screen is the normal document screen that you're used to. The bottom part of the screen is the Reveal Codes area, and it contains oodles of different-colored text in brackets.

The text in the bottom half of the screen is the same as in the top half of the screen, but it contains all the formatting codes. The different-colored text surrounded by brackets, like `[HRt]` and `[SRt]`, are the codes.

Checklist

- You can turn off Reveal Codes at any time by pulling down the **V**iew menu and choosing Reveal **C**odes. You can't use F7 or Esc to leave Reveal Codes.
- If you get begin to like Reveal Codes so much that you want to be able to turn it on at a second's notice, you can learn the shortcut key combo: Alt+F3. The same key combo also turns Reveal Codes off.
- To turn Reveal Codes on and off *really* quickly—if you have 12 function keys instead of 10—you can use F11 to turn Reveal Codes on and off.
- You can do anything within the Reveal Codes window that you can do on the document screen. For example, you can type, erase, and move around. But it's a nuisance because you have to dodge all the codes, so why bother?
- If you don't know what a code does, you're best off leaving it alone. Don't erase a code unless you know what the code does.

Moving around in the Underworld

When you've got Reveal Codes on, you suddenly have two cursors. As you use your arrow keys, your normal cursor moves around in the top half of the screen. Meanwhile, a rectangular cursor moves around in

Reveal Codes. This rectangle shows you where you are in Reveal Codes and highlights whatever character or code it's positioned on.

When you move the lower cursor to a code, the code expands and the cursor doesn't move in the top half of the screen.

The Popular [HRt] and [SRt] Codes

More than any other code, you'll see a lot of [HRt] and [SRt] codes in the Reveal Codes screen. [HRt] is the code for *hard return.* WordPerfect puts one of these in your document whenever you press Enter.

[SRt] is WordPerfect's code for a *soft return*—the end of a line. Whenever you're typing and your cursor jumps down to the next line, WordPerfect puts one of these [SRt] codes at the end of the line you just finished.

CAUTION

Don't try to delete [SRt] codes; WordPerfect put them there for a good reason. If you highlight an [SRt] code and press Delete, it's like deleting the space between two words. The words on the left and right of the [SRt] you deleted will be joined.

Housecleaning with Reveal Codes

The main reason you'll use Reveal Codes is to get rid of some formatting change that you just don't want in your document. For example, you might want to get rid of a line spacing change. To do this, you need to find the line spacing code.

Move the cursor so that it's on the code you want to erase. Press Delete. The code disappears, and the formatting it makes goes away, too.

Many of the codes in WordPerfect are called *paired codes*. These codes come in twos. The first of these two codes turns on a feature; the second turns off the feature. For example, the Bold feature uses paired codes. Before any bold text, you see `[Bold On]`. At the end of the bold text is the second of the paired code set: `[Bold Off]`. When you delete either of the paired codes, the other also disappears.

Reveal Codes Revealed

Here are some of the most common Reveal Codes:

What the code looks like	What the code means
`[HRt]`	Hard Return. You pressed Enter here.
`[SRt]`	Soft Return. WordPerfect is wrapping the line here.
`[HPg]`	Hard Page. You pressed Ctrl+Enter to end the page here.
`[SPg]`	Soft Page. WordPerfect ends the page here. Don't erase this!
`[Lft Tab]`	Text moves in one tab stop here.
`[Lft Indent]`	Paragraph is indented on tab stop here.

continues

What the code looks like	What the code means
`[Lft/Rgt Indent]`	Left and right ends of paragraph are indented on tab stop here.
`[Back Tab]`	Text moves back one tab stop here.
`[Und On][Und Off]`	Underline paired codes that mark the beginning and end of underlined text.
`[Bold On][Bold Off]`	Bold paired codes that mark the beginning and end of **bold** text.
`[Italc On][Italc Off]`	Italic paired codes that mark the beginning and end of *italic* text.
`[Small On][Small Off]`	Small text size paired codes that mark the beginning and end of small text.
`[Large On][Large Off]`	Large paired codes that mark the beginning and end of large text.
`[Very Large On][Very Large Off]`	Very Large text size paired codes that mark the beginning and end of very large text.
`[Ext Large On][Ext Large Off]`	Extra Large text size paired codes that mark the beginning and end of extra large text.

What the code looks like	What the code means
`[Cntr on Mar]`	A centered line begins here.
`[Flsh Rgt]`	A line begins here that is flush with the right margin.
`[Just:Right]`	All text is flush with the right margin until further notice.
`[Just:Full]`	All text is flush against both margins until further notice.
`[Just:Cntr]`	All text is centered between left and right margin until further notice.
`[Just:Left]`	All text is flush with left margin—but not the right margin—until further notice.
`[Just:Full, ALL]`	All text is evenly spaced between margins including the last line of a paragraph or a heading.

`[Lft Mar:1.5"]`
`[Rgt Mar:1.5"]`
`[Top Mar:1.5"]`
`[Bot Mar:1.5"]`
	New margin goes into effect here. The number is the new margin. (Note that your on-screen numbers might be different.)

`[Tab Set:Rel; 0.25"]` (big string of numbers here)]	New tab set goes into effect here. The numbers are the tab stop locations and are almost impossible to decipher.
`[Center Cur Pg: On]`	Page is centered between top to bottom margins.

continues

What the code looks like	What the code means
`[Header A:All Pages;` (First part of first line of header goes here)`]`	Header A begins here (A similar code also is available for footers.)
`[Pg Num Pos:TopRight]`	Page numbering goes into effect here.
`[Font:Times]`	Indicated font starts here.
`[Font Size:12pt]`	New font size starts here.

TIP

Every document begins with an `[Open Style: Initial Codes]` code. Don't bother trying to get rid of that. You can't. It's just there, and no amount of pressing Delete and Backspace will do anything to change it. This is the code that tells WordPerfect any special permanent changes you've made to your line spacing, margins and so forth.

PART IV

Files

Includes:

CHAPTER 14

More on Printing (Forget about the Paperless Office)

IN A NUTSHELL

- Get your printer ready
- Preview your document
- Print the whole document
- What to do when the document won't print
- Print some pages but skip others
- Print only one page
- Print only a block of text
- Print several copies of your document
- Stop a document from being printed
- Set up (install) your printer

The main reason that most of us use WordPerfect is to make the process of getting words onto paper a little easier. This chapter shows you how to deal with that all-important step in using WordPerfect: printing your documents.

Is Your Printer Ready to Print?

From your viewpoint, printing with a typewriter might seem infinitely easier than printing with a computer. With a typewriter, you punch a key, you get a character. But things *will* be easier with a computer after you print that first document and figure out how to set up everything. (Say this with your fingers crossed.)

The first step is to install your printer. With a little luck, your printer is already installed. If not, flip to the last section in this chapter, "Setting Up a Printer." The next step in the printing process is to get your printer ready:

- Check that the printer is turned on and is on-line. (To put a printer on-line, press the On Line button on the printer's panel so that the On Line light is lit. Your printer will probably be on-line when you turn it on.)

- Check that the printer has paper in it. If you have a laser printer (these printers look like copy machines), just put paper in the tray and slide the tray into the printer. If you have a dot-matrix printer (these printers look like a big fancy typewriter), you'll have to loop and weave and wind the paper through its proper contortions. Get help from someone in the know.

How Will My Document Look on Paper? (Sneak preview)

Before you print, you can take a sneak preview of how the document will appear on paper by using the Print Preview feature. It shows you an on-screen picture of how your document will look when printed, including headers, footers, page numbers and the other stuff you usually don't see while typing. To preview your document, make sure that the document you want to preview is on-screen. (Chapter 4 is the place to go if you don't know how to get a document on-screen.)

If you want to look at a certain page first, move the cursor somewhere on that page. Pull down the **F**ile menu, and then choose Print Preview to see a sneak peek of your document. The Print Preview screen appears, showing a page from your document. Be patient. It may take a moment or two to come up on-screen. When you finish looking at Print Preview, pull down the **F**ile menu, and then choose **C**lose.

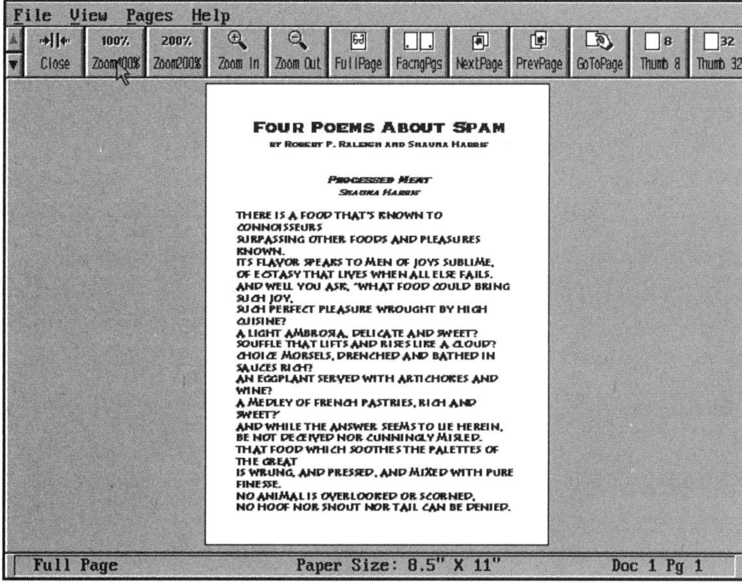

Print Preview gives you a snapshot-view of how your document looks.

Checklist

- Move from page to page by pressing Page Up (to go to the previous page) or Page Down (to go to the next page).
- To see the document at actual size, pull down the **V**iew menu and choose **1**00%. If you want to see it *really* big, pull down the **V**iew menu and choose **2**00%. At these sizes, you won't be able to see the whole page at one time. You can look at different parts of the page by pressing Home and then any arrow key. (Press the arrow key that points in the direction that you want to look.)
- When you want to see the whole page at once, pull down the **V**iew menu and choose **F**ull Page. To see facing pages (this is useful if your document will eventually be bound like a book and people will see your pages side-by-side), pull down the **V**iew menu and choose Fa**c**ing Pages.
- Jump to any page in the document by pressing Ctrl+Home, typing the page number you want, and pressing Enter.
- The lower-right corner of the screen tells you which document and page you're currently looking at in Print Preview.
- If everything looks good in Print Preview, pull down the **F**ile menu and choose **C**lose to return to the editing screen.

EXPERTS ONLY

Under my thumbnail

Sometimes it's helpful to see several pages at once so that you can tell if your page numbers, headers, and footers are starting and stopping where you want them to. WordPerfect lets you take what's called a "thumbnail" view of just about

any number of pages in your document. But bear in mind that when you look at a "thumbnail" view of a page, it's just to get an idea of how the text looks—you can't possibly make out words, or even letters.

From the Print Preview screen, you can see a thumbnail sketch of your document by pulling down the **V**iew menu, choosing **T**humbnails, and then choosing the number of pages you want to see. If you choose **O**ther, WordPerfect prompts you to type the number of pages you need. Then choose OK.

When you are in Thumbnail view mode, you can use your arrow keys to move a red border from page to page (you can also click your mouse on any of the thumbnail pages to move the red border to that page). Then, if you want to see a more close-up preview of that page, you can pull down the **V**iew menu and choose **F**ull Page, **1**00% View or **2**00% View—WordPerfect will zoom in on that page.

Printing the Whole Thing

To print, make sure that your printer is ready to go and has enough paper to print the document. Then pull down the **F**ile menu and choose **P**rint. The Print dialog box appears. Full Document is automatically selected, so just choose P**r**int.

WordPerfect goes back to the document screen, and you can go back to work. Meanwhile, your document starts printing.

Checklist

- The quick keyboard shortcut for retrieving the Print dialog box is Shift+F7.
- Don't exit WordPerfect when a document is still printing. If you do, WordPerfect asks whether you want to cancel all print jobs. Choose **N**o and wait until WordPerfect finishes printing. Then you can exit.
- If you want to print several documents at once, check out Chapter 15, which tells you how to accomplish this magical feat.
- WordPerfect stops printing any time you're in Print Preview. So if you've got a document that you need printed right away, stay out of the Print Preview feature until the job is completely printed.

My Printer Won't Print!

You're finished with that report. What a relief. Now you can print it, mail it, and take off for an early weekend. You send the document to the printer and ... nothing. Or maybe something comes out, but it's horribly mangled. What do you do when things go wrong with your printer? Try the suggestions in this section. If you still can't get things going, find someone who knows about computers and beg him to help you. You can also call WordPerfect Customer Support at 1-800/541-5170 if you have a laser printer, or 1-800/541-5160 if you have any other kind of printer.

You Can Print, but It Looks All Wrong

If the letters print on top of each other or are crammed too close together, one of three things has probably happened:

- If you're using a laser printer that uses font cartridges, someone might have taken out the font cartridge that you need. Find somebody who understands your printer and ask him to put the cartridge you need back into the printer.
- Your printer might be using something called *soft fonts* and they're not loaded. Find the person who knows the most about the printer and ask him whether the fonts have been loaded.
- If strange symbols and characters print in your document or the printer spits out page after page with only a couple of lines on each piece of paper, you've probably got the wrong printer driver selected. To check which printer driver is selected, pull down the **F**ile menu and choose **P**rint to bring up the Print dialog box. Look at the name of the printer in the Current Printer box, which is at the very top of the dialog box. If the name of the printer in this menu doesn't match the name of your printer, choose **S**elect Printer. A list of printers appears, and your printer should be one of them. (If it isn't, find someone who *really* knows WordPerfect and ask him to help you install a printer driver.) Use the arrow keys to highlight your printer. Choose Select, and then try printing again.

Nothing Prints At All

Diagnosing the problem when a printer doesn't print at *all* can be a real chore. Try the following solutions in order. After trying each suggestion, try printing again. If you still don't have any luck, call WordPerfect Customer Support at 1-800/541-5170 if you have a laser printer, or 1-800/541-5160 if you have any other kind of printer. They'll be happy to help you work through the problem.

- Make sure that your printer is on, is on-line, and has paper in it. Also, make sure that the cable that connects your printer to your computer is firmly connected. If you're not sure which cable this is, hunt down somebody who likes to fiddle with computers and ask him.

- Clear out your printer queue. Do this by pulling down the **F**ile menu, choosing **P**rint, and then choosing **C**ontrol Printer to go to the Control Printer dialog box. Choose **4** (Un)mark All, then choose **C**ancel Job. WordPerfect asks whether you want to cancel all the print jobs—choose **Y**es. Look at the instructions by Action: (the sixth item down in the Current Job box). Follow any instructions this line gives you. Choose Close to return to your document screen.

- Go to a blank document screen, type a few words, and try to print them. If they print, something's wrong with your document. To fix the problem, clear the document screen, and then open the document that you had trouble printing. Turn on Block by pulling down the **E**dit menu and choosing **B**lock, and then go to the bottom of the document (Home, Home, down-arrow key). Delete the block (this is temporary, I promise) by pressing Delete. Press F7, N, N to clear your document screen. Press Esc, then press R to magically restore your document to the screen. Try printing it again.

- Leave WordPerfect and try printing from another program. If you can't print from *any* of your programs, there's a problem with either the printer, the cable, or your computer.

- Turn off your printer, wait for a few seconds, and then turn on the printer again. Sometimes printers can crash, just like your computer does. By turning the thing off and back on, you clear the printer's memory.

Printing a Few Pages (Picky, picky, picky)

You don't have to print the entire document. In some cases, you might just want to print a few pages. Or just one page. Or just one paragraph. WordPerfect can accommodate you.

To print only certain pages from your document, make sure that your printer is set up and that the document is on-screen. Pull down **F**ile and choose **P**rint to make the Print dialog box appear. Then choose **M**ultiple Pages to bring up the Print Multiple Pages dialog box.

Choose **P**age/Label Range, type the page numbers you want to print; press Enter, and then choose OK. Choose P**r**int to print those pages. WordPerfect returns to the document screen and only the pages you specified are printed. (This procedure works even if you didn't add page numbers to the document.)

Checklist

- If you want to print a sequence of pages, type the first page to be printed, a hyphen, and then the last page to be printed. For example, if you want to print from page three to page eight, type **3-8**.
- You also can print individual pages. To do this, type each page number to be printed, separated by commas. For example, if you want to print pages 4, 9, and 12, type **4,9,12**.
- You can combine the two ways of printing certain pages. For example, if you want to print pages 1 through 3, as well as pages 8 and 10, type **1-3,8,10**.
- If you want to print from the beginning of the document to a certain page, type a hyphen, and then type the last page you want. For example, if you want to print from the beginning of the document to page 13, type **-13**.
- You can print from a certain page to the end of the document by typing the page number followed by a hyphen. For example, to print from page eight to the end of the document, type **8-**.

Print Only One Page

If you need only one page of a document, just print one page of it. Move your cursor to the page you want to print. It doesn't matter where the cursor is on the page: it can be at the top, bottom, or anywhere in between. You might want to check Pg status line (bottom-right corner) to be sure that you've got the cursor on the right page.

After you're on the right page, pull down the **F**ile menu, and then choose **P**rint to bring up the Print dialog box. Choose **P**age, then choose P**r**int. WordPerfect returns you to the document screen and prints the page.

Printing Only a Block of Text

Suppose that you don't even want to print an entire page; you just want to print a paragraph or two—or a single sentence. If that's the case, move the cursor to the beginning of the block that you want to print, pull down the **E**dit menu, choose **B**lock, and then move the cursor to the end point of the block. As you move the cursor, the text you want to print is highlighted. Pull down the **F**ile menu and choose **P**rint to bring up the Print dialog box. Lo and behold, the **B**lock option is automatically selected; you just need to choose P**r**int.

TIP

The block of text you print appears in the same place on the page as it would if you printed the entire page. Any page numbers, headers, and footers you have set up also print.

Printing Several Copies of Your Document (The photocopier effect)

If you like your document enough to want to pass it out to friends, coworkers, and people you meet waiting for the subway, you can print multiple copies.

TIP

> If you have a photocopier handy, use that instead of your printer to make the copies. Photocopiers are faster and cost less per page than running multiple copies off your printer. Plus, using a photocopier saves wear and tear on the printer.

Here's how you print several copies of a document:

1. Make sure the document you want to print is on-screen.

2. Pull down the **F**ile menu, then choose **P**rint to bring up the Print dialog box.

   Or, if you have a thing for function keys, just press Shift+F7.

3. Choose **N**umber of Copies.

   The cursor moves under the number that follows the words `Number of Copies`.

4. Type the number of copies you want; then press Enter.

   The printing doesn't start yet. You've got a couple more decisions to make.

5. Choose Generated By.

   A menu appears, with two options: **W**ordPerfect and **P**rinter. If you choose **W**ordPerfect, the copies will be collated but will come out more slowly. (*Collated* means that one whole copy of the document—from the first to the last page—is printed, and then another whole copy of the document is printed, and so on.)

   If you choose **P**rinter, the copies may come out more quickly, but will not be collated; instead, all the page 1s will print, then all the page 2s will print, and so on. You'll have to arrange the documents in the proper order (sort of like when you helped your third-grade teacher assemble stacks of handouts).

6. Choose **W**ordPerfect or **P**rinter.

7. Choose P**r**int.

WordPerfect goes back to the document screen, and your printer begins printing ... and printing ... and printing ....

Stop Documents from Being Printed (Stop the presses!)

You send your print job, fully expecting the printer to make printing noises, and...nothing. What's going on? Or more to the point, what's *not* going on? Somewhere along the line, the printer got stuck. You'll have to let WordPerfect know by canceling the print job.

Or maybe you sent a long document to the printer and realized: *Hey! I don't want to print that document. What was I thinking?*

You can cancel print jobs from the Control Printer screen. Here's how:

1. Pull down the **F**ile menu, choose **P**rint to bring up the Print dialog box, and then choose **C**ontrol Printer.

   The Control Printer dialog box appears, vaguely resembling NASA control center.

2. Choose **4** (Un)mark All, and then choose **C**ancel Job.

   When one print job gets jammed, any other print jobs that come after it have to sit idly by. It's easier to cancel all the print jobs and start over than to try to cancel one job at a time.

   A box appears in the middle of the screen, asking if you want to cancel all the print jobs.

3. Choose **Y**es.

WordPerfect tries desperately to clean up the mess, but it may need a little help. Check to see if there are any instructions by Action in the Current Job box. Press whatever strange letters WordPerfect tells you to. If Action says `None`, (which it usually does), you're in the clear. Choose Close to return to your document screen.

TIP

Your printer may have some remnants of the bad print job remaining. To clear everything, cancel the print job, turn off the printer, wait a couple seconds, and then turn on the printer. Your printer should now be cleared of the bad print job.

Setting Up a Printer

If you've just bought a new printer or if you haven't gone through the heart-wrenching process of installing a printer, you need to do so. (It's part of the WordPerfect initiation process.) In techie terms, you need to "install a printer driver." This intimidating task should not be attempted alone by mere mortals.

Instead, butter up a WordPerfect buddy and ask him to do it for you. Or make a call to the Customer Support people at WordPerfect. They'll step you through this complex process. You can call these folks at 1-800-541-5160. But before you make the call, have these things ready:

Checklist

- Have the disks that came with WordPerfect on hand. You'll need at least some of them.
- Know the name of your printer, including the make and model. It's not good enough to know just the type or printer. You need to know who made it and what model it is. On most printers, the name (make and model) of the printer is stamped on the printer.
- Be at your computer when you make the phone call.
- Know which directory your WordPerfect program is kept in, such as C:\WP60.

CHAPTER 15

Working with Documents (WordPerfect's Answer to the Overstuffed Filing Cabinet)

IN A NUTSHELL

- Decipher DOS path names
- Display a list of files
- View a document before retrieving it
- Open a file for editing
- Find files
- Print a single document
- Print many documents
- Delete files you no longer need
- Copy files
- Move files between directories
- Create directories
- Change directories
- Use QuickList to change directories fast

When you work with WordPerfect, you've got to learn something about managing files. *Files* are the documents you've named and put on your hard disk (and floppy disks, too). They're sitting on your hard disk right now, seemingly multiplying at a furious rate. To keep them from getting out of control, you're going to have to pay a little attention to them.

To begin, you need a small dose of DOS. This chapter starts by explaining *paths* and *directories*, as they relate to files. You probably should read this section.

Then this chapter covers the stuff you can do to a file: open it, print it, delete it, curl it, clip it, brush it, snip it. Skim the headings to find procedures that interest you. File management isn't a daily task, but it is something you should know how to do.

Files, Directories, and Paths! Oh My!

Files are the individual documents that you store on a disk. Rather than lump all files in one pile on the hard disk, you can—and should—divide the hard disk into sections. These sections are called *directories*.

One main directory, called the *root directory*, houses all the other directories. You can have many directories within the root directory. You can also have directories within directories within directories. (Sometimes the term *subdirectory* rather than *directory* is used; a subdirectory is a directory that is nested under another directory. The two terms mean the same thing.)

BUZZWORDS

DIRECTORY

A directory is a section of your hard disk. If your hard disk is an entire house, a directory is one room. The path tells you how to get to that room: go through the dining room to the kitchen.

The route through all the directories is called the *path*. For instance, decode this path:

```
C:\WPDOCS\RECIPES\COOKIE.DOC
```

- C: indicates the drive (in this case, drive C).
- \ (backslash) is the name of the root directory.
- WPDOCS is the first directory.
- RECIPES is a directory within WPDOCS.
- COOKIE.DOC is the file name.

Why is all this information important? When you start to organize your files into directories and you can't find a file that you're sure you saved, you'll need some clues to decode the path and the directory structure.

Starting File Manager (Unlock the file cabinet)

WordPerfect's File Manager feature does just what its name implies: it helps you manage your files. File Manager shows you lists of files on-screen; then you can select the appropriate file and open it, print it, copy it—whatever you want.

To display the File Manager, pull down the **F**ile menu and choose **F**ile Manager.

TIP

> You can simply press F5 to display the File Manager using function keys.

A Specify File Manager List dialog box appears, and the prompt appears in the middle of the screen, showing the path for the files you're about to look at—something like this:

```
C:\WPDOCS\*.*
```

Choose OK. The File Manager comes up.

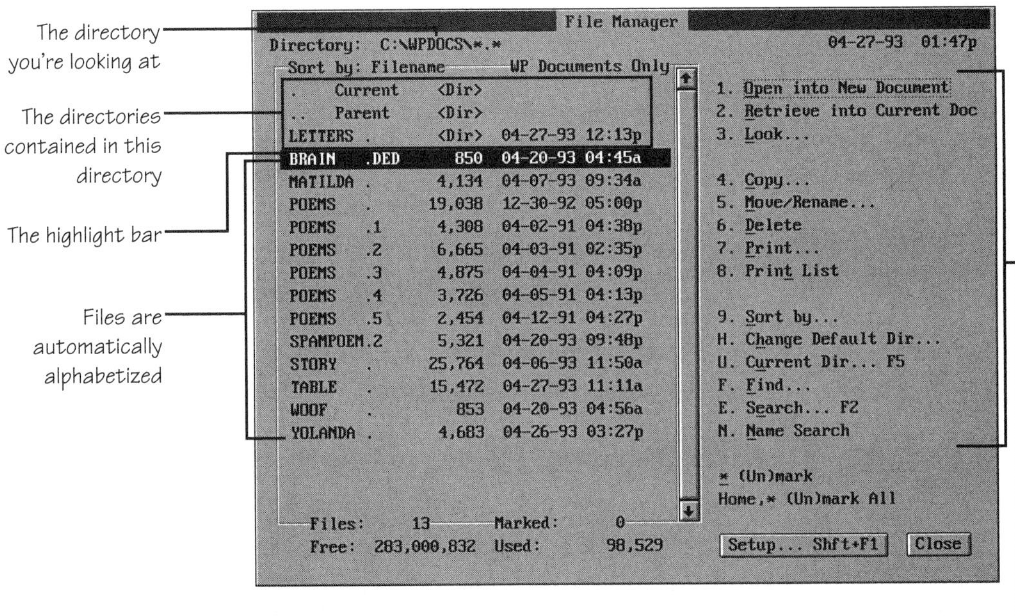

Checklist

▼ Directories are at the top of the screen and have a `<Dir>` to the right of the directory name. The directories you see are housed in the directory you're currently listing.

- Files are sorted alphabetically in the File Manager.
- The file names, at the left side of the column, are the most important part of the information on each line. The numeric information includes how big the file is and when you last worked on it. You'll hardly ever look at these numbers.
- When you're in the File Manager, you move a highlight bar to select the file (or files) that you need to do something with (like print, move, or delete). Use the arrow keys and the Page Up and Page Down keys to move the highlight bar. You can move to the bottom of the list by pressing Home, Home, down-arrow key; move to the top of the list by pressing Home, Home, up-arrow key.
- When you want to leave the File Manager, choose Close. Or, if you're more at home with the keyboard, press Esc or F7. That's right, you have a veritable bonanza of ways to leave the File Manager.

Preview a Document (The Peeping Tom feature)

You've managed to get into the File Manager. You've got a document highlighted. You even think it's the one you want to work on—but you're not sure. If only you could take a look at the file. With WordPerfect, you can.

To peek at the file (that is, to use the Look feature), simply highlight the file in the File Manager and choose Look.

Checklist

- When you're finished looking at the document, choose **O**pen to open the document or choose OK to go back to the File Manager screen.
- If the first screen of the document isn't enough to tell whether you've got the correct file, press Page Down to see another screen of text. You can continue this process through the whole document, if that's the kind of thing you enjoy.
- You can't edit the document in Look.
- The Look feature is good, but it's not exact. It can't display things like fonts, graphics, tables, and text emphasizers.
- If you find that the document you're looking at isn't the one you need, you can look at the next or previous document just by choosing **N**ext or **P**revious.

Open a Document (Open sesame!)

The main reason that you use the File Manager is to open a document that you need. To open a document, start with a blank document screen. Then go to the File Manager (pull down the **F**ile menu, choose **F**ile Manager, and then choose OK).

Highlight the file you want. Choose **O**pen into New Document. The document appears on-screen, and you're ready to go.

TIP

If you like maneuvering around in the File Manager with your mouse, you can open a file by double-clicking on it with your mouse.

EXPERTS ONLY

The document combo platter

Once in a while, you might want to insert one document into another document. Begin by opening the first document. Move the cursor to where you want to insert the second document. Pull down the **F**ile menu, choose **F**ile Manager, and then choose OK to go back into the File Manager. Highlight the document that you want to insert, and choose **R**etrieve into Current Doc. The second document is plopped right into the first document, beginning at the cursor location. You then save the combined document with a new name.

Selecting a File Name Quickly

Before long, you'll have hundreds of documents. When that happens, using your arrow keys to highlight the one particular file you need gets to be a real nuisance ... especially when the file starts with a V or some other letter far down in the alphabet. You can speed up the process by using the File Manager's Name Search feature. Here's how:

1. From the File Manager, choose **N**ame search.

   A text box appears in the lower-left corner of the File Manager. You'll type the name of the file you're looking for in this box.

2. Type the first character of the file you're looking for.

   The highlight bar quickly jumps down to the first file that begins with that letter (or number). You can continue typing the file name and WordPerfect keeps searching for the closest match to those letters.

3. After you find the file, press Enter (or any of the arrow keys) to turn off Name Search.

4. Choose **O**pen into New Document.

Checklist

- If you make a typo while using Name Search, press Backspace to erase characters; then retype the characters.

- One of the most common mistakes when using Name Search is to forget to turn it off after you find the file you want. If you highlight a file by using Name Search and then try to do something with that file—such as press R for **R**etrieve or O for **O**pen—Name Search starts looking for a different file. Press Backspace to go back to the file you want, and then press Enter to turn off Name Search. If you're using a mouse, simply click on **O**pen into New Document—you don't have to turn off Name Search.

What's Its Name?

When you haven't used a file in a while, you may forget its name. It's often easier to remember certain words you used frequently in the document than to remember the actual name of the document.

To look for files that contain certain words, you need to be in the File Manager. Then follow these steps:

1. Choose **F**ind.

   WordPerfect displays the Find dialog box. This dialog box shows the different parts of the document that WordPerfect can search through. The easiest and safest way to find your text is to have WordPerfect search through all the documents.

2. Choose **E**ntire Document.

   Now WordPerfect displays the Find Word in Entire Document dialog box. WordPerfect now wants you to tell it what word or phrase to search for.

3. Type the word that you want WordPerfect to look for; then choose OK.

   Actually, you can type more than one word if you like, but most people get best results when they stick to just one word. Use a word that you're sure has something to do with the file you're using. For instance, if you've just written a Master's thesis on armadillo farms, the word *armadillo* is a safe bet.

WordPerfect spins its wheels for a minute, scanning through all your files for the text you need, and then shows the File Manager again. This time, though, only the files containing the word you specified are in the list. You should be able to find the file you want from this narrowed list.

Printing a Document from File Manager (Avoid the middleman)

When it comes right down to it, the main reason you use WordPerfect is to get your words onto paper. The File Manager lets you print your documents without having to go through the hassle of opening them first.

To print a document from the File Manager, first make sure that your printer is on and set to print. Then follow these steps:

1. Highlight the file you want to print.

2. Choose **P**rint.

Make sure you choose **Print**—*not* **Print List**! They're close together and look a lot alike; it's easy to confuse the two. The only time you should choose **Print List** is if you want a listing of the names of your files printed.

The Print Multiple Pages dialog box appears.

3. Choose OK.

The document is printed.

Printing File after File after File

If you want to print several files—all the chapters in your Great American Novel—you can mark them and then print them. Here's how:

1. Go to the File Manager (pull down the **F**ile menu, choose **F**ile Manager, then choose OK).

2. Move the highlight bar to one of the files that you want to print.

3. Press the asterisk key.(It's the Shift+8 character on your keyboard and looks like this: *.) An asterisk appears beside the file. This is called *marking* the file.

   If you mark a file you don't want to print after all, move the highlight bar back onto the file and press the asterisk (*) again. This unmarks the file. If you want to unmark *all* the marked files, press Home, *.

4. Mark the other files you want to print.

5. Choose **P**rint.

   A dialog box appears, asking whether you want to print the marked files.

6. Choose **Y**es.

   The Print Multiple Pages dialog box appears.

7. Choose OK to print all of the documents.

Your printer begins grinding away.

Deleting a File

Murphy's Law: The minute after you delete a file, you'll need it. Granted, you *do* want to erase files from time to time; it keeps your hard disk from getting cluttered and gaining unsightly pounds. But be careful! If you even *suspect* that you might need a document sometime in the future, don't erase it.

Now that you're too scared to ever delete anything, here are the steps to erase a document you no longer need:

1. Start the File Manager and highlight the file to delete.

2. Choose **D**elete.

   A dialog box appears, asking if you want to delete the file.

3. Choose **Y**es.

The file's gone. I hope you don't need it in ten minutes.

Deleting for Serious Hard Disk Housecleaning

If you're really in the mood for some zealous housekeeping, you can delete a whole bunch of files at once. In the File Manager, highlight a file you don't need, and then press the asterisk (*) key—Shift+8. That marks the file for death.

Mark other files you want to get rid of. If you accidentally mark a file and want to unmark it, highlight the file and press the asterisk key again. When you've marked all the files you want to delete, choose **D**elete. WordPerfect brings up a dialog box and asks

```
Delete marked files?
```

Choose **Y**es. Just to be sure, WordPerfect brings up another dialog box and asks the same question again, phrased a little differently:

```
Marked files will be deleted.  Continue?
```

Again, choose **Y**es. The files are gone. Deleted. History.

Doing the Directory Thing (For organizational nuts)

If you are an organizational fanatic, you may want to set up directories for different types of documents: one for reports, one for memos, one for letters to Uncle Dale. In this case, read the rest of this chapter to learn about the wonderful world of directories.

Copying Files (The file photocopier)

In this wondrous computer age, people trade computer files like they used to trade baseball cards. Here's how you copy a file:

1. Start the File Manager by pulling down the **F**ile menu, choosing **F**ile manager, and then choosing OK.

2. Move to the directory that has the files you want to copy.

3. Highlight the file you want to copy.

4. Choose **C**opy.

   The Copy dialog box appears at the bottom of the screen.

5. Type the path where you want a copy of the file; then press Enter.

   For example, you might type **C:\WPDOCS\POEMS**.

The file is copied to the directory you specified.

Massive File Copying

You can copy several files at once:

1. Mark the files you want to copy.

   You *mark* a file by highlighting that file and then pressing the asterisk (*) key—Shift+8 on most keyboards. The file you highlighted then has an asterisk to its left, which means it's *marked*.

2. Choose **C**opy. WordPerfect brings up a dialog box which asks:

   ```
   Copy marked files?
   ```

3. Choose **Y**es. Now WordPerfect brings up another dialog box, asking where you want to copy the files to:

   ```
   Copy all marked files to:
   ```

4. Type the path where you want the copies of the files; then press Enter. Be sure to type the full path, such as **C:\WPDOCS\LETTERS**.

5. Choose Close to leave the File Manager.

Moving Files

When you're ready to roll up your sleeves and do some serious hard disk housecleaning, the File Manager's Move feature can be a big help. It moves files from one place to another. For instance, you might want to move all the chapters of your Great American Novel into their own directory. Heres how you do it:

1. Bring up the File Manager by pulling down the **F**ile menu, choosing **F**ile manager, and then choosing OK.

2. Move to the directory that has the files you want to move.

3. Highlight the file you want to move.

4. Choose **M**ove/Rename.

   WordPerfect brings up a dialog box which asks:

   ```
   New Name:
   ```

5. Type the path you want the file to go to, such as **C:\WPDOCS\LETTERS**. Then choose OK.

Checklist

- ▼ You can type a different file name after the path name, such as **C:\WP51\DOCS\LETTERS\NEWNAME.DOC**. This moves and renames the document.
- ▼ If you just want to change the document's name, type a new file name. Don't type a path. WordPerfect renames the file and leaves it in the current directory.

If you aren't into directories, you can skip the rest of this chapter. You won't need to do the directory hop.

Creating a New Directory

Few things in life make you feel so organized and purposeful as when you create a new directory for a certain type of document. After all, out of the chaos of the hard disk you've made an organized home for a specific type of file, like letters or memos.

The nice thing about creating new directories in WordPerfect is that it's easy. Just follow these steps from a document screen:

1. Pull down the **F**ile menu, choose **F**ile manager, and then press = (the equal sign).

The Change Default Directory dialog box appears, asking you to type a new directory.

2. Type the path of the directory that you want to create.

   For example, if you want a LETTERS\ directory in your C:\WPDOCS\ directory, type **C:\WPDOCS\LETTERS**.

3. Choose OK.

   A new dialog box appears, asking whether you *really* want to create this new directory:

   ```
   Create C:\WPDOCS\LETTERS?
   ```

4. Choose **Y**es.

   Now you're back at the Specify File Manager List dialog box. Your directory has been created.

5. Choose Cancel to return to your document screen.

   If you want to go into the File Manager at this point, you can choose OK instead of Cancel.

Checklist

- If you're already in the File Manager and want to create a new directory, choose C**h**ange Default Dir; then follow Steps 2-4. You'll end up back at the File Manager after creating the directory.
- The directories you create must be in directories that already exist. You can't create a C:\DREAMS\STRANGE\ directory unless the C:\DREAMS\ directory already exists. You would need to create a C:\DREAMS\ directory, and then put the STRANGE\ directory inside it.

- Directory names follow the same rules as file names: they should have eight or fewer characters and use only letters and numbers. If you make your directory names short—six or fewer characters—you don't have to type as much when you want to move from one directory to the next.

Moving around Directories

If you've taken the plunge and created a whole bevy of directories that you want to keep various types of documents in, you need to know how to move from one directory to the other.

Go to File Manager (pull down the **F**ile menu, choose **F**ile Manager, then choose OK). At the top of the list (just below where it reads `Current` and `Parent`), you see all the directories within the current directory. (Incidentally, directories have a `<Dir>`, whereas files have a number.)

Go to a directory

To go to one of the listed directories, move your highlight bar to that directory, and then press Enter. For example, suppose that you're in the C:\WPDOCS\ directory, but you want to be in the C:\WPDOCS\LETTERS\ directory. Just move the highlight bar to LETTERS and press Enter. Easy.

TIP

You also can move to a directory by double-clicking on it with your mouse.

Go from a directory to its parent directory

How about when you want to move back a level? Say, for example, you're in the file Manager and want to move from C:\WPDOCS\LETTERS\ to C:\WPDOCS\. Just highlight the *Parent* directory (at the top of the list), and then press Enter.

PARENT DIRECTORY

For some reason known only to a few key programmers, a directory that contains another directory is called a *parent* directory. So, C:\WPDOCS is the parent directory to C:\WPDOCS\LETTERS.

Go to a different drive

To list files on a floppy disk, first insert the disk and choose Current Dir to bring up the Specify File Manager List dialog box. Then type **A:** and press Enter to display files on drive A. Type **B:** and press Enter to display files on drive B.

Go from one directory to a completely different directory

Sometimes you'll want to go to a completely nonrelated directory, such as the directory for a different program. Or you might want to go to a different disk, such as one of your floppy disks. Start at a document screen; then follow these directions:

1. Pull down the **F**ile menu; then choose **F**ile manager.

   The Specify File Manager List dialog box appears with a directory highlighted in the text box. The directory looks something like this:

   ```
   Dir C:\WPDOCS\*.*
   ```

2. Type the path to the directory that you want to see.

As you begin typing, the old path disappears, replaced by your new one. For example, if you want to see the list of files in the POLICIES directory on drive C, type **C:\POLICIES**.

3. Choose OK. The list of files appears.

Zipping from Directory to Directory with QuickList

If you start using a lot of different directories in which to keep different kinds of files, you can become confused. Are your letters in C:\WPDOCS\LETTERS or just C:\LETTERS? Or was it just C:\LTRS? It's tough to remember—not to mention type—those long directory names.

WordPerfect's QuickList feature makes it easy to jump to the directories you use most often. Instead of having to remember a long string of words and backslashes, you just look at a simplified list of directories, and then choose from that list. For example, in WordPerfect's QuickList, you would just choose *Letters*—you don't have to worry about the *real* directory name (C:\WPDOCS\LETTERS). WordPerfect supplies the real name.

Making a QuickList

Before you can use the QuickList, you have to create the list items:

1. Pull down the **F**ile menu; then choose **F**ile Manager.

   The Specify File Manager List dialog box appears.

2. Choose QuickList. A fast way to do this is to press F6. The QuickList dialog box appears.

3. Choose Create.

   In the grand WordPerfect tradition, another dialog box appears; this one is called Create QuickList Entry.

4. Type a short, plain-English description of the sort of files contained in a directory you use often.

   For example, if you have a C:\WPDOCS\LETTERS directory that you put all your letters in, just type **Letters** here. If you have a C:\WPDOCS\LETTERS\MILDRED directory in which you keep all your letters to Aunt Mildred, type **Letters to Aunt Mildred**. What you type doesn't matter, as long as it's short and makes sense to you.

5. Press Enter.

   The cursor moves down into the Filename/Directory text box.

6. Type the directory where these files are kept.

   This is the directory you just described in plain English. For example, you might type **C:\WPDOCS\LETTERS** or **C:\WPDOCS\LETTERS\MILDRED**.

7. Press Enter.

8. Choose OK. The QuickList dialog box reappears.

Checklist

- After you create one QuickList item, you can go back to Step 3 and create more QuickList items for other directories that you use often.
- Choose Close to return to the Specify File Manager List dialog box. From there, choose Cancel to return to the document screen.
- WordPerfect comes with some QuickList items preinstalled. These items are mostly worthless. You can remove QuickList items you don't want or need. First, go into the QuickList dialog box. Pull down the **F**ile menu, choose **F**ile Manager, and then choose QuickList. Next, highlight the QuickList item you don't need. Choose **D**elete. WordPerfect brings up a dialog box, asking if you really want to remove that item. Choose **Y**es.

Using the QuickList

Once you've described the directories you use most often, you can use QuickList to get to those directories very quickly—hence the name. Even better, you don't have to type those long directory names or even remember what the directory paths are. To use the QuickList, do this:

1. Pull down the **F**ile menu; then choose **F**ile Manager.

   This brings up the Specify File Manager List dialog box.

2. Choose QuickList.

   The QuickList dialog box appears.

3. Highlight the type of files that you want to see.

   You can use your arrow keys to highlight an item, or you can click on an item with your mouse.

4. Choose Select.

If you're using your mouse, you can just double-click on the QuickList item that you want.

The File Manager appears, showing the files you need. You can now use the File Manager as you normally would.

TIP

The fast way to jump into QuickList is to just press F5, F6 right in a row.

PART V

The Impressive Stuff

Includes:

CHAPTER 16

Speeding Up Your Work (Mousing Around)

IN A NUTSHELL

- ▼ Use the Button Bar
- ▼ Customize your Button Bar
- ▼ Use fonts fast with the Ribbon
- ▼ Use the vertical scroll bar to zip around

f you don't have a mouse or you don't like using your mouse, you may as well skip this chapter. This chapter is for people who like using the mouse or who are at least willing to give it a chance.

There are plenty of good reasons to use a mouse in WordPerfect. Some things, such as selecting text and menu commands, are easier with the mouse. WordPerfect also has lots of shortcuts that you can only take advantage of if you've got a mouse. Finally and most importantly, it's fun to make the mouse pointer dance around in little circles on the screen.

Belly Up to the Bar

WordPerfect's got a million features, but you use only a few frequently. The idea behind the Button Bar is to put a handful of the most common features on a strip of buttons across the top of the screen—right where they're easy to get to. Then, whenever you need the feature, you can just click one of those buttons.

Turning on the Button Bar

Before you can *use* the Button Bar, you've got to be able to see it. Just pull down the **V**iew menu and choose **B**utton Bar. The Button Bar appears across the top of your screen.

Checklist

▼ Each button has a picture of what the feature does, along with the name of the feature under the picture. Sometimes the feature names have to be abbreviated or otherwise squashed in order to fit them in the small space given to the button.

- After you turn the Button Bar on, it stays on. The next time you come into WordPerfect, the program remembers you had the Button Bar on and displays it for you. In fact, the Button Bar won't go away unless you tell it to (see the next item for how to do that).

- You can turn the Button Bar off in the same way that you turn it on: pull down the **V**iew menu and then choose **B**utton Bar.

Button Bar

File Edit View Layout Tools Font Graphics Window Help

File Mgr | Save As | Print | Preview | GrphMode | TextMode | Font | Envelope | Speller | QuikFndr | Grammatk | Search

Poems about Dogs and Water
By Bob Bringhurst and Robert Raleigh

Dog-
Art thou licking a bone?
Art thou Pygmalion?
Lo-

I am the dog!
The empty dish mocks me.
-Bob

The snow is falling,
The snow is falling,
Down on my head.
And I am falling too.
And I am falling too.
And I, too, am falling.
Dissonance.
-Robert

C:\WPDOCS\POEMS Doc 1 Pg 1 Ln 1" Pos 1"

"I HATE THIS!"

Where are the pictures?

If you're working in Text mode instead of Graphics mode, you won't be able to see any of the cool pictures that go along with each button—WordPerfect can't show pictures in Text Mode. In order to see the Button Bar pictures, you need to go into Graphics mode (you can do this by pulling down the View menu, and then choosing Graphics mode).

Using the Button Bar

To use the Button Bar, just move your mouse pointer to the appropriate button; then click it with your mouse. That feature jumps into action. For example, if you click the Preview button, WordPerfect goes into Print Preview. If you click the Print button, the Print dialog box comes up. If you click the Font button, the Font dialog box comes up so that you can choose a font and size. And so on and so forth.

Checklist

- Not all of the buttons on the Button Bar are all that useful. In fact, some of the buttons are strictly for computer guru types. The next section in this chapter, "Customizing the Button Bar," shows you how to display only the buttons you really want on the Button Bar.
- If you look at the very left side of the Button Bar, you'll notice that there are two small buttons on top of each other—one with an up arrow and one with a down arrow. These small buttons are available because the Button Bar can have more buttons than you can see at the same time. If you click on these small buttons, WordPerfect shows you a different part of the Button Bar.

- If the arrow on either of the small buttons is dimmed (light gray), there aren't more buttons to that side of the button bar. Clicking a dimmed button won't do anything.
- The Button Bar is off limits when dialog boxes are showing. If you try to click a Button Bar button when a dialog box is displayed, nothing at all happens.

Customizing the Button Bar

The *idea* behind the Button Bar is great, but the Button Bar itself might not suit your fancy in its current location and look. You can customize the Button Bar so that it's more to your liking. For instance, you may not like where the Button Bar appears. Under the menus is no good—it's too easy to hit a button when you want to pull down a menu and vice versa. Or you might not like the pictures shown on the buttons. Perhaps you would prefer just words. And what about those buttons you never use? Are you stuck with them? No. You can change the Button Bar as you wish.

Moving the Button Bar

You've only got a certain amount of space on your screen, and using some of that space for typing would be nice. By getting rid of the pictures on the Button Bar and making it go down the left side of the screen instead of across the top row, you can fit more buttons into a smaller space. Plus, since the Button Bar is no longer right under the menu bar, you won't have to hassle with accidentally pulling down menus when you want to click a button. Follow these steps:

1. Pull down the View menu, choose Button Bar Setup, and then choose Options.

   The Button Bar Options dialog box comes up.

2. Choose Left Side so that the Button Bar will go down the left side of the screen instead of across the top side of it.

TIP

Sometime, you may also want to experiment with putting the Button Bar on the bottom or right side of the screen. Or you may even want to put it back at the top. In Step 2, just choose **B**ottom, **R**ight, or **T**op instead of **L**eft Side.

3. Choose Text Only.

   The pictures won't be part of the button anymore.

4. Choose OK.

Your Button Bar now goes down the left side of the screen. Notice that all the buttons fit on the screen with room to spare.

"I HATE THIS!"

Now these *&$@!? buttons are too small!

The Text Only buttons aren't for everybody. If you think the buttons are easier to find and click with the little pictures, follow the same steps. However, in Step 2, you should probably choose either **T**op or **B**ottom. If the buttons have pictures on them, not many will fit going down a side. Then, in Step 3, choose **P**icture and Text and then choose OK.

File Edit View Layout Tools Font Graphics Window Help

File Mgr | Save As | Print | Preview | GrphMode | TextMode | Font | Envelope | Speller | QuikFndr | Grammatk | Search | Tbl Edit | BBar Sel | BBar Opt | Exit

Poems About Amusement Parks and Spam
By Robert Raleigh and Bob Bringhurst

Amusement Parks Can Be Hellish

It was stormy, a little after dark
When I did hie to the amusement park.
The rides exhilarated me each one
I danced, I sang, I laughed, not crying none
My joy rose from my feet up to my head
Methought I died, was buried, and lay dead
For still! The fear into my heart did cram:
The thought that in Heaven there is no Spam.
-Bob

Reflection Upon Waiting
for the Roller Coaster

I stood in line so long my feet were sore
And then I didn't want to ride no more
That seems to be the trouble with those places:
They always seem to be filled up with faces.
Those faces gen'rally accompanied
By other body parts--a cursed tide.
The others, hoping there to be amused,

C:\WPDOCS\POEMS.1 Doc 1 Pg 1 Ln 1.22" Pos 1"

Without the pictures on the buttons, the Button Bar takes much less space.

Picking Your Buttons

You don't have to stick with the buttons that come on the WordPerfect Button Bar. You can add buttons for features you use a lot, and remove those buttons that you don't have any use for. The first thing you need to do to change which buttons you have on the button bar is bring up the Edit Button Bar dialog box. Simply pull down the View menu, choose Button Bar Setup, and then choose Edit. A list of the buttons in your Button Bar appears in the dialog box, along with a half-dozen options for things you can do with those buttons.

Checklist

- ▼ To get rid of the buttons you don't use, just use your arrow keys to scroll through the list of buttons. When you find one you don't need, highlight it, then choose the **D**elete Button. A dialog box comes up, asking whether you really want to delete the button. Choose **Y**es.

- ▼ When you've cleared out the buttons you *don't* need, you should have plenty of room on your Button Bar for Buttons you *do* need. To add buttons, choose Add M**e**nu Item. You can then choose features from the menus that you use often; those features are automatically added to your Button Bar. When you're done adding items, press F7; then choose OK.

Here are a few buttons that you might find useful to have on your Button Bar.

Button name	What the button does	Follow these steps
Save	Updates your document; if you haven't named it, has you name the document.	Pull down **F**ile menu, choose **S**ave.
Cut	Cuts selected text to the clipboard.	Pull down **E**dit menu, choose Cu**t**.
Copy	Copies blocked text to the clipboard.	Pull down **E**dit menu, choose **C**opy.
Paste	Pastes text in clipboard into document.	Pull down **E**dit menu, choose **P**aste.

Button name	What the button does	Follow these steps
Sel Sent	Blocks current sentence.	Pull down **E**dit menu, choose **S**elect, choose **S**entence.
Sel Para	Blocks current paragraph.	Pull down **E**dit menu choose **S**elect, choose **P**aragraph.

Fast Fonts with WordPerfect's Ribbon

If you need to change fonts often in WordPerfect, you might want to use the *Ribbon*. This tool lets you choose a font and size without bothering to go to the Font dialog box. You just pick the font and size from a menu (the Ribbon) that's always available on-screen.

Turning on the Ribbon

You need to turn the Ribbon on before you can use it. Just pull down the **V**iew menu and choose **R**ibbon. The Ribbon appears across the top of your screen, right below the menu bar.

Checklist

▼ After you turn on the Ribbon, it stays on. The next time you come into WordPerfect, the program remembers that you had the Ribbon on and puts it on-screen for you. In fact, the Ribbon won't go away unless you tell it to (see the next item for how to do that).

▼ You can turn the Ribbon off in the same way that you turn it on: pull down the **V**iew menu and choose **R**ibbon.

Choosing a Font

To choose a font, move your cursor to where you want the new font to start, or block the text that you want to appear in the new font. Next, click your mouse pointer on the down-arrow button to the right of the current font name in the Ribbon. Your list of fonts appears.

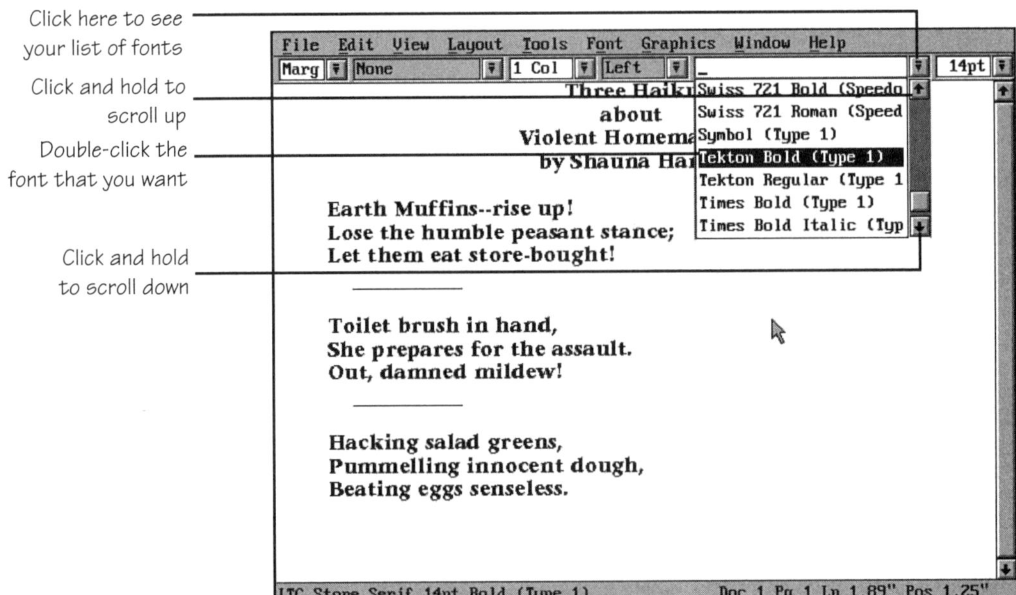

To choose a font from the list, just double-click it with your mouse.

Checklist

- If you don't see the font you want in the list, it may be because the list can't show all the fonts at the same time. Using your mouse, click and hold on the up- or down-arrow buttons at the right side of the font list. This makes the list scroll up and down. Let go when you see the font that you want; then double-click it.
- If you decide that you don't want to change the font after all, press Esc to close the list without selecting a font.
- After you've chosen a font, you also may want to set a certain size. Click the down-arrow button on the far right side of the Ribbon. If the font can have different sizes, a menu of various font sizes appears. Here you can either type a specific point size that you want and press Enter, or double-click one of the sizes from the menu.
- If you're not sure what a *point size* is, read "Giving Documents a Font Lift" in Chapter 11.

Moving Around with the Scroll Bar (Scrollin', scrollin', scrollin' ...)

One of the things your mouse is best for is editing, and one of the most important parts of editing is being able to move around in your document. You need a way to quickly move your cursor through large parts of your document. That's what the vertical scroll bar is for.

To turn the scroll bar on, pull down the **View** menu; then choose **Vertical Scroll Bar**. A bar appears on the right side of your screen.

Scrolling

- You can move the cursor up one line by clicking the up-arrow button at the top of the scroll bar, or you can move it down one line by clicking the down-arrow button at the bottom.
- You can move the cursor down one screen of text at a time by clicking anywhere in the scroll bar below the *thumb* (the box inside the scroll bar). You can move the cursor up one screen by clicking the scroll bar above the thumb.
- If you want to move the cursor an approximate amount, you can click on the thumb and drag it the distance that you want.

Click here to move up

The scroll bar thumb

Click here to move down

File Edit View Layout Tools Font Graphics Window Help

"If, as you say, the butler did it," James asked his detective friend, "how can it be that the Hotchkiss emerald was stolen three days *after* he died?"

"Hmm. A good question indeed, Bartholemew," said Magleby. "I hadn't thought of that. Maybe it wasn't the butler after all. Maybe it was the. . . the . . . the *cab driver*!"

"Not likely," said James, beginning to realize that Sherlock Magleby had a first name in common with the most famous detective in the world, but not a whole lot more. "If you'll recall, sir, the cab driver was taking *you* to the opera at the precise moment the gem was lifted. How could he have done both?"

"Good point, Bartholemew," said Sherlock. "It's for exactly this sort of common-sense faculty of yours that I keep you about. Okay, ummm, could it have been the *butler's wife*?"

"She died with the butler."

"Humph. How about the cook?"

"The cook is Hercules Poirot in disguise. I doubt he took it," said James, exasperated.

"Right. The baron's girlfriend, maybe?"

"Who?"

"Uhh, wrong case. Never mind. How about the possibility that the emerald wasn't really stolen at all, but the owner hid it and intends to collect the insurance?"

"It wasn't insured."

"Sorry, forgot about that. How about the electrician? The electrician could have found a way to disarm the alarm and took the jewel."

"But the alarm went off."

"Oh yes. The butcher, then?"

"No."

"The dentist?"

"Nope."

C:\WPDOCS\NOVEL1.DOC Doc 1 Pg 199 Ln 5.66" Pos 2.04"

TIP

After you turn on the vertical scroll bar, it stays on until you turn it off. Even leaving WordPerfect and coming back in won't turn the thing off. If you want to turn off the scroll bar, follow the same steps you used to turn it on: pull down the **V**iew menu and then choose **V**ertical Scroll Bar.

CHAPTER 17

Using Lines in Your Documents

(Line Up!)

IN A NUTSHELL

- Create lines
- Move lines with the mouse
- Change the line's length and thickness with the mouse
- Remove unwanted lines and wrinkles

One of the easiest ways to give your pages a little pizzazz is to strategically place lines on the page. Horizontal lines at the top and bottom of the page give documents a classy, typeset look. A vertical line can set one column of information off from another. You can also use lines to create unique designs that you can then sell for lots of money at local art shows. Or you can use them like this:

Starr Madding

Actress • Singer • Dancer • Waitress

509 East 52nd Street, #3G • New York, NY • 00098 Phone (382) 555-5555

Horizontal line

Objective To secure a lucrative position in either the entertainment or food services industry.

Education Received diploma from Mott High School, Waterford, Michigan

Graduated with honors from two-week advanced course at Baker Bartending School, Indianapolis, Indiana

Vertical line

Successfully completed two semesters of training at Farling Beauty College, Muncie, Indiana

Experience Nick's Cafe Russiana, September 1980 to present.

•Serve patrons food and drinks.
•Highest tip recipient on staff due to my pleasant personality and choice of attire.
•Often perform rendition of "The Rose" during weekly karoke night.
•Accidentally spilled wine on Casey Kasem, who enthusiastically promised me that I could "go places in this town."

Back of head seen prominently in ferris wheel scene of *Rocky VII.*

Played one of background crew people for Burger King "Hold the Pickle, Hold the Lettuce" stint.

Portrayed "Angry Girl In Phone Booth" in *Physical Evidence.*

Very close to getting part of show girl in *Graffiti Bridge.*

Rode up three floors on elevator with Aidan Quinn during Bloomingdale's 14-hour sale.

Making Lines

Lines are great for separating headers and footers from the rest of the document. They're useful in resumes for separating your name and address from the body of the text. They're also perfect to use if you want to show the brain activity of a rutabaga.

To create a line, follow these steps:

1. Pull down the **G**raphics menu, choose Graphics **L**ines, and then choose **C**reate.

   The Create Graphics Line dialog box appears. Here's where you make the hefty decision about whether the line should be horizontal or vertical.

2. Choose Line **O**rientation.

   A menu pops up with **H**orizontal and **V**ertical options.

3. Choose **H**orizontal or **V**ertical.

4. Make any other changes you want for the line.

   You might want to specify where the line goes, how long it is and how thick it is. (See the following checklist for instructions on changing these.)

5. Choose OK.

Checklist

- If you are making a horizontal line, by default it will run from the left to the right margin, at the baseline of your cursor (the *baseline* is the lowest point for most letters, like "a" and "x").
- If you are making a vertical line, by default it will run from the top to the bottom margin, along the left margin.
- If you want the line to be at a certain horizontal position, choose Horizontal Position, choose Set, type (in inches) the distance you want the line from the left edge of the page, and then press Enter. If you're creating a horizontal line, this position is the leftmost point of the line. If you're creating a vertical line, this position is how far from the left edge of the page the vertical line will be.
- You can set the lines vertical position, too. Choose Vertical Position, and then choose Set. Type (in inches) the distance from the top of the page you want the line to be, and then press Enter. If you're creating a vertical line, this distance is the topmost point of the line. If you're creating a horizontal line, this distance is how far from the top of the page the horizontal line will be.
- You might want to change the thickness of the line. Choose Thickness, and then choose Set from the menu that pops up. Type, in inches, how thick you want the line to be, using decimal values. A good medium thickness for lines is 0.05, and a very thick line is 0.1. Press Enter when you've typed the thickness.
- Yes, you can tell WordPerfect how long to make the line, too. Choose Length, and then type (in inches) how long you want the line to be.

- If you want a line to separate your header from the rest of the document, put the line *inside* the header. While you're in the header edit screen, create the header. (See Chapter 12 for all the dirt on creating headers.) Then press Home, Home, down-arrow key; press Enter to go to a new line; and then follow the steps to make the line. Press F7 twice to return to the document screen.
- To use a line to separate a footer from the rest of the document, you do the same thing as if you were creating a header, but you'd want the line at the *top* of the text, requiring Home, Home, up-arrow key, and then pressing Enter twice to keep the line from sitting right on top of the text.

If you want a border around the page or a paragraph, don't do it with lines. Instead, see Chapter 18. That chapter teaches you the way to make classy-looking borders.

Moving and Sizing Lines with the Mouse

With the mouse, it's a cinch to put your lines just where you want them, and just as easy to make them the right length and thickness.

Start by selecting the line: Move your mouse pointer so the tip of it is on the line, and then click. This selects the line, which makes it look like the line on the right in the screen that follows.

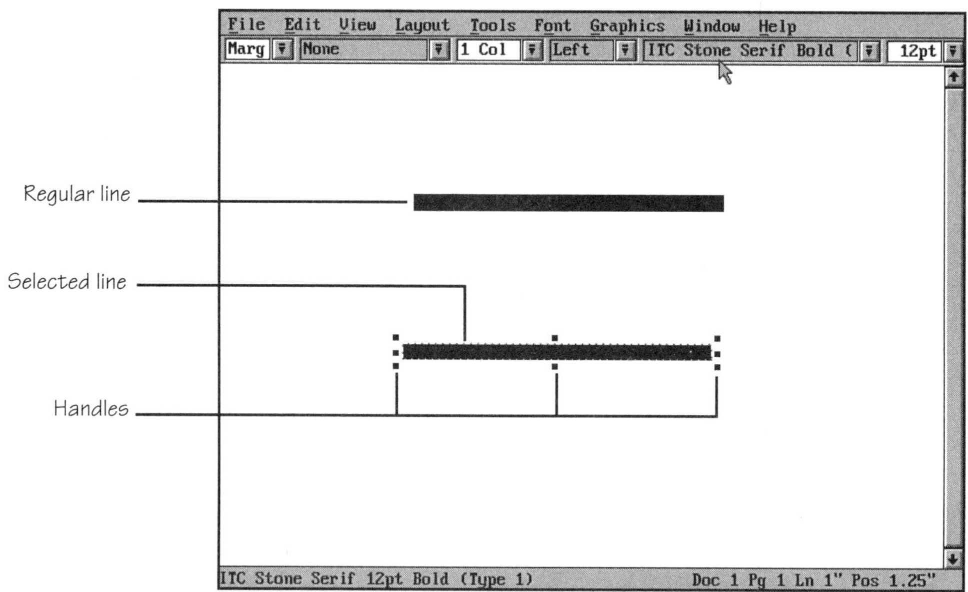

HANDLES

The little black boxes at different places around the selected line are called *handles*. By clicking on the handles and dragging, you can change the thickness and length of the line.

Checklist

- To move the line, use the mouse to drag the line to wherever you want it.
- To size the line, click on the little black handle for the direction you want to stretch the line, and then drag the mouse.

▼ If you want to change the length and thickness of a line at the same time, you need to click on one of the line's corner handles. That way, you can drag up and down, as well as left and right, to change the line's size in any way you want.

Removing the Line

When you first experiment with lines, you'll probably make some mistakes and want to start over—you'll need to get rid of your mangled line. Just select the line with your mouse, and then press Delete. A dialog box appears, asking whether you're sure you want to delete the line. Choose **Y**es to remove the line.

If you don't have a mouse and want to delete the line, it's a little trickier—you'll need to peek at Reveal Codes to find the line code.

To get rid of a line, move the cursor somewhere near the place in the document where the line appears. Then pull down the **V**iew menu and choose Reveal **C**odes. (If the screen now scares you, go back to Chapter 13, which explains all about Reveal Codes.) Look around for the `[Graph Line]` code. To delete the line, put the cursor on the code and press Delete. Turn off Reveal Codes by pulling down the **V**iew menu and choosing Reveal **C**odes.

CHAPTER 18

Using Graphics in Your Documents

(Pretty as a Picture)

IN A NUTSHELL

- Insert a graphic into your document
- Move the graphic to a different place on the page
- Change the size of the graphic
- Remove the graphic border
- Draw a border around a page
- Draw a border around a paragraph

CHAPTER 18

This chapter shows you how to add pictures (called *graphics* in computer lingo) to your document. You can add a flag to your Race Day party invitation. Or add a trophy to your Bowling League newsletter. Friends and enemies alike will be in awe of your computer prowess.

A WordPerfect document with a graphics file (GRIZZLY.WPG) to liven things up.

Come (if you dare) **To The Nelson Family Reunion**

Who: You and yer kin

Where: Wildebeast National Park, Campground Site #12

When: June 13-15— come when you can

Remember last year's reunion when Elden stumbled across the grizzly bear? Or hey, how about when Merrill accidentally set up camp over a red ant hill? He'll do anything for a laugh! This year promises to be just as much fun, so bring your camping gear, softball equipment and frisbees. We're sure to have a good time talking about old times.

If you have any questions, call Jodi at 801/773-9087. She probably won't be able to answer them, since she doesn't even realize (until now) that I've enlisted her as this year's reunion coordinator. But ask her anyway.

Can I Insert a Drawing of My Dog?

You can't create graphics in WordPerfect. Instead, you use prefab graphics. These graphics are stored in a file on disk. Quite a few come with WordPerfect. If you want more, more, more, most computer stores sell packages of graphics files (called *clip art*) on a wide range of topics.

BUZZWORDS

CLIP ART

Clip art is just any drawing or picture saved in a computerized format. You can add clip art to documents to snazz up the documents.

TIP

If you purchase a clip art package, make sure that the graphics format is compatible with WordPerfect (almost all are, because WordPerfect has a clever little program built in to convert other types of graphics into WordPerfect graphics—but you don't have to ever worry about that). Also, be aware that the quality of clip art images can vary from very good to very poor. Ask the salesperson to show you some samples printed from WordPerfect.

Using Graphics in Documents (A picture is worth ...)

There are lots of options for graphics. Do you want to mess with most of them? No. Instead, you can pop in a graphic in the default location. Here's how:

1. Decide what graphics file you want to use.

   Graphics files have file names, just like documents do. You can see what graphics are available by looking at the "Graphic Images" appendix in your WordPerfect manual. The name of the file is under the picture of the graphic. Make a note of the graphic file name you want to use. If you can't find the manual, you can find a good graphic by trial and error.

2. Move your cursor to the top of the page where you want the graphic.

   The position of the cursor in the page isn't really that critical, but the top of the page is a nice, neat place to put codes.

3. Pull down the **G**raphics menu, and then choose **R**etrieve Image.

   The Retrieve Image File dialog box comes up, which is where you type the name of the graphic you want to use.

4. If you know the name of the file, type it and choose OK.

   If you don't know the name of the file, choose File List, which brings up the Select List dialog box. Choose OK to display the File List dialog box. From this list, highlight the .WPG file you want and choose **S**elect.

On-screen, in the upper-right corner, you see your graphic. Ooooh. Aaaaah.

If you're working in Text Mode instead of Graphics Mode, all you see is a box. You'll have to use Print Preview to see the graphic. You can get to Print Preview by pulling down the **F**ile menu, then choosing Print Pre**v**iew.

Checklist

- WordPerfect automatically wraps text around your graphic. You don't have to worry about your document writing over the top of a graphic.
- You can do much more with the graphic: change its size, change its placement on the page, and on and on. Try experimenting. Or get a bigger, fatter, more expensive book on WordPerfect like, for instance, *Using WordPerfect 6, Special Edition*, published by Que. (Say—Que also published the book you're reading now. What a coincidence.)
- Graphics look their best when you print them at high resolution. When you want to print a document that contains graphics, pull down the **F**ile menu, and then choose **P**rint. At the Print dialog box, choose **G**raphics Quality, and then **H**igh. You can then continue printing as you normally do.
- If you get a `File Not Found` message when you type the name in Step 4, choose OK and try typing the name again. Be sure that you type it correctly and be sure that you type the extension. If you get the same message a second time, use the File List feature to highlight and select the file instead.
- Even though the graphics are in color on your screen, they won't be in color on your printed page, unless you're one of the few lucky stiffs who has a color printer, in which case you have permission to feel smug, knowing that I am jealous of you.

Moving and Sizing Graphics

By default, WordPerfect puts your graphic in the upper-right corner of the page. That's fine, sometimes, but you may want to move your graphic to a different part of the page once in a while. To do it, move

your mouse pointer so the tip of it is on the graphic, click the mouse button, drag the graphic to where you want it, and then let go of the mouse button. That's all.

You might want to make the graphic bigger or smaller than how it starts out. With a mouse, it's a snap—without a mouse, it's a royal pain—don't even try it. Here's how to change the graphic's size with the mouse:

1. Select the graphic by clicking on it with the mouse.

Suddenly, your graphic has little black squares—called *handles*—around it. The corner handles are the ones we're interested in.

2. Click—and hold down the mouse button—on one of the corner handles; then drag the graphic until it's the size you want.

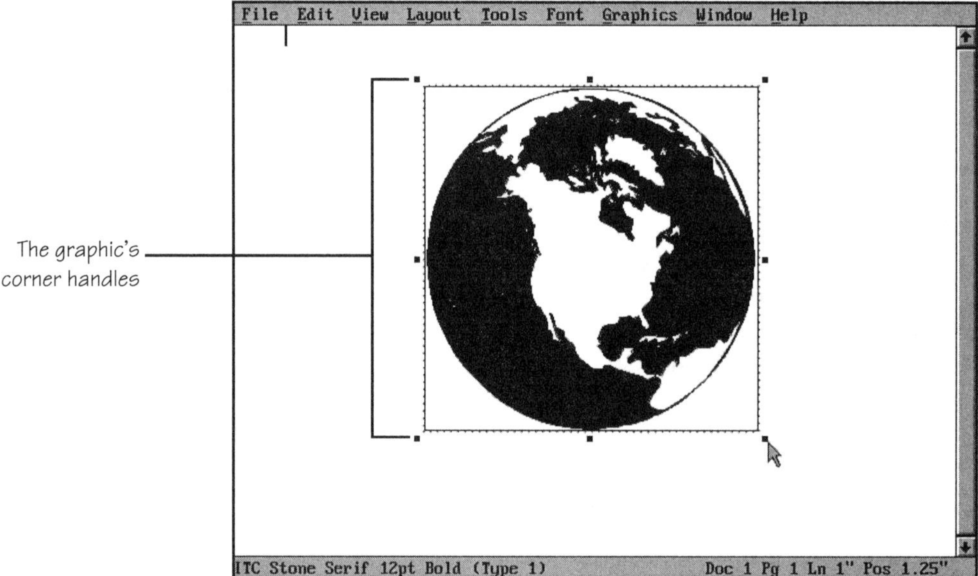

You should click on the corner you want to move. For example, if you click on the bottom-left corner, you size the graphic by moving that corner—the upper-right corner stays where it was.

3. Release the mouse button.

   Your graphic appears as the new size.

Removing the Graphic (No pictures, please)

You might change your mind and decide that you don't need that picture of a tiger's head at the top of your Master's thesis after all. It's easy to get rid of the graphic. Just select it with your mouse by clicking it; then press Delete. A dialog box appears, asking whether you're sure you want to delete the graphic. Choose Yes to remove it.

Adding a Page Border

Occasionally, you might want to put a border around your page to draw a little extra attention to your document. If you need to make your document fancy, read on. If you aren't interested, skip it.

Here are the steps:

1. Move the cursor to the page you want a border around.

   It doesn't really matter where in the page. Just somewhere in it.

2. Pull down the Graphics menu, choose Borders, then choose Page.

The Create Page Border dialog box appears. The defaults are set for a single-line border around the page, which will look just fine, thank you.

3. Choose OK.

Your border's just outside your margins. You can get a good look at it by printing your page or by using the Print Preview feature. (Flip back to Chapter 6 if you don't remember how to use Print Preview.)

Artsy page border

June 18, 1993

824 Rosedale Ct.
Grand Junction, CO 81001

Steven Schmallegar, President
New Moose Cinema, Inc.
468 S. Nixon Blvd.
Orange, CA 82599

Dear Mr. Schmallegar:

I understand that your company is currently shopping around for new scripts. I think I have something you'll like. What I mean to say is, I *know* I have it, but I think you'll like it, if you take my meaning.

I have written a screenplay based on Fyodor Dostoevsky's famous whodunnit novel *Crime And Punishment*. I know, I know, that's not exactly a new idea. But here's the twist, Mr. Schmallegar, and I think you'll agree that this is new: *It's a musical*.

"Why a musical?" you're certainly entitled to ask. Well, I've always thought that the play is just too darn dark, not to mention esoteric, for most people. Sure they want culture, but they also want entertainment—something that'll put a little bounce in their step.

Imagine Raskolnikov as he contemplates murdering the old pawnshop woman. Instead of just stewing and muttering to himself, he breaks into song, something that both conveys his inner turmoil *and* makes us want to tap our toes.

I could go on and on, Mr. Schmallegar, but I think you've got the idea. I hope you're as excited about this project as I.

Sincerely,

Howard Beighfey

P.S. Perhaps with the recent successful animated adaptations of various classic stories, we should consider making this an *animated musical*. I look forward to hearing from you.

Every page from this point forward in your document will have a border. If you don't want it that way, move your cursor to somewhere in a page where you *don't* want the border. Pull down the **G**raphics menu, choose B**o**rders, then choose P**a**ge. The Create Page Border dialog box appears. Choose **O**ff. All pages from this point forward *won't* have a border around them.

Adding a Paragraph Border

If you have a certain paragraph in your document that is absolutely, positively critically important for your audience to read, you can put a border around it. Use these steps:

1. Move your cursor so it's somewhere inside the paragraph that needs a border.

2. Block the paragraph by pulling down the **E**dit menu, choosing **S**elect, and then choosing **P**aragraph.

   Or, if you like using the mouse, skip Steps 1 and 2 and triple-click on the paragraph and drag the paragraph with the mouse. The current paragraph is blocked.

3. Pull down the **G**raphics menu, choose B**o**rders, and then choose **P**aragraph.

   The Create Paragraph Border dialog box springs up.

4. Choose OK.

You've got a border around your paragraph.

TIP

You can actually put the border around more than one paragraph. Just block any amount of text you want a border around, then follow Steps 3-4 above.

CHAPTER 19

Using Columns (Your Own Newspaper)

IN A NUTSHELL

- Set up margins to give your columns extra space
- Place a headline above your columns
- Set your document in columns
- Create columns
- Type the text

CHAPTER 19

You might get so good at WordPerfect that you'll want to set up your own press. You could publish a family newsletter, detailing how the burglary charges against Little Jimmy were dropped and how much happier Pop has been since he got those new dentures. You might set up a neighborhood newsletter, or a company newsletter, or a newsletter for cat haters. Anything you want.

You could lay out your newsletter with one plain column, but that would just announce to your family, neighbors, and coworkers that you are an amateur. Instead, use two or three columns and impress your subscribers. This document has three columns:

NEWS FROM THE BRADYS

Volume III, Issue 2 May 12, 1968

WELCOME . . .
To another edition of "News From The Bradys," the newsletter we send to all our friends and family to keep you in touch with what our ultra-normal family is doing.

Before we get started with each of the kids' antics (and believe me, they've been busy this month), I thought I'd respond to all the letters I've recently received asking about that pesky Partridge family that lives down the street.

Yes, they still practice until all hours of the night. Nobody can sleep. June Cleaver, our next door neighbor, has been especially affected by that nasty Danny Partridge's incessant drumming. She's so upset she can't eat and her hands shake. I could tell how bad she's taking all this noise when the other day I heard her shout, "Darn it Ward, how could you have *ever* come up with such a stupid name as "Beaver?!" I wouldn't be surprised if June has to make another trip to the psychiatrist before too long.

Back to the Partridges, though. No, they *still* haven't painted that horrid bus. No, Ms. Partridge *still* can't find a respectable husband—though I personally think she's in remarkable shape for having had who knows how many children.

And finally, yes, they still have that Reuben Kincaid as their manager. No, I can't figure it out either (unless *he's* the romantic interest, perish the thought). It seems that every time he finds them a gig, it winds up being in a haunted cave, a federal prison or who knows where else. Oh well. Beggars can't be choosers, I suppose.

ONE OTHER NOTE
I keep getting letters from some rather nasty relatives and even a few complete strangers wondering about my past. For those of you who are wondering who my first husband was, it's none of your business.

Now then. Let's see what everybody's been doing!

ABOUT ALICE
What would a Brady Newsletter be without a little bit about everybody's favorite housekeeper/maid/cook/auto mechanic? Yes, of course I mean our very own Alice.

I recently got a call from Richie (you know, the Cunningham boy just across town who looks so much like his younger brother, Opie). He was wondering whether Alice has a last name. That's a poser of a question if I've ever heard one.

Of course, I put the question directly to Alice and she responded, "Not as far as I know. I'm just here because I make good sandwiches and do a great job of making silly remarks, thereby setting the rest of you up for snappy comebacks." Hmmm. Alice seems a little bitter today.

MARSHA MADNESS
Now, onto our children. This issue, we'll start at the oldest—Marsha—and work down. Although now that I think about it, Greg may actually be our oldest. I can never be sure.

One thing that's been concerning me lately is the company Marsha tends to keep. I've seen her more than once with that nasty Laverne and Shirley. Imagine my humiliation—my eldest (or second eldest, see above) hanging out with a couple of *beer factory* workers. I could just die.

Aside from the company she keeps, Marsha is doing

You can use columns for anything you want, of course, but the most common reason people venture into the world of columns is because they're creating a newsletter.

Before You Begin

You're ready to type your first story about Uncle Dale and Aunt Dot's vacation in Dollywood. But wait. First, you have to ask a few questions: What kind of margins do you want around the page? Do you want a headline above the columns? How about a header at the top of each page? You should consider these issues before you start creating columns.

Make Small Margins

First, it's a good idea to use smaller margins for a document with several columns than you would for a document with only one column. With the regular 1-inch margins, you wouldn't have much space for the columns themselves. You'll want smaller page margins—probably a half inch on all four sides.

To change your margins, press Home, Home, up-arrow key to go to the top of the document. Then pull down the **L**ayout menu and choose **M**argins to bring up the Margin Format dialog box. Type **0.5** for the **L**eft, **R**ight, **T**op and **B**ottom margins (you can press Tab to move from one text box to the next), then choose OK to return to the document screen.

Now you have half-inch margins all the way around, which gives you a lot more room for your columns. The art of changing margins is more fully discussed in Chapter 11.

Making a Headline (Read All about It!)

When you use columns, you usually want a headline or banner (like the name of the newsletter) above them. This is where you can put to work all your knowledge of formatting—making text bigger, badder, bolder.

First, go to the top of the document by pressing Home, Home, up-arrow key. Pull down the **L**ayout menu, choose **A**lignment, then choose **C**enter to turn on WordPerfect's Center feature. Pull down the F**o**nt menu, choose Size/Position, then choose **E**xtra Large to turn on an extra large font for your headline. Type the name of your newsletter or your headline or the name of your master's thesis, or whatever, then pull down the F**o**nt menu and choose **N**ormal to turn off Extra Large.

You can quit here if you like. Or you can add a *subtitle*. Press Enter twice to move the cursor below the title. Type any information you want to appear below and to the left of the title, like the volume and issue number. Pull down the **L**ayout menu and choose **A**lignment, then choose **F**lush Right to move the cursor to the right edge of the page. Then insert the date by pulling down the **T**ools menu, choosing **D**ate, and choosing **T**ext from the Date submenu.

Still want more? If you want to add a line, press Enter to move below the issue number and date. Pull down the **G**raphics menu, choose Graphics **L**ines, then choose **C**reate. This brings up the Create Graphics Line dialog box. Choose OK to return to the document screen. This puts a horizontal line at the bottom of your *banner* (the name and subheading of the newsletter). For a line on using lines, read Chapter 17.

Press Enter twice to put some distance between the banner and the body of the document.

Creating the Columns (Divvying up the page)

After you've taken care of setting up the margins and banner for your document, you're all set to go with the columns. Here's what to do:

1. Move the cursor to where you want the columns to begin—generally after the banner or headline.

2. Pull down the **L**ayout menu, then choose **C**olumns.

   The Text Columns dialog box appears. This is where you tell WordPerfect how many columns you want.

3. Choose **N**umber of Columns, type how many columns you want, then press Enter.

4. Choose OK.

   If you already have text in your document, it jumps into columns. If you plan to type as you go, the text forms into columns as you type.

TIP

Limit yourself to no more than three or four columns. Otherwise, the columns start getting very narrow so that only one or two words fits on a line.

Typing the Text

The final step in creating your newsletter is typing the text. Just type away. You can move, copy, delete, make bold, and do everything you can do in a "normal" (one-column) document. The only difference

is how the text flows. When you get to the bottom of one column, WordPerfect takes you to the top of the next one. When you get to the bottom of the last column on a page, WordPerfect takes you to the beginning of the first column on the next page.

Checklist

- If you are only part-way down a column, but you want to end that column and begin the next one, press Ctrl-Enter. The cursor jumps to the beginning of the next column.
- If you're using the keyboard to move the cursor, moving from column to column can be a little tricky. To move the cursor right one column, press Alt-right arrow key. To move left one column, press Alt-left arrow key. Those keys don't work on some older keyboards, in which case you have to press Ctrl-Home, left-arrow key to move left one column. Likewise, press Ctrl-Home, right-arrow key to move right one column.
- If you don't like the text in columns and long for the old one-column format, move your cursor to where the columns begin. Turn on Reveal Codes (pull down the View menu and choose Reveal Codes) and delete the [Col Def] code. Then pull down the View menu and choose Reveal Codes again to turn off Reveal Codes.

CHAPTER 20

Using Tables
(Setting the Table)

IN A NUTSHELL

- ▼ Create a table
- ▼ Type text into a table
- ▼ Change the column width
- ▼ Add rows to a table
- ▼ Remove rows from a table
- ▼ Add a border around a paragraph

Creating a table without a special table feature is a nightmare. If you've ever typed a table, you know what I mean. You type the first column and then tab to move to the second column. You type the text for that column, but uh-oh, one of the words in column 2 wraps to the next line. You can press Tab to move it in line with the second column, but what if you add text? Who knows where anything will line up? And what if the second row is longer than the first? You'll have to readjust the second column again!

If you need to organize a lot of information so that it stays in order and is easy to find, it's time you got to know the Tables feature.

The Tables feature lets you quickly organize and categorize information.

Homes For Sale In My Price Range							
Address	**Price**	**Sq. ft**	**# bedrm**	**# bath**	**# car gar.**	**A/C**	**Rating**
974 W Bernard St	94,000	1480	3	2	2	Yes	***
8201 Hooligan Rd	88,900	1200	2	1.5	1	Yes	**
46 Townshend Circle	96,200	1360	3	2.5	2	Yes	**
232 Peach Street	102,000	1722	4	3	2	Yes	****

This chapter shows you how to make a table and make it look good. You also learn how to move around in your table once you've made it.

Creating a Table

Before you dive into the Table feature, you need to do a little planning. First, the million-dollar question: How many columns do you need? You'd better get the columns right the first time because adding them later is harder and not worth covering here. You might also venture a guess at how many rows you need, but it's pretty easy to add or remove extra rows.

CELLS

Tables are composed of columns and rows of *cells*. A column goes up and down the page. A row goes across. A cell is where the columns and rows cross. A cell looks like a rectangle and is what you type a number or word into.

After you figure out the number of columns you need, you're ready to make the table. Here's what you do:

1. Move the cursor to where you want the table.

   Make sure you move the cursor to the beginning of a blank line.

2. Pull down the **L**ayout menu, choose Ta**b**les, then choose **C**reate from the Tables submenu.

   A dialog box appears, which is where you type how many columns and rows you want. WordPerfect has already chosen the **C**olumns text box for you, so you can type how many columns you want.

3. Type the number of columns you want, then press Enter.

   Now you need to tell WordPerfect how many rows you want. Sometimes you can't tell how many rows you'll need until you've started typing all the information for your table. Just make a good guess. If you have to add more rows later, you can. If you already know how many rows you need, add one to that number so that you'll have room for the column titles.

4. Choose **R**ows, type the number of rows you want; then press Enter.

5. Choose OK.

   Now a table appears, with a complex set of options at the bottom of the screen.

The Table Editor.

```
Dutch 801 12pt Roman (Speedo)          Cell A1 Doc 1 Pg 1 Ln 1.08" Pos 1.08"
   Table_A                        Table Edit
Column Width Ctrl+Arrows  Ins  Del  Move/Copy  Calc  Names  Close
 1 Cell  2 Column  3 Row  4 Table  5 Formula  6 Lines/Fill  7 Join  8 Split
```

While you're in the Table Editor, you can't type text into the table. All you can do is change the structure of the table. You have to wait until you're out of the Table Editor before you can add text to the table.

6. Press Ctrl+right-arrow key if you want to make this column wider or Ctrl+left-arrow key if you want to make the column narrower.

   Keep using these keys until the column is as wide as you want it.

7. Press Tab to move to the next column, and then follow Step 6 again.

Use this technique to make the columns as wide or narrow as you want them. Don't worry if you're not sure about those widths; you can change them easily later.

8. Choose Close to leave the Table Editor.

The options at the bottom of the screen disappear, and the table appears in your document screen. Now you're all set to actually start putting your information into your table.

Checklist

- Tables can have a huge number of rows, but no more than 64 columns. And remember, all those columns have to fit between the left and right margins of your page, so the more columns you have, the less space you'll have in each of those columns.
- If your table will have more than 4 or 5 columns, set narrow left and right margins to make room for all those columns. You learn how to set margins in Chapter 11.

Typing Text into a Table

Now you're all set to type the information that goes in your table. Move the cursor into the top row of the table (use your mouse pointer or your arrow keys to do this). This is where the table's title goes. Center the title by pulling down the Layout menu, choosing Alignment, then choosing Center. Type the table title. The title is centered between the left and right edges of the table.

To type text into the table, move to the cell where you want to add text; then just type the text. Press Tab to move from one cell to the next. To move backward, press Shift+Tab. If you want to move up and down, just use the up- and down-arrow keys. If you're using a mouse to move the cursor around, just click in the cell you want to type in.

Checklist

- If the text in one cell has to be more than one line high, WordPerfect automatically makes the row taller to fit any new lines of text.

- If you have very narrow columns in your table, you may not be able to fit a whole word or number on a single line, in which case WordPerfect wraps your text to a new line wherever it has to. You can either make the column wider (see the section "Changing Column Width", which is coming up here quickly), or abbreviate your text to keep it from wrapping in such an odd place, like this:

ambi dextr ous

- When you move the cursor around the table, the name of the cell shows up in the status line. The columns are lettered—A, B, C, and so on—and are the first name of the cell. The rows are numbered—1, 2, 3, and so on—and are the last name of the cell. The cell name is made up of both the first and last names and looks like A1 or D27.

Changing Column Width

WordPerfect lets you easily make columns narrower or wider. To begin, move the cursor so that it's in that column; then pull down the Layout menu, choose Tables, then choose Edit to go into the Table Editor. You can now press Ctrl+right-arrow key to make the column wider, or Ctrl+left-arrow key to make it narrower.

You can only make columns wider or narrower within certain limits—the whole table can't be wider than the page margins. If you want to make one column wider, you may have to make another narrower.

When you're done changing your column widths, choose Close to return to the document screen.

TIP

If you've got one of those deluxe keyboards with 12 function keys, you can hop right into the Table Editor by pressing Alt+F11.

Adding Rows (One more for the row!)

It's hard to guess the exact number of rows you'll want in a table. You always seem to have just one more item you have to put in the table.

To add extra rows to your table, move the cursor so that it's in the row *below* where you want to add the extra rows. It doesn't matter which column the cursor is in. Pull down the Layout menu, choose Tables, then choose Edit to go into the Table Editor. Press the Insert key. (Sometimes the Insert key just has the word Ins on it. You may have to look around on your keyboard for a minute to find this key.)

The Insert dialog box appears. Choose **R**ows. Next, WordPerfect wants to know how many rows you want to add. Choose **H**ow Many, type the number of rows you want to add to your table; then press Enter. Choose OK to insert the rows, then choose Close to leave the Table Editor. Now you can fill in your new rows.

TIP

To add a single row without going into the Table Editor, move the cursor to the row *below* where you want the new row. Then press Ctrl+Insert. A new row is added.

Removing Rows (One less row to hoe)

Let's say that you enjoy adding rows so much that you go hog-wild and add a bunch more than you need. Now what? Are you stuck with extra rows? No. Just remove them.

Move the cursor so that it's at the top of the set of rows you want to delete. For example, if you want to delete four blank rows—say, rows 19, 20, 21, and 22—you'd move your cursor so it's in the top of those four rows (row 19). The other three blank rows would be beneath it. It doesn't matter which column you're in.

CAUTION

You can only use this method to delete multiple rows if the rows are next to each other. If there are extra rows between the rows that you want to delete (for example, if you want to delete rows 19, 27, 30, and 33), you cannot use this method.

Pull down the **L**ayout menu, choose Ta**b**les, then choose **E**dit to go into the Table Editor. Press Delete. The **Delete** dialog box appears. Choose **R**ows. Next, choose **H**ow Many and type the number of rows you want to delete, then press Enter. Choose OK and those unwanted cells just disappear!

Make sure that the rows are either blank or contain text that you don't want. When you delete a row, any text in that row is also deleted.

Choose Close to leave the Table Editor.

Checklist

- If you delete more rows than you bargained for, you can bring them back, but only if you act quickly. You have to be in the Table Editor to bring back deleted rows, so if you've already exited to the document screen, make sure the cursor is somewhere in the table, pull down the **L**ayout menu, choose Ta**b**les, then choose **E**dit to go into the Table Editor. Move the cursor so that it's in the row below where the deleted rows ought to go. Press Esc. WordPerfect asks whether you want to undelete those rows. Choose **Y**es.
- Yes, it's possible to add and remove columns, too. However, it's a real pain in the neck—avoid it at all costs. Make sure you get the right number of columns in your table the first time.

TIP

To remove a single row without going into the Table Editor, move the cursor so that it's in the row you want to remove. Press Ctrl+Delete. WordPerfect asks whether you want to delete the row. Choose **Yes**, and that row is now just a memory.

CHAPTER 21

Speeding Things Up with Macros

(The Not-So-Scary World of Macros)

IN A NUTSHELL

- Learn what a macro is
- Make macros
- Fix a macro you recorded incorrectly
- Use macros
- Put a signature block in the document
- Turn on double line spacing or single line spacing
- Turn on page numbering

acros. The word strikes fear into the heart of almost all WordPerfect users. And why not? *Macro* sounds like some thing a mad scientist might name his pet robot.

But when you get to know them, macros aren't scary at all. In fact, a *macro* is just a shortcut. For example, if you write a lot of letters, you might like to have a shortcut for typing your address or the signature block. This chapter shows you how to make a macro that types up your entire address when you press a keystroke combination. You also learn about several other macro shortcuts that make using WordPerfect easier.

Making and Using Macros

Creating WordPerfect macros is a lot like making audio tapes on a tape recorder. When you want to record something on a tape recorder, you follow certain steps. First, you pop a tape into the machine. Next, you press the Record button. You say what you need to say, and then you turn off the tape recorder.

Later, when you want to play back what you said, you find the tape and put it back in the machine. Then you press Play. You don't have to do anything else—just let the tape recorder do the talking.

WordPerfect macros work the same way. Instead of recording your voice, however, they record and play back actions you perform in WordPerfect.

To make a macro, you first name the macro with a keystroke combination like Alt+V—this is like popping a tape into the tape recorder and pressing Record. Next, do the steps that you want to be in your macro shortcut. For example, if you want a macro to turn on Print Preview, you press the keystrokes to turn on Print Preview. After you've done everything that you want to be part of the shortcut, you stop recording the macro.

Later, when you want WordPerfect to do those steps again, you just play the macro by pressing the same keystroke combination you used to name the macro. WordPerfect plays back the macro, doing all those steps for you—very quickly.

Recording a Macro (Record!)

Before you record a macro shortcut, you should go to a blank document screen. That way, you won't put codes and text you don't want in the document you're using right now.

If you want to automate a task you perform over and over, create a macro. Here's how:

1. Pull down the **T**ools menu, choose **M**acro, and then choose **R**ecord.

   This tells WordPerfect that you're about to create a shortcut.

   The Record Macro dialog box appears, which is where you name your shortcut. What should you name the shortcut? Pick a letter. Any letter from A-Z.

Think of a letter that you can associate with the shortcut you're creating. For example, if you want a shortcut for going into Print Preview, you might want to use V for View.

2. Hold down the Alt key and press the letter you want to use for this shortcut.

   In other words, press and hold down the Alt key. While still holding down that key, press any letter. For example, if you want to use Alt+V as a shortcut to turn on Print Preview, press Alt+V now. Remember this keystroke combo so that you can use your shortcut later.

   After you press your Alt+letter keystroke combo, ALT*X*, where *X* is the letter you pressed, appears in the Macro text box.

3. Choose OK.

   `Recording Macro` appears in the lower-left corner of the screen.

   You're all set to press the keys you want to be part of your shortcut.

4. Type the text or use the feature you want to be in your shortcut.

   For example, if you wanted to make a macro that takes you into the Print Preview feature and shows you the full page, pull down the **F**ile menu, choose Print Preview, and then pull down the Print Preview's **V**iew menu and choose **F**ull Page. As you choose these options, WordPerfect records your actions.

5. Press Ctrl+F10 to stop recording the macro.

6. If recording your macro leaves you outside the editing screen, press F7 until you're back to your document screen.

You're done.

Checklist

- You might want your macro to take you to a certain part of WordPerfect—such as Print Preview—and leave you there. That's fine. Just begin recording the macro and follow the steps you normally would to take you to the screen you want. After you're there, press Ctrl+F10 to tell WordPerfect to stop recording. You can then exit by pressing F7 until you're back at your document screen.
- You can type text for your macros or turn features on and off, or any combination of the two. For example, create a macro to make text italic, double-space a document, or add page numbers.
- When you're recording a macro shortcut, don't rush through things! WordPerfect records your mistakes as well as everything else you do. When you're recording a macro, take your time. Do everything slowly and surely.
- When you choose OK to start recording a macro in Step 3, you may see a prompt that says the macro already exists. This means you already have a macro by that name. Press Esc to cancel recording the macro (unless you *want* to replace the existing macro); then try a different Alt+letter combo.

Redoing the Macro (I goofed up!)

If you get lost or confused while creating a macro, press Ctrl+F10 to quit. Clear your screen, and then start over.

Pull down the **T**ools menu, choose **M**acro, and then choose **R**ecord. In the Record Macro dialog box, press the Alt+letter combo for the macro to be redone, and then choose OK. A prompt appears, telling you your macro already exists. Choose **R**eplace. Now you can try recording your macro again. When you finish, press Ctrl+F10 to stop recording.

Using Your Macro Shortcuts (Play!)

After you create your macro shortcut, all the hard work is done. Now you can save all kinds of time by using the macro shortcut.

Move your cursor to where you want it to be when you play back your macro shortcut.

For example, if you're about to use a macro shortcut that starts page numbering in your document, move your cursor to where you want page numbering to begin.

Press the Alt+letter keystroke combo you used to name the macro when you created it.

That's it. The macro goes to work, often finishing its task before you can blink.

"I HATE THIS!"

My macro doesn't work on Wallace's machine!

Your macro shortcuts only work on your machine. If you try them on another person's copy of WordPerfect, nothing will happen. You'll have to create the macro on the other machine as you did on your machine.

PART VI

"I Need To Do This NOW!"

Includes:

CHAPTER 22

Make a Memo

(Memo Magic)

IN A NUTSHELL

- Create an attention-getting heading
- Add the address
- Make a divider line
- Type the memo

CHAPTER 22

Business people seem to have some sort of obsession for memos. They crave writing them and are suspicious of people who don't. One employer I had would often write one memo, and then another memo detailing how the previous memo should be filed, and occasionally another memo explaining the reasons he wrote the previous two memos. He was the Memo King.

Even if you aren't memo-happy, you may have to write the occasional memo. And what you have to say is important; it shouldn't be ignored with all the other memos. To catch your audience's eye, you need memos that look professional, open, and inviting. This chapter teaches you the memo magic. Just work through the steps in this chapter, and you'll be all set, memo-making-wise.

MEMORANDUM

To: Bob Cratchit
From: Ebeneezer Scrooge
Date: December 24, 1992
Subject: The gig's up.

Remember the "vision" I had several years past that changed my life—and your income—so much? Well, surprise, surprise. Evidently they were not real ghosts. Nor were they a dream, prompted by a guilty conscience. They weren't even hallucinations brought on by food poisoning. As you well, know, Bob, they were actors—hired by *you* to trick me into increasing your salary.

Before you come running into my office protesting, you may as well know that I have irrefutable proof. I was rummaging through the cellar last week when I happened on a few old costumes, some chains, and a fog machine. Sure, everything was a little dusty, but still recognizable.

I wanted to believe that you had no part in this chicanery, but DNA tests at the lab helped me make a positive ID on several of the actors, who were quick enough to confirm everything. One of them (the Ghost of Christmas Past, apparently) even mentioned that you and she have stayed in contact. She showed me a working script you've come up with for the stage and said you hope to sell the movie rights for 1.8 million dollars soon. I went through hell, and you want to make a *movie* of it? It seems you could at least have changed my name.

You'll hear from my lawyers soon.

The heading, memo information section, and divider line all contribute to an eye-catching memo.

Creating a Heading with Punch

It should be immediately obvious to your readers that they've got a memo in their hands. So, first add all kinds of extra emphasis to the heading: make it all caps, centered, bold, and big. You also can use one other trick to make *Memorandum* extra-prominent: put a space after each letter. This makes the word unusually wide and impossible to miss.

Here's the combination platter for that attention-grabbing header. You can follow all or any of the options you want:

- To center the heading, pull down the **L**ayout menu, choose **A**lignment, and then choose **C**enter.
- To make the heading bold, pull down the F**o**nt menu; then choose **B**old.
- To make the heading extra large, pull down the F**o**nt menu, choose Size/Position, and then choose **V**ery Large.

After you add the emphasis, type the text. For example, type **M E M O R A N D U M**. Press the space bar after each letter if you want to make the word extra wide. Then press Enter. Pull down the F**o**nt menu, and then choose **N**ormal to turn off bold and extra large.

Creating the Memo's "Address"

Next you add the information that tells who the memo is from, who it's for, and what it's about. First, press Enter three times to add some room between your snazzy heading and the address.

The main goal for these lines is accessibility. You want plenty of space between lines. This is how you make a memo address:

1. Type **To:**, press F4 twice, type who the memo is to, and then press Enter twice.

2. Follow Step 1 for the *From*, *Date*, and *Subject* lines.

   When you're done, there should be a blank line below *Subject,* and your cursor should be below that blank line.

TIP

Instead of typing the date for the *Date* line, you can insert today's date by pulling down the **T**ools menu, choosing **D**ate, and then choosing **T**ext.

EXPERTS ONLY

Line 'em up

You can make the words To, From, Date, and Subject right-aligned as shown in the example at the beginning of this chapter. To do so, you need to set a right-aligned tab where you want the words to align, and then press Tab *before* you type each word.

Create a Separator Line

The last thing you do before typing the memo's message is create a *separator line*. The separator line's job is simple: it sets the preliminary information apart from the memo's message.

First, pull down the Graphics menu, choose Graphics Line, and then choose Create. This brings up the Create Graphics Line dialog box. Choose OK to create the line and return to the document screen.

Press Enter twice. This puts some space between the line and where you begin typing your message.

TIP

Before you begin typing the memo, save the framework. Save it with some generic name such as **MEMO**. Then next time you need to write a memo, you can skip all the steps you just went through. You'll just retrieve the MEMO file and change the To, Date, and Subject lines. Type the text for the memo, and then save the memo with a different name.

Typing the Memo

Now all you have to do is type your suggestions, advice, directions, party plans, or whatever you want in the memo.

SHOE®
By Jeff MacNelly
TOMORROW IS THE START OF A WHOLE NEW WEEK.

I BETTER GET MY EXCUSES ORGANIZED.

WELL, NO, I DIDN'T GET TO IT BECAUSE THE COPIER WENT DOWN YESTERDAY.

NOPE. DIDN'T GET THE MESSAGE... THERE'S SOMETHING WRONG WITH MY MACHINE.

SORRY... I MEANT TO GET IT TO YOU YESTERDAY...

BUT MY FAX IS ON THE BLINK.
I TRIED TO CALL IN FROM THE ROAD, BUT MY CAR PHONE'S IN THE SHOP.

I WOULD HAVE FINISHED IT YESTERDAY, BUT THE COMPUTER WENT DOWN...

WELL, THIS MORNING THE LASER PRINTER CRASHED,...

AND I COULDN'T GET MY MODEM ON LINE.

THAT'S THE GREATEST THING ABOUT ALL THIS HIGH-TECH EQUIPMENT:

HIGH-TECH EXCUSES.

CHAPTER 23

Write a Letter

(Build a Better Letter)

IN A NUTSHELL

- Set margins for letterhead stationery
- Add the date stamp
- Add the return address
- Add the forwarding address
- Type the letter
- Create the signature block
- Print the envelope

CHAPTER 23

A letter is probably the simplest document you can create in WordPerfect. Basically, you type. And you type. This chapter covers all the typing stuff, plus a few other tidbits on letter writing.

December 26, 1992

2323 Brazil St.
Apt. 14
East Lansing, MI 80654

Mr. Santa J. Claus
Santa's Workshop
The North Pole

Dear Mr. Claus,

Earlier this month, you and I had a discussion. At that time, you assured me I would receive a certain number of items on December the 25th. I am writing this letter to complain that I did ***not*** get a Ferrari, a speedboat, a new table saw, a laser printer or even a genuine "Indiana Jones" brand fedora.

To refresh your memory, let me tell you what I ***did*** get. I got any number of ties (none wearable), three paperback novels (which, oddly enough, I have never heard of, but my wife wanted), a cookbook, a chef's apron, and purple derby.

Mr. Claus, I was good all last year. So my question is this: What gives? What do I have to do to get things I want, and not things my wife wants for me? Is it that you like her better than me?

I anxiously look forward to your reply.

Sincerely,

Elden C. Nelson
Confused, Overgrown Child

A simple letter writing format.

Adjusting for Letterhead

If you are going to print the letter on letterhead, the first step is to change the margins. (If you aren't printing on letterhead, skip to the next section.)

When you print on letterhead, you need to start the text of the letter farther down the page. Otherwise, you'll print right on top of the "head" of the letter. To avoid this unsightly problem, change the top margin. Pull down the Layout menu; then choose Margins to bring up the Margin Format dialog box. Choose Top Margin. Press 2 and press Enter to set a 2-inch top margin. This size margin works for most letterheads. Choose OK to return to the document.

TIP

If your letter will be shorter than one page, it will look nicer if you center it between the top and bottom margins—like the letter shown in this chapter. To center the letter this way, pull down the Layout menu, choose Page, and then choose Center Current Page. Choose OK to return to your document screen. On-screen, your text won't look like it's centered between the top and bottom margins. Don't worry. It is, and it will print correctly.

The Date Stamp

The date is usually the first thing you put in a letter. With WordPerfect, you don't even have to type in the date. Just pull down the Tools menu, choose Date, and then choose Text to put the current date in your document. Press Enter twice to add some space between the date and your address.

TIP

If you want the date to be up against the right margin, instead of against the left margin, pull down the **L**ayout menu, choose **A**lignment, and choose **F**lush Right; *then* follow the steps at the beginning of this section.

Return to Sender

The return address is just your address, and nothing could be simpler than typing it. Simply type your address, pressing Enter after each line. After you're done with the last line in your address, press Enter twice to make a space between the return address and the *addressee*—the person you're writing.

Checklist

- If you're printing the letter on premade letterhead, don't include the return address. It's already in the letterhead.
- The return address part of the letter usually includes only the address—not your name. Your name will be included in the *signature block.*
- A lot of people put the ZIP code on its own line. Don't. Put the ZIP code on the same line as the city and state.

The Forwarding Address

The forwarding address is just the address of the person you're writing. Typing the forwarding address is a cinch. You simply type each line of the address, pressing Enter after each line. After you've typed the last line of the address, press Enter twice to put some distance between the address and the body of the letter.

The Body of the Letter

Writing the letter is like writing anything in WordPerfect—you just type away. Here are a couple of tricks you should know to get the best possible results:

Checklist

- To make the letter opening, type **Dear Mr. Claus,** (or whomever you're writing), and then press Enter twice to make some space between the opening and the body of the letter.
- There are a few ways you can begin new paragraphs. If you want a space between each paragraph, press Enter twice at the end of each paragraph. If you *don't* want a blank line between paragraphs, press Enter only once; then press Tab to indent the first line of the new paragraph.
- Chapter 11 shows you how you can make WordPerfect automatically put a tab at the beginning of each paragraph.

The Signature Block (Your John Hancock)

After you've penned your letter, it's time to sign your John Hancock. First, press Enter twice to put some room between the letter and the signature. Next, type the closing. You can type **Sincerely**, **Warm Wishes**, **Eat Rocks**—whatever your sentiments are at the time.

Then press Enter four times. This makes room for your signature. Type your name. If you need to put a title, press Enter and type it here.

You're all set to send the letter to the printer. When you print your letter, don't just stuff it into an envelope. Remember to sign it!

"I HATE THIS!"

My name won't fit!

One of the most frustrating things that can happen when writing a letter is getting to the end of the letter and finding that your signature block isn't going to fit on the current page. You don't want the signature block on a page of its own. What do you do? If you have any extra blank lines, delete them. If you can combine paragraphs, do so. You can also change your margins to allow more lines on the page. You might even try using a smaller font—an 11-point font will give you a few more lines per page than a 12-point font. Or, if you are really, really, really trying to cram something on the page, change the line spacing, as described in Chapter 11.

TIP

If you write a lot of letters, you can speed up creating your address and signature block by using macros. Learn how in Chapter 19.

Don't Forget the Envelope!

Before you print your letter, you can make WordPerfect print an envelope. With your letter showing on the document screen, follow these steps:

1. Pull down the **L**ayout menu and choose En**v**elope.

   The Envelope dialog box appears, and WordPerfect has typed the mailing address for you.

2. If you aren't using preaddressed envelopes, choose **R**eturn Address and type your address.

TIP

If the return address you're typing is the one you always use, choose **S**ave Return Address as Default so that WordPerfect remembers your address and automatically inserts it from now on.

3. Have an envelope ready in your printer.

4. Choose **P**rint.

The Envelope dialog box disappears, and out comes the envelope. Now you can print the letter that goes with it. If you need help printing the letter, see Chapter 6, which shows you the ropes.

TIP

Practice printing envelopes before you absolutely have to have one printed. It can be tricky to get the envelope loaded and fed through the right way, so you don't want to be under pressure the first time you try printing one.

CHAPTER 24

Create a Form Letter

(Dear Fill-in-the-Blank)

IN A NUTSHELL

- ▼ Create the form letter
- ▼ Make a list of the names and addresses of the recipients
- ▼ Merge the letter and the list

Suppose that you need to send the same letter out to lots of people. On the one hand, you don't want to send a generic letter. You want to personalize it. On the other hand, you don't want to type the same letter over and over. Is there a solution? Yes! Use WordPerfect's Merge feature.

The idea behind Merge is to write a form letter with some fill-in-the-blank parts, like the recipient's name and address. You then create another document that has a list of the information to fill in those blanks. Then, using the magic of WordPerfect's Merge feature, you combine the two documents, making a personal letter to each person.

This chapter shows you how to work the magic. If you don't need to send form letters, skip this chapter. If you do, read on. The process may seem scary, but it's much easier and less painful than typing the same letter to 50 people.

A Quick Preview

To create a personalized form letter, you need two documents: the form and the data table. The *form* contains the standard text—the text you want to send to everyone. This document also includes secret codes (called *fields*) that tell WordPerfect, "Insert something personal from the data table here."

FIELD

A *field* is a special code that you insert into your main document. The field tells WordPerfect where to insert personal text.

CHAPTER 24

Use Merge to combine a form letter and a list of names, addresses, and other information to create customized form letters.

Address	First Name	Car
Barney Davis 487 Broadway Blvd New York, NY 10302	Barney	1989 Honda Accord
Allison Stevens 898 Chicken Circle New York, NY 10800	Allison	1965 Ford Mustang
Fred Holms 123 Main Street New York, NY 10303	Fred	1972 Ford Pinto

The fill-in-the-blanks list

```
______
______

Dear ____ ,

  Thanks for buying your____ .
It's truly a magnificent car
and you'll get many years of
happy driving from it.
  If you have any friends who
are interested in purchasing a
new automobile in the near
future, I hope you'll let them
know they can find great cars
and friendly service at "Slick
Al's Used Cars."

Sincerely,

Al
```

The form letter

```
Fred Holms
123 Main Street
New York, NY 10303
```

```
Allison Stevens
898 Chicken Circle
New York, NY 10800
```

```
Barney Davis
487 Broadway Blvd
New York, NY 10302

Dear Barney,

  Thanks for buying your 1989
Honda Accord.It's truly a
magnificent car and you'll get
many years of happy driving from
it.
  If you have any friends who
are interested in purchasing a
new automobile in the near
future, I hope you'll let them
know they can find great cars
and friendly service at "Slick
Al's Used Cars."

Sincerely,

Al
```

The merged form letters

The *data table* contains all the personal information that you want to insert, such as the list of names and addresses that you'll use.

Creating the Form (The stuff you want to say to everyone)

The first part of your form letter is the form itself—the part that's going to be the same for everybody who receives a copy. You need to tell WordPerfect that you're going to create a form. To do this, you need to be at a blank document screen. Pull down the **T**ools menu, choose Merge, and then choose **D**efine. The Merge Codes dialog box appears with **F**orm already selected; all you need to do is choose OK. The Merge Codes dialog box appears. You don't need to change anything here, either. Just choose OK to close the dialog box.

After you've told WordPerfect that you're going to create the form part of the form letter, you create the form in about the same way you create any other document. Simply type away. But here's the key. Where you want to insert *personal* information, you insert a field code. You might want the letter to begin *Dear John*. Because the word *Dear* is unchanging text that will be in every letter, just type it.

However, you don't want *John* in each letter (unless, of course, everyone you're sending the letter to is named John, which isn't likely). Instead, you want WordPerfect to insert a different name for each letter. (Those names will be in the second document. More on that later.) To tell WordPerfect to insert a name from a second document, you insert a field code instead of typing **John**.

Here's how you insert field codes:

1. Move your cursor to where you want the field.

   Common places for fields are the address and the greeting.

2. Press Shift+F9.

   If you prefer using menus, you could pull down the **T**ools menu, choose M**e**rge, and then choose **D**efine. However, this process is much slower.

   The Merge Codes (Form File) dialog box appears. This dialog box is where you tell WordPerfect that you want to put in this field code.

3. Choose **F**ield.

   Another dialog box (called "Parameter Entry," and I have no idea what that means) appears with your cursor in a text box.

4. Type a word that describes the kind of information to go into this spot; then press Enter.

   Give each field a unique name so that WordPerfect can tell one field from another. Think of a word that describes the kind of information that you want to go into this spot, such as *address* or *first name*.

   The field appears in your document, looking something like the following:

   ```
   FIELD(first name)
   ```

   `FIELD` always signals the beginning of your field, and the text between the parentheses is the name of the field.

It's not good enough to just *type* **FIELD(field name)** into your document screen. You need to follow these steps or your merge won't work.

5. On a piece of paper, write the name you gave to the field you just created.

   Make sure that you copy the field name *exactly*. You'll need this field name later, when you type the list of names and addresses to go in this form.

6. Follow Steps 1-5 for each place in the letter where you want custom information. Your primary file should look something like this:

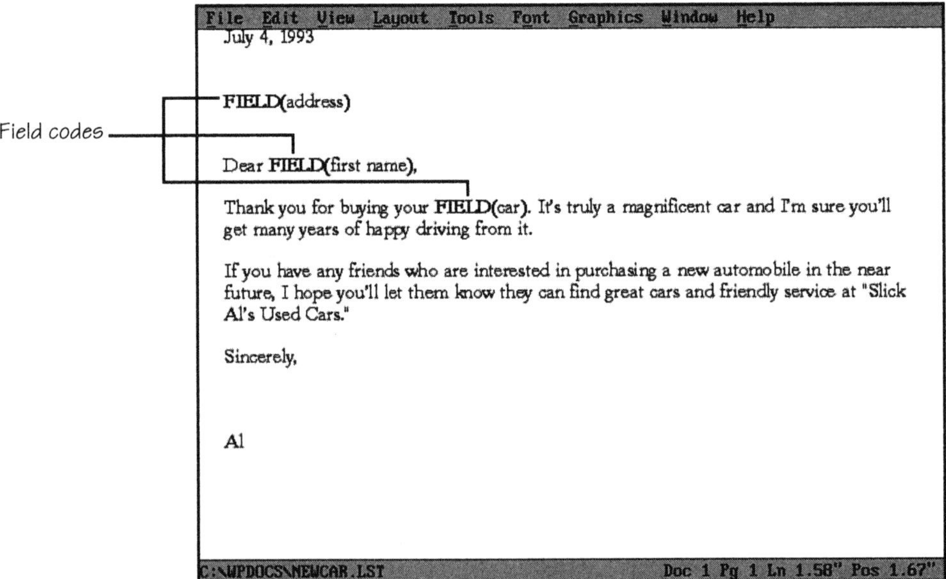

7. When you're finished creating the form letter, save it like you would any document; then clear the screen. Be sure that you remember the name you used to save this form file!

Checklist

- You can use a field more than once in a document. For example, you want to use someone's first name several times in a document. Insert a FIELD(first name) code in each place you want the first name. Sweepstakes letters often insert the name several times:

  You, `Elden Nelson`, *might have won a lot of money. That's right,* `Elden Nelson`, *you could already be a winner ...*

- A field can hold more than one line of text. For example, you'll probably want the reader's address in your form letter, but your form letter doesn't have to have separate fields for each line of the address. Just insert one field, FIELD(address), on a line by itself. The extra lines the address needs will be added when you combine this letter with your data table (the fill-in-the-blanks list).

- If you want a word to come after a field, make sure that you include a space after the closing parenthesis in your field. If you want the field to be the last thing in a sentence, make sure the period comes right after the closing parenthesis. And if you want a couple of blank lines after a field (such as the address field) make sure that you press Enter a couple of times after the field.

- If you make a mistake adding a field, just use the Delete or Backspace key to delete or change a name.

Creating the Data Table (Fill-in-the-blanks)

You've got the letter all set up. Now you have to tell WordPerfect what to insert in the blanks (fields).

There are two parts to making the fill-in-the-blanks list (the data table). First, you tell WordPerfect what you've named your fields. Second, you type the information for each person.

Before you can begin, make sure that you're at a blank document screen.

Name Your Fields (Field of dreams)

WordPerfect uses a special kind of table to hold your fill-in-the-blanks information. The first thing you do when you want to start typing this list is tell WordPerfect what information you'll be putting into the list. Heres how you do it:

1. Pull down the Tools menu, choose Merge, and then choose Define.

   The Merge Codes dialog box appears.

2. Choose Data [Table]; then choose OK.

   This brings up the Merge Codes (Table Data File) dialog box.

3. Choose Create a Table with Field Names.

   The Field Names dialog box appears with your cursor in the Field Name text box.

4. Type the field names that you wrote down, pressing Enter after each one. You don't have to type the parentheses that went around the field names in your form file. Just type the name. For instance, if you have a field named *address*, simply type **address**. You don't need to worry about having the same letters capitalized, though.

Type the field names in the order that you will enter the fields. For example, if you'll type the first name, last name, address, and then phone number, type the field names in that same order.

5. When you're finished typing the field names, choose OK.

The prompt disappears, and a table appears at the top of your screen, looking something like this:

File Edit View Layout Tools Font Graphics Window Help

address	first name	car

Dutch 801 12pt Roman (Speedo) Cell A2 Doc 1 Pg 1 Ln 1.39" Pos 1.08"

WordPerfect creates a column for each type of information that you'll have in your fill-in-the-blanks list.

TIP

Some kinds of information are wider than others. For example, your address is probably longer than your first name. You can adjust the width of your data table's columns in order to match the amount of information that needs to fit. For information on how, read "Changing Column Width" in Chapter 20.

Make the Fill-in-the-Blanks List

The ugly part is over. Now you simply type the information for each letter. (You should still be in the document with the field code cheat sheet at the top.)

Type the text for the current field. If you're not sure what field you're in, look at the top of the column. The field name appears there.

CAUTION

Don't press Enter after you type the text, unless you're typing a multiline field like an address. If you do accidentally press Enter, press Backspace to go back up to the previous line.

Also, if you are typing a multiline field, press Enter at the end of each line—except the last one.

After you type the field, press Tab. This process moves your cursor to the next column, where you're ready to enter another piece of information.

TIP

Sometimes you'll come to a column where you don't have anything to type for a certain person. When this happens, just press Tab to skip pass that column, leaving it blank.

After you've typed all the fill-in-the-blank information about one person, you're ready to start over, typing the same kind of information about the next person who will receive the letter. When you press Tab in the last column, WordPerfect creates a new row in the table so that you're ready to begin again.

Type the information for the next person in this new row.

Save the document, and then clear the screen. Be sure to save the document with a name that you will remember.

Merging the Two Letters (All together now)

So you've made your form letter and your fill-in-the-blanks list. Now you're ready to combine the two into your personalized, customized, gee-whiz, merged letters.

Make sure that you're at a blank document screen. Then follow these steps:

1. Pull down the **T**ools menu, choose M**e**rge, and then choose **R**un.

   The Run Merge dialog box appears. Here's where you tell WordPerfect the names of the form and data table files that you want to combine.

2. Choose Form File and type the name of your form letter; then press Enter.

   For example, if you were making a form letter to clients who hadn't paid up, you might have named your form letter DEADBEAT. In that case, you would type DEADBEAT here and then press Enter.

   Now WordPerfect wants to know the name of your fill-in-the-blanks list.

3. Choose **D**ata File and type your fill-in-the-blanks list file name; then press Enter.

4. Choose Merge.

A prompt appears in the bottom-left corner of the screen, counting off the form letters it's merging. This prompt is to let you know that WordPerfect is busy combining your two files and has not taken a vacation to the Bahamas.

When the merge is done, all of your personalized form letters are in one document with page breaks (shown as double bars going across the page) separating each letter.

Checklist

- If you've got an especially large fill-in-the-blanks list, the merge could take a while.
- The document created by your merge doesn't have a name. If you want to keep the document, you need to save it.

TIP

You can have WordPerfect send all of your form letters straight to the printer instead of into one giant document. Follow steps 1 through 3, choose **O**utput, and then choose **P**rinter from the menu that pops up. Choose Merge to start. Make sure that you've got plenty of paper in the printer!

PART VII

The Quick and Dirty Dozens

Includes:

12 Cool Things You Can Do in WordPerfect

12 Things You Should Never Do in WordPerfect

12 Heart-Stopping WordPerfect Messages and What To Do about Them

12 Features You Should Leave Alone unless You Have Time To Kill

12 Common Mistakes

12 Best WordPerfect Shortcuts

I HATE WORDPERFECT 6

Quick and Dirty Dozens

12 Cool Things You Can Do in WordPerfect

1. Get back, Jack.

When you're really on a word processing roll, it's easy to accidentally hit the Page Down key when you meant to simply hit Delete. Now you have to find where you were, right? Wrong. Just press Ctrl+Home twice, and your cursor jumps back to where you were typing. Just make sure you press Ctrl+Home, Ctrl+Home before you do anything else, or WordPerfect will forget where you were last working.

2. I've got your number.

You may need to insert the current page number somewhere in your text. *Don't* just type the number you see by Pg in the lower right corner of the screen. After all, that number might change when you edit. Instead, press Ctrl+P. That puts the page number at your cursor. As you edit the document, the page number automatically updates, so it's always the *right* number.

Use this Ctrl+P trick in headers and footers for page numbers, too.

3. Document dog tags.

Lots of offices keep printed copies of their documents on file. When you want to make a change to one of those documents, though, it's sometimes not so easy to remember what the document's file name is. The easy solution? Put the document's name at the bottom of the document. WordPerfect even has an easy way to do that, so if you change the name of the document, the file name at the bottom of the document changes, too. Move your cursor to where you want the name of the file (Home, Home, Down arrow key to go to the end of the document; then press Enter

a couple of times to move to a new line). Pull down the Layout menu, choose Other, and then choose Insert Filename to bring up the Insert Filename dialog box. Choose Insert Path and Filename, and then choose OK to close the dialog box. Choose OK in the Other Format dialog box to return to your document screen and see your document filename appear.

4. You can say that again.

When you're working on certain topics, chances are you'll use certain words and phrases over and over. No point in retyping them. Use the Alt+Number shortcut instead.

First, you need to tell WordPerfect what text you'll be repeating, and the keystroke combo that should put that text in the document. To do this, type the word or phrase you use often, block that text by pressing F12 or Alt+F4, and then use your arrow keys to highlight the text. Next, press Ctrl+Page Up, and then choose Assign Variable. In the Assign Variable dialog box, press a number, 0-9, and then press Enter. Whenever you need that word or phrase, hold down the Alt key and press that number. With no more effort on your part, the text appears. You can use this trick for up to 10 Alt+number combinations. Note that when you leave WordPerfect, the shortcuts are erased.

5. Math 101.

Don't go digging through your desk drawer looking for that calculator—WordPerfect has one that works just fine. Pull down the Tools menu, choose Macro, choose Play, type calc and choose OK. A calculator pops up on your screen. Press keys on your keyboard to type the numbers and operators, or click the buttons with your mouse (but that's kind of slow).

A couple of the operator keys are a little different. Use * for multiplication and / for division. Use either = or Enter to perform the calculation, and C/CA to clear the display. If you need the number in your document, Choose Ins. When you're done with the calculator, press Esc to make it disappear.

6. Find your file fast!

Instead of pulling down the File menu, choosing File Manager and choosing OK to go to the File Manager, press F5 twice to get there even faster. As an extra bonus, this trick takes you back to the same directory and file you used the last time you were in List Files. This trick is great when you've had to navigate through tons of directories to find a file, and then later found that you need to go back to that directory. F5, F5 gets you there without all the finger work.

7. Joined at the hip.

It doesn't work to have dates or proper names split across two lines by WordPerfect. You can avoid this problem by pressing Home, space bar (instead of just the space bar) between words that need to be kept on the same line. For instance, if I were Elvis Presley (and do you really know for absolutely sure that I'm *not*?) and I were typing my name, I would type Elvis, press Home, space bar, and *then* type Presley. That way, both my first and last name would stay on the same line.

8. Does anybody really know what time it is?

One of the most important questions in the world is "How long 'til 5:00?" You can use WP to quickly find the current time by pressing F5, F5 and looking in the upper-right corner, which shows the current time, date, and temperature. Okay, the temperature isn't really displayed. Choose Close (or just press F7) to go back to the document.

9. **Stuck in the middle with you.**

As you type, your cursor works toward the bottom of the screen until you're stuck at the bottom row, where lines wrap up one at a time. What a nuisance. Press Alt+F3, Alt+F3 and half the screen scrolls up so that your cursor is in the middle of the screen. Go ahead and type until you're at the bottom of the screen, and then do the trick again.

10. **Dashing dashes.**

An em-dash is, simply enough, a dash about the width of an "m." People use them when they're not sure what punctuation they *really* should be using. You'll notice them in this book—right here, for instance. When using typewriters, people would fake em-dashes by pressing the dash key (-) twice. Now that we've got computers, you can use *real* em-dashes, which look better. Just press Ctrl+A and press the dash (-) key twice.

11. **Billions and billions of fonts.**

Different projects look best in different kinds of fonts, so it's nice to know what kind of fonts you have available. WordPerfect can make a sampler of all the fonts you have. Before following these steps, make sure you're at a new document. Pull down the **T**ools menu, choose **M**acro, choose **P**lay, type **allfonts** and choose OK. A meter appears, letting you know WordPerfect's chugging away—this could take a couple of seconds or a couple of minutes. When the meter disappears, you can print the list, so you'll have a permanent record of all the fonts you have and what they look like.

12. Hide and seek.

You can hide text you're pretty sure you don't need, but make it reappear if it turns out you *do* want it.

To hide some text, pull down the Edit menu, choose **B**lock, and then use the arrow keys to highlight the text you want to hide. Pull down the F**o**nt menu, and then choose Hidden Text. In the Hidden Text dialog box, choose **H**idden Text, and make sure that Show All Hidden Text is *not* selected (if there is a check in the check box, choose **S**how, otherwise leave it alone). Choose OK. Your blocked text disappears—but you can bring it back if you want to. To make hidden text reappear, pull down the F**o**nt menu, and then choose Hidden Text. In the Hidden Text dialog box, choose **S**how All Hidden Text, so there *is* a check in the check box. Choose OK, and your questionable text magically reappears.

12 Things You Should Never Do in WordPerfect

1. No spaces!

Don't use the space bar to indent the beginning of a paragraph or to make columns.

The space bar is a tempting key—it's so much bigger than all the others. You may be in the habit of pressing the space bar five times each time you start a new paragraph, or maybe you use the space bar to line up columns of information. Get out of the habit quickly. If you use the space bar to begin paragraphs or start columns, things probably won't line up on the printed page.

Use the Tab key instead. The Tab key was made specifically for beginning paragraphs and lining up columns.

2. I said, No spaces!

Don't use the space bar to go to the next line in a document. When you need to put some space between paragraphs or lines in a document, don't lean on the space bar until you've created those lines of space. If you ever edit your work, those spaces will shift around and wreak havoc on your document. Instead, when you need to move down a line, just press Enter. If you need to move down a few lines, press Enter a few times. Don't, however, use Enter to go all the way to the next page (that's the next tip).

3. Breaking up is easy to do.

Don't use the Enter key to go to the next page. If you just finished a title page and want to begin on a fresh page for the body of your document, don't keep pressing Enter until you see that row of dotted lines. Instead, just press Ctrl+Enter.

4. I'm feeling a little off-center.

WordPerfect has a couple of ways you can center your text between the left and right margins—Center Justify and Center Alignment. Center Justification is above Center Alignment, so you'll be tempted to use it when centering titles and so forth. Don't. Center *Justify* is for when you want to center whole pages worth of stuff—not just a line or two. When you want to center a line, just press Shift+F6. It's easier than trying to remember which Center is which.

5. Replacement files.

Don't blindly replace one file with another. You've been typing away at a new document, and it's time to give it a name. You pull down the **F**ile menu, choose **S**ave, type a name, and then press Enter. WordPerfect asks:

```
Replace (your file)?
```

If you aren't intentionally replacing an old file with this new one, choose **N**o; then type a new name for your new file. Otherwise, you could erase a file that you'll need someday.

6. Proper page number etiquette.

With typewriters, you had to type page numbers on each page. If you try the same thing in WordPerfect, you'll get disastrous results. Any time you edit the document, your manually typed page numbers will shift around, winding up too far down on the page, or even somehow jumping onto the previous page.

Instead of typing page numbers, use the page numbering feature. Go to the top of the document (press Home, Home, up-arrow key), pull down the **L**ayout menu, choose **P**age, choose Page **N**umbering, and then choose Page Number **P**osition. In the Page Number Position dialog box, choose Top R**i**ght to have page numbers in the top right corner of the page. Choose OK in as many dialog boxes as you have to return to the document screen. You won't be able to see the page numbers, but they'll be added when you print.

7. I *probably* don't need this file.

Don't delete files you don't understand. When you look in your WordPerfect directory (usually C:\WP60), you notice a lot of files. If you're ever in the mood to clear up some space on your hard drive, you may be tempted to delete some of those files. Well, look elsewhere, my friend. Most of those files are critical to run WordPerfect smoothly. Be especially careful not to delete any files that end with .EXE, .COM, .FIL, .PRS, .ALL, CVX, VRS, .DRS, or .FRS.

8. Security clearance.

Don't use the Password Protect feature. I didn't cover the Password Protect feature in this book on purpose because it's too tempting.

The thought of having your own secret, private files that nobody but you can read is just too mysterious to resist. You'll probably eventually find the Password feature on your own and want to try it out. Well, chances are that somebody who's *really* serious about reading your files could get right past your password. Besides, the chances of you forgetting your password (so you can't retrieve your own file) are much greater than the chances of somebody else wanting to read your diary.

9. Practice makes perfect.

Don't experiment with new features while you're working on actual real-world work. If something gets messed up, you don't want to have to try to root through your document looking for whatever bizarre codes this strange feature-creature might have inserted. Instead, the first time you try something new, try it on either a blank document or an unimportant one. Don't use the feature in a real document until you've got a handle on how it works.

10. Save, save, save, and save again.

Don't type a document without frequently saving it. When your typing is really on a roll, it's easy to forget to update your document from time to time. That's a big mistake. You wouldn't like it if all those brilliant paragraphs were to suddenly go to the great computer graveyard in the sky. But it could happen unless you save your documents early, and save them often. Read Chapter 3, "Save Your Work," to learn how to save and update your document.

11. Exit stage right.

Don't turn off your computer without exiting WordPerfect first. When the whistle blows, you want to turn off the computer and get out of the office as fast as you can. It's almost enough to make you want to just turn off your computer before you exit WordPerfect. Don't do it.

When you exit WordPerfect, it does some important file housecleaning. If you turn off your computer before you exit WordPerfect, the next time you try to use it, WordPerfect will ask you all kinds of strange and time-consuming questions before you can get to work.

12. **Can't touch this.**

As you get better at WordPerfect, you might feel the urge to explore this strange new program. That's fine. There are, however, a few features that you just aren't very likely to ever need, and I recommend staying away from them. When you see these options in menus and dialog boxes, just ignore them: Hypertext, Equations, Sound Clips, Gradient Fills, Math, Fill Styles, Table of Authorities (unless you're a lawyer, in which case you won't pay attention to anything I say anyway), Spreadsheet. There are more, but most of them are safely tucked away where you won't likely ever see them.

12 Heart-Stopping WordPerfect Messages and What To Do about Them

1. **`Backup File Exists`**

This dialog box, along with a long message, appears every once in a while when you start WordPerfect. The best thing to do is choose the last of the three options: Open. A document appears in WordPerfect—probably one you recognize and should save.

Why does this message come up? The last time you used Word-Perfect, you didn't exit correctly. Either the computer hung up, the power went out, or you just turned off the machine before exiting WordPerfect. So, the next time you start WordPerfect, WordPerfect wants to know if anything is amiss. The file you opened was the file you were working on last when you shut off the computer.

2. `File not found – `*`your file`*

This message appears when you try to open a document by pulling down the **F**ile menu, choosing **O**pen, typing a file name, and choosing OK. The message means that you made a mistake when typing the file name. When you get this message, choose OK to return to the Open Document dialog box. Look carefully at the file name you typed. If you see the mistake, correct it, and then choose OK. If you get the message again, choose File Manager and open the document from the File Manager list of files.

3. `Macro interpreter error`

This dialog box pops up with the message macro file not found when you press an Alt+letter key combo that doesn't either pull down a menu or start a macro. Press Esc to make the message go away, and then try a different key combo.

4. `Unknown file format`

This message just means that you've tried to open a file that Word-Perfect can't read. For example, youll get this message if you try to retrieve a program. Choose OK to make this message disappear.

Don't bother trying to retrieve the file again; you won't have any better luck the second time. Try opening a different file. If this really is the file you need to work on, you'll need to get a computer guru—a really good one—to help you out. You'll need a special computer program to either repair or convert the file, which is way, way, way beyond the scope of this book.

5. `Too much text`

This message happens when you try to put more information in a header or footer than will fit. Usually this means that you were making a header or footer, and then forgot and started typing the rest of the document. When you finally tried to exit, WordPerfect gave you this error. To take care of the problem, either delete or cut some of the text in the header or footer, and then leave the header or footer. You can now paste or restore the text you had to remove. (For information on deleting and restoring text, see Chapter 2. For information on cutting and pasting, see Chapter 8.)

6. `Cancel all print jobs?`

You've sent one or more print jobs to the printer, and now you want to leave WordPerfect. Problem is, WordPerfect's not done printing. If you really have decided that you don't want to print after all, choose **Y**es to cancel all your print jobs and leave WordPerfect. Otherwise, choose **N**o to return to the WordPerfect screen.

7. `ERROR: Access denied`

This nasty-sounding message reads as though you've just tried to break into NASA's main computer. Nothing so glamorous here. Instead, this message probably means one of three things. It could be that you tried to save a document with a name that already

exists; the file with that name has been protected from being overwritten. Or you might have tried to give a document the same name as a directory. Finally, the disk you're trying to save to might be full. Choose OK, and then try saving with a different name. If that doesn't work, you may need to delete some other documents from your hard disk before you can save this one.

8. `Replace (filename)?`

You've just tried to name a document with the same name as a file that already exists. If you're just updating a document, this is no big deal. Just choose **Y**es and get back to work. If you're doing a first save on your document, however, you might be about to erase a file you don't want to lose. Choose **N**o, type a different file name, and then press Enter again to save the document with the different file name.

9. `Directory not empty. Cannot delete.`

You're getting just a touch to zealous in your hard disk housecleaning. You just tried to delete a directory that still has files in it. WordPerfect can't allow that. Choose OK to make the message go away. If you really want to delete a directory, you need to remove all the files from that directory first.

10. `Write protect error writing drive A. Press any key to continue.`

The disk you're trying to save a file on has been fixed so that you can retrieve information from it, but you can't put new files on it. The best solution is to take the floppy disk out of the drive and use a different floppy disk. Whoever doesn't want you putting files on that disk probably has a pretty good reason.

If you must put a file on that floppy disk, first take it out of the drive. If it's a 5.25-inch disk, there's probably a piece of tape covering up a notch on the right edge of the disk (that is, the right side when you're reading the disk label). Remove that piece of tape, insert the disk into the floppy drive, press a key to make the Write protect error message disappear, and then try saving to the floppy disk again.

If you were trying to save to a 3.5-inch disk, remove the disk from the drive, turn it over, and slide the little plastic square (in the upper left corner of the disk) so you can't see a hole through that corner. Put the disk back into the floppy disk drive, press a key to make the Write protect error message disappear, and then try saving to the floppy disk again.

11. `Drive A Not Ready. 1 Retry; 2 Cancel`

You're trying to save a document to your floppy drive, but there's no floppy diskette in there, the disk is damaged, or the drive door isn't closed. Make sure you've got a disk in the drive, close the door, and press 1 to try saving again.

12. `ERROR: Invalid drive/path specification`

You're trying to save or retrieve a file to a certain directory, but that directory doesn't exist. This almost always means that you typed the name of the directory wrong. Choose OK to make the message go away, and then take a look at the directory the way you typed it, fix whatever you mistyped, and choose OK to try again.

12 Features You Should Leave Alone Unless You Have Time To Kill

1. Advanced advance.

You can make your cursor magically move to any point on the page by using the Advance command. This is nice if you need to put a word exactly 2.75 inches from the top of the page or 1.89 inches from the left side of the page. If you need WordPerfect to print on pre-printed forms, you may need to deal with Advance.

Pull down the **L**ayout menu, choose **O**ther, and then choose **A**dvance to bring up the Advance dialog box.

Choose From **T**op of Page if you want to specify how far from the top of the page (not margin) you want your text to be, or choose **F**rom Left Edge of Page to tell WordPerfect how far from the left side of the page you want the text to be. Type the measurement you want; then press Enter. Choose OK twice to return to the document screen.

2. Where's the end of the paragraph?

When you're using WordPerfect, it's sometimes handy to know where you've pressed Enter. If you want a symbol to appear on-screen at the end of paragraphs, pull down the **V**iew menu; then choose Scree**n** Setup to bring up the Screen Setup dialog box. Choose **D**isplay Characters, and then **H**ard Return Character. Here's where you can type the character that you want to show up whenever you press Enter. I recommend the paragraph symbol (¶).

To insert this, press Ctrl+W; then type 4,5 (don't forget the comma between the 4 and 5) and press Enter. Choose OK to return to your document screen. Now, when you press Enter at a document screen, the end of your paragraph is signaled by a paragraph symbol. This symbol only shows up on-screen, not on the printed page.

If you decide you don't like having an end-of-paragraph marker after all, pull down the View menu, choose Screen Setup, choose Display Characters, and then Hard Return Character. Then press the space bar to get rid of the character. Choose OK to return to your document screen.

3. I see clearly now.

Most people work in WordPerfect's Graphics mode. This lets you see your fonts, graphics and attributes while you type. There's another view mode for the ultra-finicky: The Page Mode. If you turn the page mode on, you can see your margins, headers, footers, page numbers and everything else as you type. To turn this mode on, pull down the View menu and choose Page Mode.

4. Overstrike! Overstrike!

Some day, a crazy notion to print two characters on top of each other may come into your head. For instance, you may want a zero with a slash through it (Ø) to make sure that nobody mistakes it for a capital O. The Overstrike feature lets you put two characters on top of each other. Pull down the Layout menu, choose Character, choose Create Overstrike. In the Create Overstrike dialog box, type the two characters you want printed on top of each other. Press Enter, and then choose OK to return to your document screen. On the WordPerfect screen, your overstrike character may not look that magnificent. It should look fine, though, on the printed page.

5. Outlines made easy.

Outlines are nice when you've got to make an agenda for a meeting or an outline for a book or report. WordPerfects Outline feature puts an adjustable outline level on-screen whenever you press Enter.

To turn on Outline, pull down the **T**ools menu, choose **O**utline, choose **B**egin New Outline. At the Outline Style List dialog box, highlight the item that says Outline in the leftmost column, and then choose **S**elect. Press F4 so that all your outline text will be indented at the same level; then type your text for that level. Press Enter to go to the next outline item, and then press F4 to indent the text for that level.

If you want to move down an outline level, press Tab. If you want to move up a level, press Shift-Tab. Each time you press Enter, WordPerfect goes to the previous outline level.

6. Initial codes unlimited.

If you use certain margins or line settings all the time in WordPerfect, you can set them to be the defaults. Pull down the **L**ayout menu, choose **D**ocument, and then choose Initial Codes Se**t**up. This brings you the Initial Codes Setup dialog box, which is similar to a regular editing screen. Set the margins, justification, line spacing and whatever other formatting you want in each document as you normally would. Press F7 twice to return to your document screen. The settings you just made will apply to all the documents you create from now on.

7. Etch-A-Sketch.

This is a silly little feature you might play with when you feel like doodling. Make sure you're at a blank screen before doing this. Choose a mono-spaced font—one that has "10cpi" or "12cpi" as

part of the name. Next, pull down the Graphics menu and choose Line Draw. Now, when you press your arrow keys, you make a line. Guess what—WordPerfect has just become an Etch-A-Sketch. You can change to a double line by pressing 2. When you're finished with this nonsense, choose Close to leave Line Draw, and be sure to clear the screen before your boss comes in and screams at you to quit fiddling around.

8. Talking to yourself.

If you want to make a remark to yourself in a document, but don't want that remark to print, try out the Comments feature. Move the cursor to where you want the comment to appear. Then pull down the Layout menu, choose Comment, and then choose Create. The cursor appears in a box, where you can type away. Press F7 when you're done. Your comment appears in a box on-screen, but it won't print.

9. Dates your way!

Usually, WordPerfect's automatic date feature puts the date in like this: July 4, 1993. If you would prefer something different (such as 04/03/93), you can customize the date. Pull down the Tools menu, choose Date, and then choose Format to bring up the Date Formats dialog box. Choose any of the example formats listed in the dialog box, and then choose OK. You can then insert the date by pulling down the Layout menu, choosing Date, and then choosing Text.

10. Happy hyphenation.

WordPerfect ordinarily keeps entire words together on a line, but you can have it hyphenate automatically as you write. This is most useful if your documents are full-justified. Move the cursor to where you want WP to begin hyphenating words. Then pull down the Layout menu, choose Line, and then Hyphenation. Choose OK to return to the document screen.

11. **Redecorating WordPerfect.**

What?! You don't like the plain-gray menu bar or the blue-collar dialog boxes? You can change your WordPerfect screen colors to something more festive, if you want. Pull down the **F**ile menu, choose Se**t**up, and then choose **D**isplay to go to the Display dialog box. Choose **G**raphics Mode Screen Type/Colors. In the Graphics Mode Screen Type/Colors dialog box, choose **C**olor Schemes, highlight one of the items in the list, and then choose **S**elect. Choose Close to return to your document screen. If you're like me, you'll think all the alternatives are much uglier than the default colors. In that case, follow these steps again, selecting the [WP Default] option in the Color Schemes list.

12. **Document bonanza.**

WordPerfect's really like having nine typewriters at once—you can work on nine documents at the same time. Any time you want to work on a different document, just pull down the **F**ile menu and choose **N**ew. You can switch between your documents by pulling down the **W**indow menu, choosing Switch to, and then choosing the number by the name of the document you want to work on. Each document works exactly the same. Make sure you've got all your documents named and updated before you exit WordPerfect.

12 Common Mistakes

1. **Saving takes too long.**

When you first name a document, you should pull down the **F**ile menu and choose Save **A**s. Here you'll get a chance to type a name for the document and choose OK to save it. And, since that's how you saved the document the first time, you may think that's how you should update your documents, too. Well, it's much easier than

that. After you save the document this first time, you should update it by pulling down the **F**ile menu and choosing **S**ave. This way, WordPerfect automatically updates your document and you don't have to do any mucking around with hard-to-answer questions like `Replace (your file)`?

2. Hey! Where'd the menu bar go?

WordPerfect's menu bar is probably the easiest way to get around WordPerfect, and many people would feel lost without it. What a shame, then, that it's so easy to accidentally turn off. If you pull down the View menu and choose Pull-Down Menus, the menu bar suddenly disappears! Ack! Without being able to use the menu bar, how do we turn the menu bar back on? It's truly a philosophical blockbuster.

If you have a mouse, the answer's easy. Click the right button on your mouse and the menu bar comes back. Now, before it goes away again, pull down the **V**iew menu and choose **P**ull-Down Menus. Choose OK twice to get back your menu bars.

If you *don't* have a mouse, getting the menu bar back is a bit trickier. Press Ctrl+F3, and then Shift+F1 to bring up the Screen Setup dialog box. Choose **S**creen Options, and then choose **P**ull-Down Menus. Choose OK twice to get back your menu bars.

3. Oops! I forgot to turn on my printer.

It doesn't matter how long you've worked with computers; you'll still occasionally do this one. You send a print job to your printer, but haven't bothered to turn on the printer. If you turn on the thing now, your backlogged print jobs should start rolling out in just a couple of minutes.

4. **How do I open this stupid file?**

Name Search is a nice feature to have in the File Manager, but it's easy to forget that you have to turn it off once you've found the file. Here's what usually happens You're in the File Manager and want to look for a certain file. You choose **N**ame Search and start typing the name of the file. After you type just a few characters, WordPerfect highlights the file you want, so you press O to open the document. Nothing happens. You press O again, this time a little harder. Then you start hammering on O for Open, wondering what's wrong with your stupid computer.

Well, WordPerfect's still in Name Search mode, so pressing O so many times doesn't do any good—WordPerfect just thinks that "o" is part of the name you're looking for. As soon as you've highlighted the list item you want, press *Enter*—not another letter.

5. **Toto, I don't think we're in WordPerfect 6 anymore....**

You start WordPerfect from a DOS prompt and find you're in some strange program that doesn't act or look like the WordPerfect 6 you know and love. What happened? Well, a lot of people have more than one version of WordPerfect and *all* DOS versions of WordPerfect can be started by typing WP at a DOS prompt. You're probably in an old version. Get out by pressing F7, N, Y. Find an expert to help you get started on the right version of the program, and take notes so you know what to do in case you wind up in some other version sometime again.

6. **Where am I?**

With just a slight slip of the mouse, it's easy to choose the wrong option in a menu or dialog box, putting you in some strange, foreign-looking dialog box, full of ominous messages and sinister

voices. How can you get out without bungling your mission-critical document? Press Esc, or choose Cancel if the dialog box has a Cancel button. *Don't* choose any of the OK keys—that's the same thing as giving WordPerfect the go-ahead to do whatever it wants with your document.

7. Non-system disk? What?

You're starting a new day of work. You turn on your computer, only to get this message:

```
Non-System disk or disk error

Replace and strike any key when ready
```

The cause of this problem is easy: you have a floppy disk in your A drive. Remove the floppy disk, press the space bar, and get back to work.

8. mY tEXT lOOKS wEIRD.

If you're transcribing from something printed, you may not notice accidentally pressing your Caps Lock key when you meant to hit Shift. Now all the characters that you want uppercase are lowercase, and vice versa. You don't have to retype the mess, however. Just move your cursor to the first character where things started being backward. Turn on Block by pulling down the **E**dit menu, choosing **B**lock, and then move the cursor just after the last character you need fixed. Now pull down the **E**dit menu, choose Convert Case, and then **L**owercase. This makes everything except the beginning of sentences lowercase. You might need to go and fix proper names, but that's easier than retyping the whole mess.

9. **Backspace vs. Delete**

Pressing Backspace erases the character to the *left* of your cursor. Pressing Delete erases the character to the *right* of the cursor. It's that simple, but it's hard to remember. If you've erased in the wrong direction, press Esc, then R right away to restore the lost text.

10. **Did I say Tab? I meant indent.**

If you need a paragraph further to the right than the surrounding text, it's tempting to press tab at the beginning of each line. Don't. When you edit the paragraph, the tabs will no longer always be at the beginning of each line, and the paragraph becomes a shambles. Instead, right at the beginning of the paragraph, press F4. The entire paragraph is now indented over one tab stop.

11. **I inserted my *own* hyphen.**

If you're at the end of a line and are about to type a long word (such as *terpsichorean*), you might want to break it up with a hyphen. That way the whole word doesn't wrap to the next line, leaving the previous line looking short. Most people hyphenate the word by moving to the point they want to break the word, pressing the hyphen key (-), and then pressing the space bar.

If you edit the paragraph so that the whole word fits on a single line, you now have something that looks like *terpsi-chorean*. Instead, when you want to hyphenate a word, move to where you want the word to break, and then press Ctrl+hyphen to insert the hyphen. If you later edit the paragraph so that the whole word fits on a line, the hyphen automatically disappears.

12. **Numbers mysteriously appear in my document.**

Whenever you first start WordPerfect, the Num Lock key is on automatically. If you want to go to the top of the document and press what you think is Home, Home, up-arrow key, you've actually just typed 778 because the keys are acting as numbers.

12 Best WordPerfect Shortcuts

1. **Save painlessly.**

Here's a tip that makes saving your documents easy. Press Ctrl+F12 to save. The first time you save your document, this keystroke combo has you name the document normally. After that, pressing Ctrl+F12 just updates your document in a flash, without bothering you with any pesky questions.

2. **Lists with a bullet.**

Bullet lists are one of the mainstays of word processing. They're just lists with little black circles at the beginning of each item. They look good, but they've traditionally been hands-off for normal people because nobody knows how to make those little black circles. Well, it doesn't have to be difficult. Just type your list *without* the bullets, pressing Enter after each item in the list. When you're done with the list, move your cursor to the beginning of the first item in the list, pull down the Edit menu, choose Block, and move your cursor to the end of the last item in the list. This blocks your whole list. Next, press Alt+F10, type *bullet* and press Enter (these are the shortcut keystrokes for starting a macro). The Bullet Inserter dialog box appears. Choose Insert bullet, wait a second, and behold—your list is bulleted.

3. No-stress numbered lists.

The problem with typing numbered lists is that you always remember that there should have been a list item that goes between number 3 and 4. So now you've got to renumber the whole thing. Well, not with this trick. Move your cursor to a new line where you want to start the numbered list, and then press Ctrl+T. A number appears, and you can start typing your list, pressing Enter after each item. If you remember some item that needs to go between two other items, move your cursor so it's at the *end* of the two items you want your new item between, press Enter, and type your new line. For example, if you want a new item between items 2 and 3, move your cursor so it's at the end of item 2, press Enter, and type the new item. All the other items automatically renumber.

When you're done with the list, move your cursor to the bottom of the list, press Enter to go to a new line below the list, and press Ctrl+T to turn off the list maker.

4. From here to there in nothing flat.

When you need to move to a certain page in WordPerfect, there's no need to press down on arrow keys, waiting endlessly to finally get to the page you need. Instead, press Ctrl+Home, type the page number you want to move to, and press Enter. You're there. Period. This feature is also handy for moving to the top or bottom of the current page. To go to the beginning of the page, press Ctrl+Home, up arrow key. If you want to go to the end of this page, press Ctrl+Home, down arrow key.

5. You turn me off.

WordPerfect's got a lot of funky things you can do to make your text look different. You can underline it, double-underline it, bold it, italicize it, put a strikethrough line through it, make it large,

make it small, and much, much more. Each of these tricks has to be started in its own way. However, you can use the same shortcut to turn all of them off: Press Ctrl+N. No matter what text emphasizer you're using, you can quickly switch it off with this keystroke combo.

6. Oops! I didn't mean to do that!

Accidents happen. Luckily, WordPerfect gives you a couple of easy shortcuts for fixing them. If you just deleted text that you didn't want to delete, press Esc, R—and do it right away. If you sorted something that didn't come out right, or spell-checked something and it only made it worse, or cut when you should have copied, press Ctrl+Z to undo the action. Remember these two shortcuts—they're lifesavers.

7. Block it again.

When you block text and turn some feature—like Bold—on, WordPerfect takes the highlight off the block. Sometimes, though, you'll want to do more than one thing to that block. For example, you might want to make it bold *and* italic. Well, after you've turned on one feature for the blocked text, press Alt+F4, Ctrl+Home, Ctrl+Home to reblock the text so you can turn on another feature.

8. Back to work.

Often, the last document you work on in WordPerfect on one day will be the *first* document you work on the next day. Here are the quick steps you can follow to quickly open the document you worked on most recently: Press Shift+F10, down arrow key, Enter. This brings up your most recent document. You can now make your cursor zip to where it was when you last used the document by pressing Ctrl+F (when you press Ctrl+F, you're using a feature called QuickMark, which is the topic of the next shortcut).

9. **I'll be back.**

WordPerfect has a feature called QuickMark, which is good for when you need to move around in your document, but want to be able to return to a certain part very fast. To use QuickMark, move your cursor to the point you want to return to, and then press Ctrl+Q—this places the QuickMark, which is like a bookmark in your document. You can then move around in your document as much as you please, returning to that spot immediately whenever you press Ctrl+F, which finds the QuickMark.

10. **I'll take this word, please.**

Of all the things you select in WordPerfect, you'll probably select a single word most often. If you've got a mouse, it's incredibly easy to do. Just move the mouse pointer so it's anywhere on the word you want to block, then double-click. (This means you should press your mouse button twice in a row without moving the mouse—it takes practice, but you'll get the hang of it.) You can use a similar trick to block a whole sentence— triple-click anywhere in the sentence. Finally, you can quadruple-click anywhere in a paragraph to block the paragraph.

11. **Get me out, NOW!**

Getting in and out of WordPerfect dialog boxes is such a chore. You can at least speed up the process of getting out of those boxes—and back to your document screen—by using this shortcut.

Before you can use the shortcut, you have to do a little preparation work. Don't worry, you'll only have to do this part once. Press Alt+F10, and then press F5 three times to go to the File Manager. Press N for Name Search, and then type EXITALL.WPM to highlight EXITALL.WPM. Press Enter. Press C for Copy, type

ALTX.WPM, and then press Enter. Press Esc three times to return to your document screen.

Now, after you finish making changes in a dialog box, just press Alt+X to zip back to your document screen, without the usual hassle of having to choose OK and close several times.

12. A capital shortcut

I probably don't need to tell you why this one's useful, but I will anyway. If you forget to capitalize a word, you've got to go back, delete the old letter and retype the capital version. Save the effort by moving your cursor anywhere within the word and using this shortcut.

Like the previous shortcut, you've got to do a little one-time work before you can use this shortcut. Press Alt+F10, and then press F5 three times to go to the File Manager. Press N for Name Search, and then type INITCAPS.WPM to highlight INITCAPS.WPM. Press Enter. Press C for Copy, type ALTC.WPM, and then Enter. Press Esc three times to return to your document screen.

Now whenever you've got a non-capitalized word that needs capitalizing, just move your cursor anywhere into the word and press Alt+C. WordPerfect capitalizes the first letter of the word for you, no questions asked.

I HATE

Index

Symbols

A

B

C

I HATE WORDPERFECT 6!

D

I HATE WORDPERFECT 6!

I HATE WORDPERFECT 6!

E

F

I HATE WORDPERFECT 6!

K

L

M

N

O

P

Q-R

S

I HATE WORDPERFECT 6!

T

U–V

W–Z